MW01229047

Copyright   2023
All rights reserved.
Printed in the United States of America

First Edition

Author: One Exam Prep (1-877-804-3959)
www.1examprep.com

VISIT US HERE FOR EXCLUSIVE OFFERS

Unleashing the Power Of Digital Marketing For Your Contractor Business

- Company Branding
- Contractor Website
- Social Media Templates
- 1-on-1 Marketing Consultations
- Google Search Optimazation

W W W . 1 5 4 A G E N C Y . C O M

TABLE OF CONTENTS

PRACTICE EXAMS

Modern Masonry, 9th Edition
Questions and Answers

1. In masonry work, _____ is used to make long horizontal joints.

    A. Sled runner
    B. Joint raker
    C. Line jointer
    D. Line runner

2. Concrete should be compacted or vibrated when layers or lifts are up to a maximum _____ inches thick in reinforced concrete.

    A. 8
    B. 10
    C. 12
    D. 14

3. _____ brick is used in dry conditions and exposed to freezing weather.

    A. Grade SW
    B. Grade MW
    C. Grade NW
    D. Grade FBX

4. Brick that will come in contact with ground water and freezing conditions should be _____.

    A. Grade MW
    B. Grade NW
    C. Grade SW
    D. Type FBA

5. With masonry, _____ inch is the unit of measure used in a modular grid system.

    A. 1
    B. 3
    C. 4
    D. 5

6. _____ is the nominal size of a modular brick.

    A. 2" x 2 1/3" x 8"
    B. 3" x 2 2/3" x 8"
    C. 4" x 2 1/3" x 8"
    D. 4" x 2 2/3" x 8"

7. _____ percent of a brick must be solid for it to be considered solid.

    A. 95
    B. 85
    C. 75
    D. 65

8. _____ is the white powder that forms on a masonry wall after exposure to moisture.

    A. Efflorescence
    B. Chalk dust
    C. Fluoropolymer
    D. Sodium bicarbonate

9. Five stretcher courses of brick with one header course describes a _____ bond.

    A. Running
    B. Flemish
    C. English
    D. Common

10. When laying brick and all the vertical joints align, this is a _____ bond.

    A. Dutch
    B. Stack
    C. Flemish
    D. American

11. Which brick pattern is considered the weakest bond?

    A. English cross bond
    B. Common bond
    C. Stack bond
    D. Running bond

12. What type of mortar joint is recommended in areas exposed to high winds and heavy rains?

    A. Weathered
    B. Concave
    C. Troweled
    D. Raked

13. What type of facing tile is used when a high degree of mechanical perfection is required?

    A. FTX unglazed
    B. FTS unglazed
    C. SCR acoustile
    D. SCR unglazed

14. _____ aggregate is expanded shale or clay, expanded slag, coal cinders, pumice, and scoria.

    A. Normal weight
    B. Dense
    C. Lightweight
    D. Coarse

15. The openings in blocks are called _____.

    A. Cross web
    B. Cells
    C. Face shell
    D. Lintels

16. _____ means the quicklime has been formed into putty by combining it with water.

    A. Plasticity
    B. Repointing
    C. Bleeding
    D. Slacked

17. _____ inch is the standard size of a mortar joint when using standard concrete masonry units.

    A. 1/8
    B. ¼
    C. 3/8
    D. ½

18. What is not an advantage of a two-core block CMU versus a three-core block design?

    A. Reduced heat conductor
    B. Lighter
    C. More space for placing conduit
    D. The shell is narrower at the center web

19. A _____ block is used the same way as the corner block but has a rounded corner.

    A. Double corner
    B. Bullnose
    C. Pier
    D. Stretcher

20. A standard glass block mortar joint is _____ inch thick.

   A. 1/8
   B. ¼
   C. ½
   D. 1/3

21. To prevent moisture from entering the top of a masonry wall, you should use _____ copings.

   A. Ceramic tile
   B. Plaster
   C. Wood
   D. Stone

22. What is the best stone to protect against moisture on sills?

   A. Limestone
   B. Granite
   C. Sandstone
   D. Slate

23. Mortar is mainly composed of which cementitious material?

   A. Blended cement
   B. Portland cement
   C. Hydrated lime – Type S
   D. Ground limestone

24. What type of lime is used in mortar?

   A. Type N hydrated
   B. Type M hydrated
   C. Type S hydrated
   D. Type K hydrated

25. What is the primary aggregate used in mortar?

   A. Sand
   B. Quartz
   C. Crushed oyster shells
   D. Gravel

26. To avoid hardening due to hydration, mortar should be used _____ hour(s) after mixing.

   A. 1
   B. 1 ½
   C. 2
   D. 2 ½

27. What type of mortar is best suited for use below grade?

   A. Type S
   B. Type N
   C. Type M
   D. Type O

28. What is the most important property of hardened mortar?

   A. Compressive strength
   B. Bond strength
   C. Durability
   D. Weatherability

29. Which of the following is not a masonry mortar?

   A. Type P
   B. Type O
   C. Type K
   D. Type N

30. What is added to mortar to increase strength?

   A. Admixture
   B. Cement
   C. Aggregate
   D. Polymer

31. What type of mortar is used where wind speeds will exceed 80 miles per hour?

   A. Type K
   B. Type O
   C. Type M
   D. Type N

32. What type of mortar is used for interior non-load bearing partitions where high strength is not needed?

   A. Type S
   B. Type M
   C. Type N
   D. Type K

33. A 10ft x 100ft single wythe brick wall is to be constructed and will have 655 non modular brick per 100 sq ft and 3/8-inch mortar joints. _____ cubic feet of mortar will need to be purchased.

   A. 32
   B. 34
   C. 50
   D. 58

34. _____ are strips of metal or metal wire used to tie masonry wythes together or to tie masonry veneer to a concrete frame or wood frame wall.

    A. Wall ties
    B. Anchors
    C. Joints
    D. Jambs

35. The maximum height of grout lifts is _____ feet.

    A. 3
    B. 5
    C. 7
    D. 9

36. With masonry, what gage wire is ordinarily used for continuous horizontal joint reinforcement?

    A. 5, 6, 7 & 8
    B. 6, 7, 8 & 9
    C. 7, 8, 9 & 10
    D. 8, 9, 10 & 11

37. The closest an adjustable truss type brick tie should be from the edge of the brick is _____ inch.

    A. 3/8
    B. ¾
    C. 5/8
    D. ½

38. When bearing walls intersect, they may be connected with a _____.

    A. Strap anchor
    B. "L" bent bar anchor
    C. Hex coupling
    D. Acorn nut

39. When the cut edge will be hidden by the mortar, which hand tool is used to cut brick?

    A. Masonry saw
    B. Brick hammer
    C. Brick trowel
    D. Brick set chisel

40. When laying brick, what area of the building contains the leads?

    A. The foundation
    B. The first course
    C. The corners
    D. None of the above

41. Wall ties in a brick masonry cavity wall should be placed _____ inch from either edge of the masonry unit.

    A. 3/16
    B. 3/8
    C. 5/8
    D. ½

42. _____ the joint helps the mortar and masonry unit bond together and provide the best moisture protection.

    A. Weathering
    B. Toweling
    C. Raking
    D. Tooling

43. The recommended air pressure setting when using abrasive blasting to clean brick is _____ psf.

    A. 50 – 100
    B. 80 – 120
    C. 60 – 100
    D. 75 – 150

44. When blocks are laid, they are positioned _____.

    A. Narrow flange on top
    B. Wide flange on bottom
    C. Wide flange on top
    D. Narrow flange on bottom

45. _____ is the best cleaning chemical for brick.

    A. Hydrochloric acid
    B. Sulfuric acid
    C. Diluted bleach
    D. Diluted ammonia

46. A two-wythe wall allowing each wythe to react independently to stress known as a _____ wall.

    A. Solid masonry
    B. Cavity
    C. Composite
    D. Reinforced concrete masonry

47. When using 9 gage ties in a composite wall, what is the proper separation of ties?

    A. One for every 4 1/4 square feet
    B. One for every 2 1/2 square feet
    C. One for every 4 1/2 square feet
    D. One for every 2 2/3 square feet

48. When constructing a cavity wall, each wythe is separated by a continuous air space that is at least _____ inch(es) wide.

   A. 1
   B. 1 ½
   C. 2
   D. 2 ½

49. _____ units are masonry units that have been designed for aesthetic appeal.

   A. Ground face
   B. Architectural concrete masonry
   C. Prefaced concrete masonry
   D. Split face masonry

50. What is used to anchor brick veneer to the structure?

   A. Corrugated metal ties
   B. Strap anchors
   C. Flat head anchor
   D. Veneer nails

51. When laying an 8 inches concrete block wall, string out the blocks for the first course without mortar to check layout. Allow for _____ inch each mortar joint.

   A. ¼
   B. ½
   C. 3/8
   D. 5/8

52. The lead corner is usually laid up _____ courses high.

   A. Two to three
   B. Three to four
   C. Four or five
   D. Five to six

53. A _____ inch diameter bar is used to make a 3/8 inch concave mortar joint.

   A. 1/8
   B. 3/8
   C. 5/8
   D. 1/4

54. What type of footings are used for free standing columns or piers?

   A. Stepped
   B. Isolated
   C. Combined
   D. Continuous

55. Foundation walls that are being dampproofed should be parged _____ inches above the finish grade.

    A. 6
    B. 5
    C. 8
    D. 10

56. Masonry exterior non-load bearing walls not supported at each story are known as _____ wall.

    A. Panel
    B. Cavity
    C. Curtain
    D. Solid masonry

57. If the outer wythe of a cavity wall on each side of an external corner extends more than _____ feet, expansion joints are recommended.

    A. 30
    B. 50
    C. 60
    D. 65

58. _____ units are widely used as facing veneer. The veneer is attached to backing but does not act structurally with the rest of the wall.

    A. Brick and stone
    B. Brick and mortar
    C. Stone and concrete
    D. Concrete and glass

59. _____ are placed over an opening in a wall used to support the loads above that opening?

    A. Chases
    B. Recesses
    C. Lintels
    D. Stirrups

60. Welded wire reinforcement for masonry should be lapped to what minimum distance?

    A. One full stay plus 1 inch
    B. Two full stay plus 1 inch
    C. One full stay plus 2 inches
    D. Two full stay plus 2 inches

61. Terrazzo toppings are typically _____ inch thick.

    A. ¼
    B. ½
    C. 3/8
    D. ¾

62. Filling voids in masonry with fresh mortar is known as _____.

    A. Tuckpointing
    B. Joint tucking
    C. Re-grouting
    D. Joint pointing

63. What type of float is used to float large flat slabs?

    A. Hand float
    B. Bull float
    C. Power float
    D. None of the above

64. Open, unsupported stacks of brick should not exceed _____ feet in height.

    A. 5
    B. 6
    C. 7
    D. 8

65. To use a ladder safely be sure it extends at least _____ feet above the point where you plan to step off.

    A. 2
    B. 2.5
    C. 3
    D. 3.5

66. If a plan is drawn 1/4" = 1'0" scale, how long on the drawing would a 40-foot wall be?

    A. 5 inches
    B. 10 inches
    C. 15 inches
    D. 20 inches

67. If a plan is drawn to 1/4 inch size, how long on the drawing would a 40-foot wall be?

    A. 10 feet
    B. 20 feet
    C. 20 inches
    D. 10 inches

68. A hollow masonry unit is one whose cross-sectional area in any plane is less than _____% solid material.

    A. 85
    B. 80
    C. 75
    D. 70

14

69. The _____ are the tops and bottoms of the bricks or blocks.

    A. Bearing surfaces
    B. Splits
    C. Openings
    D. Bats

70. The simplest mortar joint to make is the _____ joint.

    A. Flush
    B. Rough cut
    C. Raked
    D. Both A and B

71. Hollow load bearing block, ASTM C90, Grade N will have an average minimum compressive strength of _____ psi (individual unit).

    A. 600
    B. 800
    C. 900
    D. 1000

72. An 8" x 8" x 16" block has actual dimensions of _____.

    A. 7 5/8" x 7 5/8" x 15 5/8"
    B. 7 5/8" x 7 3/8" x 15 7/8"
    C. 7 3/8" x 7 3/8" x 15 3/8"
    D. 7 15/16" x 7 15/16" x 15 15/16"

73. Stone is divided into three categories. They are all of the following EXCEPT _____.

    A. Metamorphic
    B. Quartzite
    C. Igneous
    D. Sedimentary

74. Mortar can be retempered by adding water but must be used within _____ hour(s) after original mixing.

    A. 1
    B. 1 ½
    C. 2
    D. 2 ½

75. What ASTM type mortar is used for general use in above ground exposed masonry?

    A. Type N
    B. Type O
    C. Type S
    D. Type M

Please see Answer Key on the following page

3/15/23

Modern Masonry, 9th Edition
Questions and Answers
Answer Key

Q	Answer	Page #	Index
1.	A	27	Jointers
2.	C	431	Concrete – placing and finishing
3.	B	116	Brick – classification
4.	C	116	Brick – classification
5.	C	119	Brick – sizes
6.	D	120	Brick – sizes
		Figure 7-14	
7.	C	123	Brick – weight
8.	A	124	Efflorescence
9.	D	129	Pattern bond
10.	B	130	Stack bond
11.	C	130	Stack bond
12.	B	131 – 132	Concave joints
13.	A	137	Unglazed facing tile
14.	C	154	Lightweight aggregate
15.	B	160	Concrete block – block terminology
16.	D	187	Hydrate lime
17.	C	157	Concrete block – sizes and shapes
18.	D	157	Concrete block – sizes and shapes
19.	B	157	Concrete block – uses
20.	B	170	Glass block
21.	D	181	Stone - applications
22.	A	181	Stone - applications
23.	B	187	Mortar – cementitious materials
24.	C	187	Mortar – cementitious materials
25.	A	188	Sand
26.	D	191	Mortar – hardened
27.	C	191	Type M mortar
28.	B	191	Mortar – properties
29.	A	191 – 193	Mortar – proportions and uses

<u>Q</u>	<u>Answer</u>	<u>Page #</u>	<u>Index</u>
30.	B	191	*Mortar – properties*
31.	C	191 – 192	*Type M mortar*
		Figure 10-8	
32.	D	193	*Type K mortar*
33.	D	197 - 198	*Mortar – estimating quantities*
		Figure 10-11	

Choose the row with 655 per 100 square ft and would require 5.8 cuft per 100 sq ft of mortar

5.8 cuft / 100 square ft x (10 ft x 100 ft) = 58 cubic feet

<u>Q</u>	<u>Answer</u>	<u>Page #</u>	<u>Index</u>
34.	A	204	*Wall ties*
35.	B	199	*Grout – placement*
36.	D	206	*Metal ties*
37.	C	209	*Adjustable ties*
		Figure 11-11	
38.	A	212	*Anchors*
39.	B	223	*Brick – cutting*
40.	C	230	*Brick walls – laying common*
41.	C	244	*Brick walls – tie place/joint replacement*
42.	D	244	*Brick walls - tooling*
43.	C	254	*Abrasive blasting*
44.	C	266	*Block – handling*
45.	A	252	*Brick – cleaning*
46.	B	260	*Cavity wall*
47.	D	261	*Composite wall*
48.	C	260	*Cavity wall*
49.	B	161	*Concrete block – decorative block*
50.	A	261	*Veneered walls*
51.	C	268	*Block – laying concrete block walls*
52.	C	270	*Block – laying concrete block walls*
		Step #7	
53.	C	272	*Block – laying concrete block walls*
		Step #11	
54.	B	312	*Isolated footing*
55.	A	316	*Dampproofing*

Q	Answer	Page #	Index
56.	C	328	*Curtain wall*
57.	B	332	*Masonry walls and components – hollow*
58.	A	332	*Wall systems – masonry walls and components*
59.	C	348	*Lintels*
60.	C	396	*Concrete – reinforced*
61.	B	444	*Decorative special finishes – concrete flatwork*
62.	A	193	*Tuckpointing*
63.	B	42	*Bull float*
64.	C	58	*Safety – handling and storing materials*
65.	C	60	*Safety – ladder*
66.	B	69-70	*Construction drawings*

Plan scale is ¼" = 1 ft

¼ = .25" = 1 ft

.25"/1 ft = x / 40ft

X = 40 (.25")

X = 10 inches

67.	A	69-70	*Construction drawings*

40 ft x ¼ = 10 ft

68.	C	123	*Hollow masonry units*
69.	A	123	*Bearing surfaces*
70.	D	132	*Flush joint*
71.	B	154, 156	*Grade N*
		Figure 8-8	
72.	A	157	*Concrete block – sizes and shapes*
73.	B	174	*Stone – classification*
74.	D	190	*Retempering*
75.	A	192	*Type N mortar*

Modern Masonry, 8th Ed.
Questions and Answers

1. In masonry work, what tool is used to make long horizontal joints?

    A.   Sled runner jointer
    B.   Joint raker
    C.   Line jointer
    D.   Line runner

2. Concrete should be compacted or vibrated when layers or lifts are up to a maximum____ inches thick in reinforced concrete.

    A.   8 inches
    B.   10 inches
    C.   12 inches
    D.   14 inches

3. What type of brick is used in dry conditions and exposed to freezing weather?

    A.   SW
    B.   MW
    C.   NW
    D.   FBX

4. Brick that will come in contact with ground water and freezing conditions should be type_____.

    A.   MW
    B.   NW
    C.   SW
    D.   FBA

5. With masonry, what unit of measure is used in a modular grid system?

    A.   1"
    B.   3"
    C.   4"
    D.   5"

6. What is the nominal size of a modular brick?

    A.   2" x 2 1/3" x 8"
    B.   3" x 2 2/3" x 8"
    C.   4" x 2 1/3" x 8"
    D.   4" x 2 2/3" x 8"

7. What percentage of a brick must be solid for it to be considered solid?

    A.   95%
    B.   85%
    C.   75%
    D.   65%

8. What is the white powder that forms on a masonry wall after exposure to moisture?

    A.   Efflorescence
    B.   Chalk dust
    C.   Fluoropolymer
    D.   Sodium bicarbonate

9. Five stretcher courses of brick with one header course describe what type of bond?

    A.   Running
    B.   Flemish
    C.   English
    D.   Common

10. When laying brick and all the vertical joints align, this is a_____.

    A.   Dutch bond
    B.   Stack bond
    C.   Flemish bond
    D.   American bond

11. Which brick pattern is considered the weakest bond?

  A. English cross bond
  B. Common bond
  C. Stack bond
  D. Running bond

12. What type of mortar joint is recommended in areas exposed to high winds and heavy rains?

  A. Weathered joint
  B. Concave
  C. Troweled joint
  D. Raked joint

13. What type of facing tile is used when a high degree of mechanical perfection is required?

  A. FTX unglazed
  B. FTS unglazed
  C. SCR acoustile
  D. SCR unglazed

14. What is the weight of an 8 x 8 x 16 CMU made of sand & gravel?

  A. 28 lbs.
  B. 35 lbs.
  C. 40 lbs.
  D. 42 lbs.

15. What is the highest strength aggregate in an 8 x 8 x 16 CMU?

  A. Shale
  B. Sand and gravel
  C. Expanded slag
  D. Scoria

16. Which CMU weighs the least per cubic foot of concrete?

  A. Sand
  B. Limestone
  C. Air-cooled slag
  D. Pumice

17. What is the standard size of a mortar joint when using standard concrete masonry units?

   A.   1/8"
   B.   ¼"
   C.   3/8"
   D.   ½"

18. What is not an advantage of a two-core block CMU versus a three-core block design?

   A.   Reduced heat conductor
   B.   Lighter
   C.   More space for placing conduit
   D.   The shell is narrower at the center web

19. The nominal size of an 8-inch stretcher block is_____.

   A.   6 x 6 x 18
   B.   8 x 8 x 16
   C.   8 x 8 x 12
   D.   10 x 10 x 18

20. A standard glass block mortar joint is how thick?

   A.   1/8 inch
   B.   ¼ inch
   C.   ½ inch
   D.   1/3 inch

21. To prevent moisture from entering the top of a masonry wall, you should use_____.

   A.   Ceramic tile copings
   B.   Plaster copings
   C.   Wood copings
   D.   Stone copings

22. What is the best stone to protect against moisture on sills?

   A.   Limestone
   B.   Granite
   C.   Sandstone
   D.   Slate

23. Mortar is mainly composed of which cementitious material?

    A.   Blended cement
    B.   Portland cement
    C.   Hydrated lime – Type S
    D.   Ground limestone

24. What type of lime is used in mortar?

    A.   Type N hydrated
    B.   Type M hydrated
    C.   Type S hydrated
    D.   Type K hydrated

25. What is the primary aggregate used in mortar?

    A.   Sand
    B.   Quartz
    C.   Crushed oyster shells
    D.   Gravel

26. To avoid hardening due to hydration, mortar should be used within what time span after mixing?

    A.   1 hour
    B.   1 ½ hours
    C.   2 hours
    D.   2 ½ hours

27. What type of mortar is best suited for use below grade?

    A.   Type S
    B.   Type N
    C.   Type M
    D.   Type O

28. What is the most important property of hardened mortar?

    A.   Compressive strength
    B.   Bond strength
    C.   Durability
    D.   Weather ability

29. Which of the following is not a masonry mortar?

    A.   Type P
    B.   Type O
    C.   Type K
    D.   Type N

30. What is added to mortar to increase strength?

    A.   Admixture
    B.   Cement
    C.   Aggregate
    D.   Polymer

31. What type of mortar is used where wind speeds will exceed 80 miles per hour?

    A.   Type K
    B.   Type O
    C.   Type S
    D.   Type N

32. What type of mortar is used for interior non-load bearing partitions where high strength is not needed?

    A.   Type S
    B.   Type M
    C.   Type N
    D.   Type K

33. How many cubic feet of mortar are required for a single wythe brick wall that measures 200 square feet, has 3/8" mortar joints and has 655 non-modular brick units per 100 square feet?

    A.   6.8 cubic feet
    B.   11.6 cubic feet
    C.   12.8 cubic feet
    D.   14.4 cubic feet

34. Per 100 sq ft, using a 3/8" mortar joint, you will need how many brick and how many cubic feet of mortar?

      A.   655 brick and 5.8 cubic feet of mortar
      B.   616 brick and 7.2 cubic feet of mortar
      C.   470 brick and 5.8 cubic feet of mortar
      D.   432 brick and 4.5 cubic feet of mortar

35. The maximum height of grout lifts is usually how high?

      A.   3 feet
      B.   5 feet
      C.   7 feet
      D.   9 feet

36. With masonry, what gauge wire is ordinarily used for continuous horizontal joint reinforcement?

      A.   5, 6, 7 & 8
      B.   6, 7, 8 & 9
      C.   7, 8, 9 & 10
      D.   8, 9, 10 & 11

37. What is the closest an adjustable truss type brick tie should be from the edge of the brick?

      A.   3/8"
      B.   ¾"
      C.   5/8"
      D.   ½"

38. When masonry walls intersect, they may be connected with a?

      A.   Strap anchor
      B.   "L" bent bar anchor
      C.   Hex coupling
      D.   Acorn nut

39. When the cut edge will be hidden by the mortar, which hand tool is used to cut brick?

      A.   Masonry saw
      B.   Brick hammer
      C.   Brick trowel
      D.   Brick set chisel

40. When laying brick, what area of the building contains the leads?

    A.   The foundation
    B.   The first course
    C.   The corners
    D.   None of the above

41. Wall ties in a brick masonry cavity wall should be placed what distance from either edge of the masonry unit?

    A.   3/16"
    B.   3/8"
    C.   5/8"
    D.   ½"

42. Which masonry joint provides the best moisture protection?

    A.   Weathered joint
    B.   Toweled joint
    C.   Raked joint
    D.   Tooled joint

43. What is the recommended air pressure setting when sandblasting brick with a ¼" nozzle?

    A.   50 – 100 psf
    B.   80 – 120 psf
    C.   60 – 100 psf
    D.   75 – 150 psf

44. When blocks are laid, they are positioned how?

    A.   Narrow flange on top
    B.   Wide flange on bottom
    C.   Wide flange on top
    D.   Narrow flange on bottom

45. What is the best cleaning chemical for brick?

    A.   Hydrochloric or muratic acid
    B.   Sulfuric acid
    C.   Diluted bleach
    D.   Diluted ammonia

46. What is a two-wythe wall allowing each wythe to react independently to stress known as?

    A.   Solid masonry wall
    B.   Cavity wall
    C.   Composite wall
    D.   Reinforced concrete masonry wall

47. When using 9 gage ties in a composite wall, what is the proper separation of ties?

    A.   One for every 4 1/4 square feet
    B.   One for every 2 1/2 square feet
    C.   One for every 4 1/2 square feet
    D.   One for every 2 2/3 square feet

48. When constructing a two wythe wall, what is the most common cavity size?

    A.   1"
    B.   1.5"
    C.   2"
    D.   2.5"

49. What type of CMU is commonly used with reinforcement?

    A.   Double bull nose block
    B.   2 core block
    C.   3 core block
    D.   Sash block

50. What is used to anchor brick veneer to the structure?

    A.   Corrugated metal ties
    B.   Strap anchors
    C.   Flat head anchor
    D.   Veneer nails

51. When laying an 8" concrete block wall, string out the blocks for the first course without mortar to check layout. Allow for _____ each mortar joint.

    A.   ¼"
    B.   ½"
    C.   3/8"
    D.   5/8"

52. The lead corner is usually laid up how many courses high?

    A.   Two to three courses
    B.   Three to four courses
    C.   Four or five courses high
    D.   Five to six courses

53. What diameter bar is used to make a 3/8" concave mortar joint?

    A.   1/8 inch
    B.   3/8 inch
    C.   5/8 inch
    D.   1/4 inch

54. What type of footings are used for free standing columns or piers?

    A.   Stepped
    B.   Isolated
    C.   Combined
    D.   Continuous

55. Foundation walls that are being damp-proofed should be parged how many inches above the finish grade?

    A.   6"
    B.   5"
    C.   8"
    D.   10"

56. What are masonry exterior non-load bearing walls not supported at each story?

    A.   Panel wall
    B.   Cavity wall
    C.   Curtain walls
    D.   Solid masonry wall

57. How long must the outer wythe of a cavity wall be on each side of an external corner before expansion joints are recommended?

    A.   30 feet
    B.   50 feet
    C.   60 feet
    D.   65 feet

58. A brick veneer wall will not support loads.

    A.   True
    B.   False

59. What masonry structural member is placed over an opening in a wall used to support the loads above that opening?

    A.   Chases
    B.   Recesses
    C.   Lintel
    D.   Stirrups

60. Welded wire mesh for masonry should be lapped to what minimum distance?

    A.   One full wire grid spacing plus 1 inch
    B.   Two full wire grid spacing plus 1 inch
    C.   One full wire grid spacing plus 2 inches
    D.   Two full wire grid spacing plus 2 inches

61. How thick are terrazzo toppings typically?

    A.   ¼"
    B.   ½"
    C.   3/8"
    D.   ¾"

62. What is filling voids in masonry with fresh mortar known as?

    A.   Tuck pointing
    B.   Joint tucking
    C.   Re-grouting
    D.   Joint pointing

63. What type of float is used to float large flat slabs?

    A.   Hand float
    B.   Bull float
    C.   Power float
    D.   None of the above

64. Open, unsupported stacks of brick should not exceed _____ feet in height.

    A.   5"
    B.   6"
    C.   7"
    D.   8"

65. To use a ladder safely be sure it extends at least _____ feet above the point where you plan to step off.

    A.   2"
    B.   2.5"
    C.   3"
    D.   3.5"

66. If a plan is drawn 1/4" = scale, how long on the drawing would a 40' wall be?

    A.   10 feet
    B.   10 inches
    C.   4 feet
    D.   4 inches

67. If a plan is drawn to 1/4" **size**, how long on the drawing would a 40' wall be?

    A.   10 feet
    B.   10 inches
    C.   4 feet
    D.   4 inches

68. A hollow masonry unit is one whose cross-sectional area in any plane is less than _____ % solid material.

    A.   85
    B.   80
    C.   75
    D.   70

69. The term that describes a white powder or salt like deposit on masonry walls is _____.

    A.   Efflorescence
    B.   Chalk dust
    C.   Fluoropolymer
    D.   Sodium bicarbonate

70. The simplest mortar joint to make is the _____ joint.

    A.   Flush
    B.   Rough cut
    C.   Raked
    D.   Both A and B

71. Hollow load bearing block, ASTM C90, Grade N will have an average minimum compressive strength of _____ psi (individual unit).

    A.   600
    B.   800
    C.   900
    D.   1000

72. An 8" x 8" x 16" block has actual dimensions of _____.

    A.   7 5/8" x 7 5/8" x 15 5/8"
    B.   7 5/8" x 7 3/8" x 15 7/8"
    C.   7 3/8" x 7 3/8" x 15 3/8"
    D.   7 15/16" x 7 15/16" x 15 15/16"

73. Stone is divided into three categories. They are all of the following EXCEPT:

    A.   Metamorphic
    B.   Quartzite
    C.   Igneous
    D.   Sedimentary

74. Mortar can be retempered by adding water but must be used within _____ hour(s) after original mixing.

    A.   1 hour
    B.   1.5 hours
    C.   2 hours
    D.   2.5 hours

75. What ASTM type mortar is used for general use in above ground exposed masonry?

    A.   Type N
    B.   Type O
    C.   Type S
    D.   Type M

Please See Answer Key on following page
ALH 11/13/2019

1 Exam Prep
Modern Masonry
Questions and Answers

ANSWER KEY

<u>Answer</u>	<u>Section/Page#</u>
1. A	Page 6
2. C	Page 379
3. B	Page 82
4. C	Page 82
5. C	Page 85
6. D	Page 87
7. C	Page 91
8. A	Page 92
9. D	Page 96
10. B	Page 97
11. C	Page 97
12. B	Page 99
13. A	Pages 104
14. C	Page 119
15. B	Page 119
16. D	Page 119
17. C	Page 122
18. D	Page 128
19. B	Page 123
20. B	Page 132
21. D	Page 144
22. A	Page 143
23. B	Page 148
24. C	Page 148
25. A	Page 149
26. D	Page 152

Answer	Section/Page#
27. C	Page 152
28. B	Page 152
29. A	Page 153
30. B	Page 153
31. C	Page 154
32. D	Page 154
33. B	Page 159, (refer to figure 8-8, double the amount).
34. A	Page 159
35. B	Page 161
36. D	Page 167
37. C	Page 169
38. A	Page 173
39. B	Page 182
40. C	Page 187
41. C	Page 200
42. D	Page 200
43. C	Page 210
44. C	Page 220
45. A	Page 208
46. B	Page 214
47. D	Page 216
48. C	Page 214
49. B	Page 216
50. A	Page 216
51. C	Page 222
52. C	Page 224
53. C	Page 225
54. B	Page 262
55. A	Page 268
56. C	Page 278
57. B	Page 283

Answer	Section/Page#
58. A	Page 283
59. C	Page 283
60. C	Page 346
61. B	Page 393
62. A	Page 485
63. B	Page 14
64. C	Page 26
65. C	Page 29
66. B	Page 36
67. A	Page 36
68. C	Page 91
69. A	Page 92
70. D	Page 99
71. B	Page 121
72. A	Page 122
73. B	Page 135
74. D	Page 133
75. A	Page 154

Pipe and Excavation Contracting
Questions and Answers

1. A method of projecting a straight line for precise centerline transfer when using a laser is to use _____.

   A. Parallax
   B. Crossing coordinates
   C. Preset hubs
   D. Offset hubs

2. The first priority for underground excavation in any developed area is _____.

   A. Notify all owners
   B. Notify Sunshine
   C. Locate existing ground utilities
   D. Site preparation and material layout

3. When excavating asphalt always allow a swell factor of _____.

   A. 1.7
   B. 1.5
   C. 1.0
   D. .5

4. The fast pumping of ground water will cause _____.

   A. A shallow angle of depression
   B. A deep angle of depression
   C. A cone of depression
   D. Cave in

5. When calculating the force of a ram multiply the area of the piston by the pressure of the _____.

   A. Sheep
   B. Oil
   C. Hydraulic force exertion
   D. Resistance

6. A backhoe is best when working within _____ percent of its maximum digging depth.

    A. 50
    B. 60
    C. 70
    D. 80

7. A slope of .38% equals _____ inches of slope in 250 feet.

    A. 11.4
    B. 95.0
    C. 7.9
    D. 0.9

8. Doubling the pipe diameter of a clay pipe increases carrying capacity _____ times.

    A. 2
    B. 4
    C. 6
    D. 8

9. A common test used to determine if a pipe has flattened or deflected under backfill and compaction is the _____ test.

    A. Mandrake
    B. Pull
    C. Compression
    D. Mandrel

10. The _____ test is not an acceptable method for testing sewer piping.

    A. Lamp
    B. Water
    C. Sniff
    D. Air

11. Testing by isolating portions of the line and filling the manholes with water is known as _____.

    A. Mandrel
    B. Exfiltration
    C. Infiltration
    D. Water

12. The invert elevation of a 400-foot pipe with a fall of .002 and station elevation of 92.6 is _____.

    A. 399.2
    B. 400.8
    C. 93.4
    D. 91.8

13. A six-foot wide sheep foot roller, .75 operator skill, .83 efficiency, 12 inch fill layers compacted to 8 inch layers requiring eight passes of the roller at the speed of 2.5 miles per hour. Using only the given information, according to Pipe and Excavating Contracting, the maximum number of cubic yards is _____.

    A. Less than 155
    B. Between 155 and 160
    C. Between 160 and 165
    D. More than 165

14. A small stake driven into the ground to identify a reference point is known as a _____.

    A. Stake
    B. Hub
    C. Reference grade
    D. Marker

15. The hub's elevation and situation in relation to the pipeline will be on a _____.

    A. Surveyor's sheet
    B. Reference hub
    C. Reference stake
    D. Line marker

16. An elevation of 2,400.08 is referenced on the plans and the C marker is 9.5, The flow line is _____.

    A. 2,390.58
    B. 2,400.08
    C. 2,409.58
    D. 9.5

17. The RP information stake shows 7 feet. The hub is _____.

    A. 7 feet above the pipe
    B. Offset 7 feet from the pipe
    C. Offset 7 feet from the centerline
    D. The flow line is 7 feet below the pipe

18. A telescope is mounted on a tripod is a/an _____.

    A. Level
    B. Laser level
    C. Theodolite
    D. Optical level

19. Information given on a stake can n also be found _____.

    A. On a cut street
    B. In the engineer's notes
    C. In the contact
    D. In the reference

20. The uphill invert is 203.77. The grade is .5 percent. The pipe is 240 feet long. The downhill invert is
    _____.

    A. 202.57
    B. 323.77
    C. 215.77
    D. 191.77

21. The excavation is 15 feet by 36 feet. The corner heights are 15 feet, 13 feet, 7 feet and 19 feet. The excavation is on a hillside. The cubic yards to be excavated is _____.

    A. Less than 200
    B. Between 200 and 250
    C. Between 250
    D. More than 300

22. A hub is a _____.

    A. Wheel support for a tire
    B. Central point of activity
    C. Support for a cap
    D. A small stake driven in the ground

23. Stake information is also available on the _____.

    A. Cut sheet
    B. Field report
    C. Supervisor's log
    D. Test report

24. A .75 percent rise indicates a rise of _____.

    A. 75 feet in 100 feet
    B. 7.5 feet in 100 feet
    C. .75 feet in 100 feet
    D. 75 inches in 100 feet

25. The effect of a charge depends on all of the following except the _____.

      A. Amount of the explosive
      B. Powder of the explosive
      C. Resistance of the explosive
      D. Power of the explosive

26. The advantage of the wheeled backhoe is _____.

      A. It can double as a loader
      B. Most people know how to drive a wheeled backhoe
      C. The large rubber tires provide comfort to the driver
      D. The size of the bucket is not limited

27. Trenches over _____ feet deep should be provided with some kind of cave-in protection.

      A. 4
      B. 5
      C. 8
      D. 10

28. The Proctor test measures the _____.

      A. Relationship of air to moisture
      B. Relationship of the soil to moisture
      C. Relationship between soil's density, its moisture content and the amount of compaction effort needed
      D. Density of the soil

29. The advantage of polyethylene is _____.

      A. Flexibility
      B. Its ease of cutting
      C. The lack of joints
      D. Its compaction factor

30. The base area is 47 feet by 58 feet. Elevations show corner heights of 3 feet, 5 feet, 9 feet and 7 feet. The cubic yards of excavation is _____.

      A. Less than 600
      B. Between 600 and 610
      C. Between 610 and 620
      D. More than 620

31. The most practical maximum range of most lasers is about _____ feet.

      A. 40
      B. 400
      C. 4,000
      D. 40,000

32. The total compactive effort used in the standard Proctor test (AASHTO test) is _____ foot-pounds.

    A. 56,200
    B. 48,250
    C. 18,640
    D. 12,400

33. The water capacity of 18-inch ID pipe per linear foot is _____ gallons.

    A. 35.23
    B. 1902.46
    C. 52.84
    D. 13.21

34. A fast-wheeled backhoe with a 14 ft. hoe in an eight-foot-deep trench with hard dry loam is to be used. _____ equipment cycles per hour will be achieved.

    A. 150
    B. 225
    C. 300
    D. 360

35. A backhoe is used for the following excavation:

Six-foot-deep by 3-foot-wide trench loamy soil conditions
Cycle time is 15 seconds
Machine cycle time 20 seconds
Heaped bucket capacity is 8 loose cubic feet
Ten-foot sets

The linear feet of trench production per hour is _____.

    A. 78.4
    B. 82.6
    C. 91.8
    D. 99.3

36. The rise over a distance of 97 ¾ ft. and a grade of .0090 is _____ inches.

    A. 10
    B. 10 ½
    C. 11
    D. 11 ½

37. A 6-foot sheepsfoot roller is traveling at a speed of 1.25 miles per hour. The 12-inch lifts take 8 passes of the roller for 8-inch compaction. The human efficiency is 83 percent and the operator correction factor is 75 percent. The hourly production is _____.

    A. Less than 30 cubic yards
    B. Between 30 and 60 cubic yards
    C. Between 60 and 90 cubic yards
    D. More than 90 cubic yards

38. The _____ does not determine the rate of flow for a sewer pipe.

    A. Pipe diameter
    B. Pipe material
    C. Slope
    D. Pipe fitting

39. For the _____ test, portions of the line are isolated, and the manholes are filled with water.

    A. Exfiltration
    B. Air
    C. Mandrel
    D. Hydrostatic

40. A wheeled backhoe with a 14' hoe in a four-foot deep trench with hard dry loam is to be used. The cycle time is 12 seconds. _____ equipment cycles per hour will be achieved.

    A. 150
    B. 225
    C. 300
    D. 360

41. A 480' long run of 21" PVC is placed between two manholes. The invert elevation of the pipe at manhole Number One is 100.00'. The grade from the Number Two manhole is .42 percent. The low-end invert has a _____.

    A. 2.01 Fall
    B. 2.01 Rise
    C. .42 Fall
    D. .42 Rise

42. A 300 cubic yard volume of loose soil with a load factor of 0.769 is to be moved. The average hourly production rate to be expected is _____ cubic yards.

    A. 390.1 bank
    B. 390.1 loose
    C. 230.7 bank
    D. 230.7 loose

43. The gallon capacity of 12" 1D pipe per linear foot is _____.

   A. 9.17
   B. 4.07
   C. 2.61
   D. 5.87

44. Bank cubic yards refers to soil that is _____.

   A. Disturbed
   B. Natural
   C. Compacted
   D. Drawing interest

45. Soil that is excavated from its original state, increases in volume due to swell and is called _____.

   A. Loose
   B. Medium consistency
   C. Cycled
   D. Useable

46. Projecting a concentrated beam of light in a straight line for several hundred feet is done with the use of a _____.

   A. Level and Rod
   B. Strong "Q" beam
   C. Reflector
   D. Pipe laser

47. A backhoe is used for the following excavation:

   Four foot deep by 2-foot wide trench
   Moist sandy soil swell conditions of 17 percent
   Cycle time is 12 seconds
   Machine cycle time 15 seconds
   Heaped bucket capacity is 8 loose cubic feet
   Eight-foot sets

   The linear feet of trench production per hour is _____.

   A. 200
   B. 226
   C. 210
   D. 214

48. The advantages of a wheeled backhoe are _____.

   A. Ease of operation and reasonable cost
   B. Ease of operation and use as a loader
   C. Ease of operation and load capability
   D. Easy to maneuver and use as a loader

49. The rise is over a distance of 62 1/2" and a grade of .0030 is _____ inches.

    A. 2
    B. 2 ¼
    C. 2 ½
    D. 2 ¾

50. The Proctor Test is the relationship of all except _____.

    A. Moisture
    B. Density
    C. Repose
    D. Compactive effort

51. A 6-foot-wide sheepsfoot roller travels at 1.25 miles per hour. The 12-inch lifts will be compacted to 8 inches. There will be 8 passes of the roller. Machine efficiency is 83 percent and there is an operator correction factor of 75 percent. Hourly production should be _____ cubic yards.

    A. 115
    B. 102
    C. 51
    D. 77

52. The total compactive effort of the Standard Proctor test is _____ foot-pounds.

    A. 56,200
    B. 48,250
    C. 18,640
    D. 12,400

53. The single cut is good for felling trees up to _____.

    A. 4
    B. 6
    C. 8
    D. 12

54. The effect of a charge depends on all except the _____.

    A. Length of the fuse
    B. Power of the explosive
    C. Resistance encountered
    D. Amount of the explosive

55. The purpose of soil compaction is to _____.

    A. Tighten up
    B. Reduce air voids
    C. Increase stability
    D. Reduce sinking

56. Peter is working in coarse sandy soil. Peter should use _____.

    A. Pumps
    B. Well points
    C. Swales
    D. Drainpipes

57. At Station A (0+40) there is a 12-inch valve. At Station B (3+20) there is a 12-inch tee. At Station C (4+40) there is a 90-degree elbow with a thrust block. The distance between the 12-inch valve and the 90-degree elbow is _____ feet.

    A. 280
    B. 400
    C. 440
    D. 360

58. The "STA" is 3+25. The "EI" is 54.00. The "C" is 8. The reference hub is located next to the information stake. The elevation of the flow line of the pipe is _____.

    A. 46
    B. 51.25
    C. 62
    D. 48

59. _____ is not a function of the control fitting.

    A. Interruption of flow
    B. Ability to gradually increase pressure when required
    C. Reduce water pressure
    D. Shut off flow

60. In a direct tap the corporation stop is _____.

    A. Threaded
    B. Placed at a 45-degree angle to the pipe
    C. Placed at a 90-degree angle to the pipe
    D. Installed with a compression fitting

61. The backhoe operator can make 61 cycles per hour. The trench is 2 feet wide and 7 feet deep. The backhoe has a 1 ½ yard bucket. The hourly production is _____ cubic yards.

    A. 61
    B. 91.5
    C. 320
    D. 480

62. A laser may not be reliable because _____.

    A. They are useful only up to 500 feet
    B. They are useful only up to 200 feet
    C. Temperature and density changes in the air can refract the beam
    D. Dust in the air can cause malfunctions in the equipment

63. A fire hydrant will be likely to have adequate pressure if it _____.

    A. Is the sole outlet on that main
    B. Is at the dead end of the main
    C. Has adequate thrust blocking
    D. Is fed from more than one direction

64. According to *Pipe and Excavation Contracting*, when dewatering a trench, the contractor should _____ to prevent the blockage of a pump's intake hose from drain rock and silt.

I. weld a mesh screen on the end of the last pipe
II. use a dewatering bag
III. filter the water through a baffle tank or sump before it's discharged to the pump

    A. I only
    B. II only
    C. I and II
    D. I and III

65. To reduce pressure in a line, _____ should be used.

    A. Proctor valve
    B. Corporation stop
    C. Force reduction valve
    D. Pressure reducing valve

66. The cone of a manhole is usually _____ feet high.

    A. 1-2
    B. 2-3
    C. 3-4
    D. 5-6

67. A bulldozer going downhill at a 30 percent grade should push _____ of dirt.

    A. Double the normal amount
    B. One half the normal amount
    C. One third the normal amount
    D. 150 percent more

68. The first thing to do upon arriving at the job locale is _____.

    A. Take roll
    B. Locate existing utilities
    C. Notify the building department
    D. Set up traffic cones and barricades

69. An underground utility contractor is preparing a bid for the amount of bedding he will need to fill a trench on a road slide project. In addition to the exact amount required, he always uses a 10% waste factor in calculating his total cost. If the trench is 30 feet long, 3 feet wide and bedding depth of 2 feet, the contractor will require _____ cubic yards of bedding. Select the closest answer.

    A. 7.2
    B. 7.4
    C. 7.6
    D. 7.8

70. Increasing pipe diameter by twice as much increases the capacity by _____ as much.

    A. Twice
    B. Three times
    C. Four times
    D. Eight times

71. Water service lines are generally made of all the following except _____.

    A. Wood
    B. Copper
    C. PVC
    D. CPVC

72. The best way to remove a tree on a utility job is to _____.

    A. Use a backhoe
    B. Hire a tree surgeon
    C. Remove the roots
    D. Use the Humbolt method

73. The best joint to use for immediate use of pipe is the _____.

    A. Flanged
    B. Mechanical
    C. Slip on
    D. Push on

74. A mechanical joint is made up of _____.

    A. Nuts and bolts
    B. Nuts, bolts, followers and a gasket
    C. Gaskets and bolts
    D. Gaskets and followers

75. The difference between a Proctor test and the modified Proctor test is _____.

    A. The modified Proctor test has 3 layers and the standard Proctor test has 5 layers
    B. The modified Proctor test has 5 layers and the standard Proctor test has 3 layers
    C. The standard Proctor test uses a 10 pound hammer
    D. The modified Proctor test uses a 5.5 pound hammer

76. The cone of depression is _____.

    A. The feeling you get when opening your test booklet
    B. The presence of ground water and its behavior
    C. An excavation process used to alleviate undue pressure on the drill
    D. An excavation term describing the burring of drill bits

77. Well point sub jet well holes should be placed at intervals of _____ feet.

    A. 2
    B. 10
    C. 15
    D. 20

78. When the main is under pressure, tapping machines allow the installation of _____.

    A. Stops
    B. Corporation stops
    C. Implants
    D. Water taps

79. A backhoe is most efficient when working within a maximum digging depth of _____.

    A. 60 percent
    B. 70 percent
    C. 6 feet
    D. 7 feet

80. Water mixing with granular soil causing the soil to run is called _____.

    A. Puddling
    B. Flowing sand
    C. Flooding
    D. Blowout

81. The main purpose of an air relief valve is to _____.

    A. Allow easy access to pressure determination
    B. Allow for the monitoring of air pressure
    C. Allow for the escape of air
    D. Provide relief in the event of excess oil

82. The top section of a manhole is the _____.

    A. Cone
    B. Cone of depression
    C. Hub
    D. Lid

83. Laser alignment is especially critical when used in _____.

    A. Large diameter pipe
    B. Medium diameter pipe
    C. Small diameter pipe
    D. Ductile iron pipe

84. The outward force of water pressure on pipe is known as _____.

    A. Pressure
    B. Thrust
    C. Outward pressure
    D. Resultant force

85. The rate of fall is 12 feet per mile. The uphill invert is 26.29. The downhill invert at 2,650 feet is _____.

    A. 26.28
    B. 32.31
    C. 20.27
    D. 6.02

86. The uphill invert is 92.00. The downhill invert is 91.04. The distance from the uphill invert to the downhill invert is 240 feet. The percentage of fall is _____.

    A. .96
    B. 2.3
    C. 4
    D. .4

87. The downhill invert is 36.09. The rate of rise is 6 feet per 225 feet. The pipe is 350 feet long. The percent of rise is _____.

    A. 1.55
    B. 64.28
    C. 2.67
    D. 9.33

88. There is a spoil stack of 1,000 cubic yards of dry loam. The bank cubic yards is _____.

    A. 660
    B. 769
    C. 1,000
    D. 1,350

89. Broad form indemnification holds the _____.

    A. Contractor harmless for negligence of the owner
    B. Owner harmless for negligence of the contractor
    C. Contractor harmless for negligence of the contractor
    D. Owner harmless for negligence of the owner

90. It is standard practice to show horizontal distances in multiples of _____.

    A. 10
    B. 100
    C. 500
    D. 1,000

91. The effect of a charge depends on all except the _____.

    A. Amount of the explosive
    B. Amount of the resistance
    C. Length of the fuse
    D. Power of the explosive

92. An area of sitework where a contractor should be over prepared is _____.

    A. Workers compensation
    B. Drilling insurance
    C. Groundwater knowledge
    D. Hidden utilities

93. Fast pumping at the cone of depression gives a _____ angle of depression.

    A. Steep
    B. Shallow
    C. Flat
    D. Narrow

94. _____ work best in unstable soil.

    A. Steel sheets
    B. Trench boxes
    C. Shoring jacks
    D. Angle of repose

95. _____ is best joint for immediate use.

    A. Mechanical
    B. Push on
    C. Flanged
    D. Slip

96. _____ is not recommended for service lines.

    A. Polyethylene
    B. Galvanized
    C. Copper
    D. Cast iron

97. _____ does not determine the rate of flow.

    A. Diameter
    B. Slope
    C. Material
    D. Pressure

98. A _____ cone is used for shallow manholes.

    A. Depression
    B. Concentric
    C. Eccentric
    D. Steep

99. The point where cut and fill areas meet is known as the _____.

    A. Zero line
    B. Level point
    C. Cumulative point
    D. Base line

100. A pipe one mile long has a downhill slope of .4%. The amount of fall is _____ feet.

    A. 211.2
    B. 21.12
    C. 241.6
    D. 24.16

101. The benchmark is 37.89. A back sight reading of 4.8 is taken. A front swing of 9.8 is also taken. The elevation at the second reading is _____.

    A. 32.89
    B. 52.49
    C. 23.29
    D. 42.89

102. The invert elevation of the pipe is 32.65 at station 0+00. Downhill at station 2+25 the invert elevation assuming a .4 percent grade is _____.

    A. 31.75
    B. 23.65
    C. 32.64
    D. 32.56

103. A pipe has an invert elevation of 32.00. The invert elevation 400 feet downstream is 28.00. The fall or rise in feet of the invert elevation is _____.

    A. 4 feet of rise
    B. 4 feet of fall
    C. 16 feet of rise
    D. 16 feet of fall

104. A pipe has an invert elevation of 42.00. Two hundred feet uphill the invert elevation is 46.00. The rise or fall per loot is _____.

    A. .2 fall
    B. .2 rise
    C. .02 fall
    D. .02 rise

105. A pipe has an invert elevation of 40.00. The invert elevation 450 feet downstream is 36.00. The percentage of fall per foot is _____.

    A. .08
    B. .8
    C. .88
    D. 88

106. The cut stake is + 12.99. The rod reading is 5.26. The difference between the flow line and the top of the pipe is 2.15. The rod reading on top of the pipe opposite the hub is _____.

    A. Less than 16
    B. Between 16 and 16.5
    C. Between 16.5 and 17
    D. More than 17

107. A light, powerful and highly efficient tool to remove trees is the _____.

    A. Bulldozer
    B. Chain saw
    C. Backhoe
    D. Humboldt undercut

108. Wellpoints work well in _____ soil.

    A. Sandy
    B. Clay
    C. Loam
    D. Rock

109. When working in firm soil the best choice of shoring is _____.

    A. A repose angle of 45 degrees
    B. Shoring jacks
    C. Benching
    D. Firm soils do not require shoring

110. The relationship between soil density and moisture is measured by _____.

    A. Gamma rays
    B. The Standard Proctor test
    C. X rays
    D. Weight to volume ratios

111. The outward force of water pressure is called _____.

    A. Thrust
    B. Pressure
    C. Density
    D. PSI

112. The easiest joint to install is the _____.

    A. Roll your own
    B. Push
    C. Pull
    D. Compression

113. The manhole cone is usually _____ feet high.

    A. 2 or 4
    B. 3 or 4
    C. 2 or 3
    D. 5

114. A test used to determine if a pipe has flattened during backfill is the _____ test.

    A. Backfill
    B. The mandrel
    C. The exfiltration
    D. The infiltration

115. A hub is a _____.

    A. Wheel support for a tire
    B. Central point of activity
    C. Support for a cap
    D. A small stake driven in the ground

116. Stake information is also available on the _____.

    A. Cutsheet
    B. Field report
    C. Supervisor's log
    D. Test report

117. A .75 percent rise indicates a rise of _____.

    A. 75 feet in 100 feet
    B. 7.5 feet in 100 feet
    C. .75 feet in 100 feet
    D. .75 inches in 100 feet

118. The effect of a charge depends on all of the following except the _____ of the explosive.

    A. Amount
    B. Powder
    C. Resistance
    D. Power

119. The advantage of the wheeled backhoe is _____.

    A. It can double as a loader
    B. Most people know how to drive a wheeled backhoe
    C. The large rubber tires provide comfort to the driver
    D. The size of the bucket is not limited

120. Trenches over _____ feet deep require some kind of cave-in protection?

    A. 4
    B. 5
    C. 8
    D. 10

121. The Proctor test measures _____.

    A. The relationship of air to moisture
    B. The relationship of soil to moisture
    C. The relationship between soil density, moisture content and compaction effort
    D. The density of the soil

122. The advantage of polyethylene is _____.

    A. Flexibility
    B. Its ease of cutting
    C. The lack of joints
    D. Its compression factor

123. The base area is 47 feet by 58 feet. Elevations show corner heights of 3 feet, 5 feet, 9 feet and 7 feet. The cubic yards of excavation required is _____.

    A. Less than 600
    B. Between 600 and 610
    C. Between 610 and 620
    D. More than 620

124. The practical maximum range of most lasers is _____.

    A. One mile
    B. 600 feet
    C. 400 feet
    D. 250 feet

125. An 8-foot-wide sheepsfoot roller travels 1.5 miles per hour. The 12-inch lifts will be compacted to 6 inches. There will be 4 passes of the roller. Machine efficiency is 83 percent and there is an operator correction factor of 95 percent. Hourly production should be _____ cubic yards.

    A. 293
    B. 243
    C. 463
    D. 231

126. The effect on a charge depends on the _____.

    A. Amount of the explosive
    B. Compaction of the explosive
    C. Length of the fuse
    D. Type of explosive

127. Wellpoint systems work very well in _____.

    A. Sandy soils
    B. Clay soils
    C. Concrete
    D. Low lying areas

128. A common visual test is called _____.

    A. Lamping
    B. Shinning
    C. Mandrel
    D. Mandrake

129. The best way to remove trees is to use _____.

    A. The Humbolt cut
    B. A chainsaw
    C. A backhoe
    D. A bulldozer

130. The invert at Station 5+ 10 is 62.4. The pipe is falling at a rate of .46%. The invert reading at Station 9+10 is _____.

    A. 246.4
    B. 64.24
    C. 60.56
    D. 58.21

131. Pressures in backhoe hydraulic systems usually range from _____ pounds.

    A. 2,000 to 3,000
    B. 1,500 to 5,000
    C. 3,000 to 5,000
    D. 10,000 to 15,000

132. _____ is not a common method for testing pipe.

    A. Lamping
    B. Sounding
    C. Water
    D. Mandrel

133. A station number of 2+80 means the mark is _____.

    A. At elevation 2.80 feet
    B. 2.80 feet from the starting point
    C. 2.80 mile from the starting point
    D. 280 feet from the starting point

134. The manhole invert is +63.7. The rim elevation is +71.35. The distance to the bottom of the manhole is _____.

    A. -7.65
    B. + 7.95
    C. -8.15
    D. + 8.65

135. The ram is most efficient at the _____.

    A. Source of the travel
    B. Middle of the travel
    C. End of the travel
    D. Source of the hydraulics

136. The purpose of the air relief valve is to _____.

    A. Reduce pressure in the line
    B. Allow air to escape from the main line when there is no other escape
    C. Allow air to release from the branch lines
    D. Stabilize the pressure in all the lines

137. The Proctor test with a compaction effort of 12,400 foot pounds is the _____.

    A. Standard Proctor test
    B. Modified Proctor test
    C. Ambivalent Proctor test
    D. Heimlich Proctor Maneuver

138. The best technique for cutting trees 6 inches in diameter or less is the _____.

    A. Humbolt
    B. Single cut
    C. Undercut
    D. Backhoe push

139. Mechanical joints though less likely to come apart than slip joints they still require _____.

    A. Mechanical fasteners
    B. Bonding adhesives
    C. Blocking
    D. Directional boring

140. _____ is not a physical test.

    A. Lamping
    B. Air
    C. Mandrel
    D. Water

141. A tracked backhoe can revolve a total of _____ degrees.

    A. 90
    B. 180
    C. 270
    D. 360

142. A benchmark is a/an _____.

    A. Point of known distance
    B. Point of known elevation
    C. Grade stake gradient
    D. Topographic mark

143. A sheepsfoot roller is 9 feet wide, speed 2.5 mph, thickness of the compacted lift is 9 inches, there will be 5 passes of the roller, operator correction factor is .8. Using a job efficiency factors of 0.83, the compaction output should be _____ cubic yards.

    A. Less than 400
    B. Between 400 and 425
    C. Between 425 and 450
    D. More than 450

144. The first thing to consider when laying pipe is _____.

    A. Safety
    B. Time
    C. Cost
    D. Scheduling

145. _____ not an important relationship when dealing with soils.

    A. Density
    B. Color
    C. Moisture
    D. Amount of compaction effort needed

Please see Answer Key on the following page
2/8/23

Pipe and Excavation Contracting
Questions and Answers
Answer Key

	Answer	Page#	
1.	D	122	
2.	C	137	
3.	A	138	
4.	B	196	
5.	B	143	
6.	C	150	
7.	A	118 – 119	250 X .38% X 12 = 11 .4
8.	B	219	
9.	D	248	
10.	C	248 – 249	
11.	B	249	
12.	D	120	400 X .002 = .8
			92.6 - .8 = 91.8
13.	A	192 – 193	6 x 2.5 x 8 x 16.3 ÷ 8 x 83% x .75 = 152.2
14.	B	113	
15.	C	113	
16.	A	113	2,400.8 – 9.5 = 2,390.58
17.	C	113	
18.	D	114	
19.	A	113	
20.	A	120	240 X .5% Yields 1.2
			203.77 – 1.2 = 202.57
21.	C	256	Average depth X L X W ÷ 27 = cubic yards
			15 + 13 + 7 + 19 ÷ 4 X 36 X 15 ÷ 27 = 270
22.	D	113	
23.	A	113	
24.	C	119	
25.	B	287	
26.	A	149	

	Answer	Page#
27.	B	171
28.	C	183
29.	A	301
30.	B	256

Average depth X L X W ÷ 27 = cubic yards

3 + 5 + 9 + 7 ÷ 4 X 58 X 47 ÷ 27 = 605.7

	Answer	Page#
31.	B	122
32.	D	183
33.	D	207

3.14 x 9 in x 9 in ÷ 144 = 1.766

1.766 x 7.48 = 13.21

Note: Pipe radius is equal to one-half of the pipe diamter

	Answer	Page#
34.	C	65

60 X 60 ÷ 12 = 300

	Answer	Page#
35.	A	146 – 147

Set = length of trench a backhoe can excavate from one position = 10 ft

Swell Factor for loamy soil = 30%

Bank cubic feet = 6 ft x 3 ft x 10 ft (length of set) = 180 ft^3

Loose cubic feet = 6 ft x 3 ft x 10 ft x 1.3 = 234 ft^3

Volume of dirt in set / dirt moved per cycle = digging cycles per set

234 ft^3 / 8 ft^3 = 29.25 digging cycles per set

Digging cycles per set x average cycle time = time required to excavate a set

29.25 x 15 seconds/cycle = 438.75 seconds add 20 seconds to move the machine

438.74 + 20 = 458.75 seconds / 60 seconds per minute = 7.65 minutes

How many sets in a hour = 60 minutes per hour / 7.65 minutes each set = 7.84 sets/hour

7.84 sets/hour x 10 ft per set = 7.84 ft per hour

	Answer	Page#
36.	B	118 – 120

97.75 X .009 X 12 = 10.55"

	Answer	Page#
37.	C	192 – 193

6' wide x 1.25mph x 8" lift x 16.3 = 978

978/8 passes = 122.25 CCY per hr. production rate

122.25 x .83 human efficiency x .75 operator correction = 76.1 CCY hr.

	Answer	Page#
38.	D	219
39.	A	248 – 249
40.	C	65

60 X 60 ÷ 12 = 300

	Answer	Page#
41.	A	120

	Answer	Page#	
42.	C	66	300 X .769 = 230.7
43.	D	207	
44.	B	60	
45.	A	61	
46.	D	121	
47.	B	146 – 147	

Set = length of trench a backhoe can excavate from one position = 8 ft

Swell Factor for sandy soil = 17%

Bank cubic feet = 4 ft x 2 ft x 8 ft (length of set) = 64 ft^3

Loose cubic feet = 4 ft x 2 ft x 8 ft x 1.17 = 74.88 ft^3

Volume of dirt in set / dirt moved per cycle = digging cycles per set

74.88 ft^3 / 8 ft^3 = 9.36 digging cycles per set

Digging cycles per set x average cycle time = time required to excavate a set

9.36 x 12 seconds/cycle = 112.32 seconds add 15 seconds to move the machine

112.32 + 15 = 127.32 seconds / 60 seconds per minute = 2.122 minutes

How many sets in a hour = 60 minutes per hour / 2.122 minutes each set = 28.27 sets/hour

28.27 sets/hour x 8 ft per set = 226.16 ft per hour

48.	D	149	
49.	B	119 – 120	62.5 X .003 X 12 = 2.25'
50.	C	183	
51.	D	192 – 193	6 X 1.25 X 8 X 16.3 ÷ 8 X 83% X 75% Yields 76.1
52.	D	183	
53.	B	132	
54.	A	287	
55.	B	182	
56.	B	294	
57.	B	111	
58.	A	113	54 – 8 = 46
59.	B	316	
60.	A	204	
61.	B	146 – 147	61 X 1.5 = 91.5

	Answer	**Page#**	
62.	C	121	
63.	D	195	
64.	D	292	Note: the question asks both "drain rock and silt"
65.	D	196	
66.	B	245	
67.	D	84	
68.	B	137	
69.	B	60 – 63	(30 ft x 3 ft x 2 ft) $\div$ 27 ft^3 cyd x 1.10 = 7.33 cyd
70.	C	219	
71.	A	298 / 301 / 303 / 308	
72.	A	131	
73.	A	315	
74.	B	315	
75.	B	183	
76.	B	296	
77.	B	293	
78.	B	204	
79.	B	150	
80.	B	291	
81.	C	314	
82.	A	245	
83.	C	244	
84.	B	196	
85.	C	118 – 120	12 $\div$ 5,280 X 2,650 = 6.02
			26.29 – 6.02 = 20.27
86.	D	118 – 120	92 – 91.04 $\div$ 240% Yields .4
87.	C	118 – 120	6 $\div$ 225 X 350 = 9.33 $\div$ 350% Yields 2.67
88.	B	60 – 61	1,000 $\div$ 1.3 = 769
89.	D	52	
90.	B	113	
91.	C	287	
92.	C	290	
93.	A	296	

	Answer	**Page#**	
94.	B	172	
95.	C	315	
96.	D	300	
97.	D	219	
98.	B	246	
99.	A	259	
100.	B	111	5,280 X .4% Yields 21.12'
101.	A	114 – 115	BM + BS – FS = Elevation
102.	A	120	225 X .4 % Yields .9
			32.65 - .9 = 31.75'
103.	B	118/120	32-28 = 4' of Fall
104.	D	118/120	46 – 42 ÷ 200 = .02 Rise
105.	C	118/120	40 – 36 ÷ 450% Yields .88
106.	B	113	5.26 + 12.99 – 2.15 = 16.1
107.	B	132	
108.	A	294	
109.	B	172	
110.	B	183	
111.	A	196	
112.	B	314	
113.	C	245	
114.	B	248	
115.	D	113	
116.	A	113	
117.	C	120	
118.	B	287	
119.	A	149	
120.	B	171	
121.	C	183	
122.	A	301	
123.	B	256	Average depth X L X W ÷ 27 = cubic yards
			58 X 47 X 6 ÷ 27 = 605.7
			3 + 5 + 9 + 7 ÷ 4 = 6

Answer		Page#	
124.	C	122	
125.	D	192 – 193	8 X 1.5 X 6 X 16.3 ÷ 4 X 83% X 95% Yields 231.3
126.	A	287	
127.	A	294	
128.	A	248	
129.	C	131	
130.	C	120	910 – 510 X .46% Yields 1.84
			62.4 – 1.84 = 60.56
131.	A	143	
132.	B	248 – 249	
133.	D	111	
134.	A	111	63.7 – 71.35 = -7.65
135.	B	144	
136.	B	314	
137.	A	183	
138.	B	132	
139.	C	315	
140.	A	248	
141.	D	163	
142.	B	111	
143.	C	192 – 193	9 X 2.5 X 9 X 16.3 ÷ 5 X 83% X .8 = 438.3
144.	A	227	
145.	B	183	

2012 Residential Building Contractor Practice Exam

1. Insulation materials used for wall assemblies, roof assemblies and crawl spaces shall have a MAXIMUM flame spread index of

    1. 25.
    2. 75.
    3. 200.
    4. 300.

2. A detached one- and two-family dwelling in Seismic Design Category D, E or F with a maximum height of 3 stories constructed with stud bearing walls can have plain concrete foundations and basement walls provided the MINIMUM thickness is

    1. 6.5".
    2. 7.0".
    3. 7.5".
    4. 8.0".

3. What is the MINIMUM thickness of a solid masonry wall for a single story dwelling?

    1. 6"
    2. 8"
    3. 10"
    4. 12"

4. What MAXIMUM height off the finished floor can the sill of an emergency egress window be installed?

    1. 44"
    2. 45"
    3. 46"
    4. 47"

5. What is the MINIMUM thickness of foundation walls built with rubble stone?

    1. 12"
    2. 14"
    3. 16"
    4. 18"

6. What is the MINIMUM uniformly distributed live load for a sleeping room in a residential dwelling?

   1. 10 psf
   2. 20 psf
   3. 30 psf
   4. 40 psf

7. What MIMIMUM distance clearance shall be maintained from combustible materials around the outside surfaces of a masonry heater?

   1. 36"
   2. 40"
   3. 44"
   4. 48"

8. A 6 mil vapor retarder shall be installed under which one of the following concrete floors?

   1. Garages
   2. Basement floors
   3. Utility buildings
   4. Accessory structures

9. Exterior insulation finishing systems ("EIFS") when installed on a home shall terminate what MINIMUM distance above the finished ground?

   1. 3"
   2. 4"
   3. 5"
   4. 6"

10. When admixtures are used for water reduction and setting time modification, they shall conform to which one of the following Standards?

   1. ASTM C260
   2. ASTM C494
   3. ASTM C845
   4. ASTM C1017

11. Foam plastic spray insulation applied to a sill plate and header shall have a MAXIMUM thickness of

   1. 2.75".
   2. 3.00".
   3. 3.25".
   4. 3.50".

12. When 29 gage steel siding is installed horizontally, what is the MAXIMUM fastener spacing?

    1. 12"
    2. 14"
    3. 16"
    4. Same as stud spacing

13. What is the MINIMUM width of the material used for lining an open valley on a residential roof?

    1. 18"
    2. 24"
    3. 30"
    4. 36"

14. When handrails are being installed in a residential home, at what height shall the handrails be mounted?

    1. 30" to 34"
    2. 32" to 36"
    3. 33" to 37"
    4. 34" to 38"

15. When a permit application is submitted, what is the MINIMUM number of sets of construction documents required to accompany the application?

    1. 1 set
    2. 2 sets
    3. 3 sets
    4. 4 sets

16. What MINIMUM amount of under-floor space ventilation is required for the area between the floor joists and the earth below with no vapor barrier?

    1. 1 sq. foot for each 100 sq. feet of under-floor area
    2. 1 sq. foot for each 150 sq. feet of under-floor area
    3. 1 sq. foot for each 175 sq. feet of under-floor area
    4. 1 sq. foot for each 200 sq. feet of under-floor area

17. What shall be the MAXIMUM outside diameter of Type I round handrails installed in a dwelling?

    1. 1-1/4"
    2. 1-1/2"
    3. 1-3/4"
    4. 2"

18. What is the net cross-sectional area of a 12" x 16" rectangular flue in a masonry chimney?

    1.   131 sq. inches
    2.   173 sq. inches
    3.   181 sq. inches
    4.   222 sq. inches

19. Weepholes will be provided in the outside wythe of exterior masonry walls with a MAXIMUM spacing of

    1.   27" on center between holes.
    2.   30" on center between holes.
    3.   33" on center between holes.
    4.   36" on center between holes.

20. What MAXIMUM size floor joists can be used for a dwelling before they must be supported laterally with solid blocking or diagonal bridging?

    1.   2" x 6"
    2.   2" x 8"
    3.   2" x 10"
    4.   2" x 12"

21. Water-resistant gypsum board is being used for the ceiling in a shower with 16" on center framing spacing. What is the MINIMUM thickness of gypsum board required?

    1.   3/8"
    2.   1/2"
    3.   5/8"
    4.   3/4"

22. What is the MINIMUM distance that the foundation anchor bolts should be embedded into the concrete or grouted cells of the concrete masonry units?

    1.   6"
    2.   7"
    3.   8"
    4.   9"

23. What MINIMUM thickness roof sheathing should be used when rafters are spaced 24" apart?

    1.   1/2"
    2.   5/8"
    3.   3/4"
    4.   1"

24. What is the MINIMUM thickness of the concrete footings required for a masonry chimney?

    1. 12"
    2. 14"
    3. 16"
    4. 18"

25. Fire escapes shall be designed to what MINIMUM amount uniformly distributed live load?

    1. 10 psf
    2. 20 psf
    3. 30 psf
    4. 40 psf

26. What MINIMUM distance above finished grade shall a concrete or masonry foundation extend at all points?

    1. 3"
    2. 4"
    3. 5"
    4. 6"

27. What is the MINIMUM nominal thickness in the least dimension for wood framing supporting gypsum board?

    1. 1"
    2. 2"
    3. 3"
    4. 4"

28. When glazing is used in walls, enclosures or fences of saunas, whirlpools and hot tubs, if the bottom of the exposed edge of the glazing is located less than what MINIMUM distance (measured vertically) above the standing surface, it shall be considered a hazardous location.

    1. 48"
    2. 54"
    3. 60"
    4. 66"

29. What is the MINIMUM nominal size wood column used for support in a residential house?

    1. 4" x 4"
    2. 4" x 6"
    3. 6" x 6"
    4. 6" x 8"

30. What is the MAXIMUM span of a 2" x 10" Southern pine #1 grade floor joist used for a residential sleeping area with joist spacing of 16" and a dead load of 20 psf?

    1. 14' 4"
    2. 15' 2"
    3. 16' 1"
    4. 17' 11"

31. What is the MAXIMUM smoke-developed index for 6" thick foam plastic insulation?

    1. 350
    2. 400
    3. 450
    4. 500

32. What is the MINIMUM thickness of a masonry chimney wall built with solid masonry units or hollow units filled with grout?

    1. 4"
    2. 6"
    3. 8"
    4. 10"

33. When drilling or notching a top plate more than 50% of its width, a galvanized metal tie shall be fastened across the opening and shall have a MINIMUM width of

    1. 1".
    2. 1-1/4".
    3. 1-1/2".
    4. 2".

34. Mechanical and gravity outdoor air intakes shall be located what MINIMUM distance from any hazardous or noxious contaminants?

    1. 10 feet
    2. 15 feet
    3. 20 feet
    4. 25 feet

35. All of the following information should be included in roof truss design drawings EXCEPT the

    1. location of all joints.
    2. name of designer and license number.
    3. required bearing widths.
    4. lumber size, species and grade for each member.

36. How many coats of exterior portland cement plaster shall be required when applied over metal lath?

    1. Not less than 2 coats
    2. Not less than 3 coats
    3. Not less than 4 coats
    4. Not less than 5 coats

37. A dwelling unit separation wall between townhouses that has no plumbing, mechanical, ducts or vents in the wall shall be a MINIMUM

    1. 1.0 hour fire-resistance rated wall.
    2. 1.5 hour fire-resistance rated wall.
    3. 2.0 hour fire-resistance rated wall.
    4. 2.5 hour fire-resistance rated wall.

38. What is the MINIMUM size access opening through a perimeter wall to the under-floor areas of a residential house?

    1. 16" x 24"
    2. 18" x 26"
    3. 20" x 30"
    4. 22" x 36"

39. What MINIMUM number of fasteners shall be used per wood shake when attached to the roof sheathing?

    1. 1 fastener
    2. 2 fasteners
    3. 3 fasteners
    4. 4 fasteners

40. In a building when making the truss to bearing wall connection, what number and size of screws should be used in each truss?

    1. 1 No. 8 screw
    2. 2 No. 8 screws
    3. 1 No. 10 screw
    4. 2 No. 10 screws

41. What is the MINIMUM thickness of standard unit glass masonry blocks for wall construction?

    1. 3"
    2. 3-1/8"
    3. 3-7/8"
    4. 4"

42. When an emergency situation requires the replacement or repair of equipment, how soon must the permit application be submitted to the building official?

    1. Within the next working day
    2. Within 2 working days
    3. Within 3 working days
    4. Within 4 working days

43. If ambient temperatures on a job are above or below the recommended temperature for placing and curing concrete, a record shall be kept of the protection used for the concrete. What is the temperature range?

    1. 35°F to 90°F
    2. 40°F to 95°F
    3. 45°F to 90°F
    4. 50°F to 95°F

44. What is the MAXIMUM spacing between screws on 1/2" gypsum used for wall board without adhesive and studs that are 24" on center?

    1. 10"
    2. 12"
    3. 14"
    4. 16"

45. Each end of a ceiling joist or rafter that is bearing on a concrete or masonry surface shall have what MINIMUM amount of bearing on that surface?

    1. 1-1/2"
    2. 2"
    3. 2-1/2"
    4. 3"

46. Wood foundation walls below grade shall have a moisture barrier installed. What thickness polyethylene film should be applied?

    1. 3 mil
    2. 4 mil
    3. 6 mil
    4. 8 mil

47. What type of valley lining material has a MINIMUM thickness of 0.027"?

1. Aluminum
2. Copper
3. Lead
4. Zinc alloy

48. Which one of the following building projects is required to have a permit?

1. New deck, 300 square feet and 5 feet off the ground
2. New one story accessory building, 180 square feet
3. New privacy fence, 6 feet tall
4. New retaining wall, 2.5 feet tall

49. What is the MINIMUM thickness lumber used for floor sheathing when joist or beam spacing is 16" and sheathing is installed diagonal to the joist?

1. 1/2"
2. 5/8"
3. 3/4"
4. 11/16"

50. Light-weight concrete shall contain aggregate that meets the density specifications determined by

1. ASTM C33.
2. ASTM C330.
3. ASTM C496.
4. ASTM C567.

51. What is the MINIMUM ceiling height for a bathroom in a residential home?

1. 6' 6"
2. 6' 7"
3. 6' 8"
4. 6' 9"

52. Which of the following jobs requires the contractor get a permit for the work?

1. Fences less than 7 feet tall
2. Retaining walls not over 4 feet tall
3. One-story detached accessory buildings less than 200 sq. feet
4. Installing a new shingle roof

53. What is the MAXIMUM allowed length of a building built with structural insulated panel ("SIP") construction?

    1. 60 feet
    2. 70 feet
    3. 80 feet
    4. 90 feet

54. What is the MINIMUM depth of a masonry or concrete fireplace firebox?

    1. 18"
    2. 19"
    3. 20"
    4. 21"

55. A window well used for emergency escape and rescue shall have a permanently affixed ladder if the vertical depth is greater than

    1. 40".
    2. 44".
    3. 48".
    4. 52".

56. What is the MINIMUM size access opening to the attic of a dwelling with a combustible ceiling?

    1. 22" x 30"
    2. 24" x 30"
    3. 30" x 30"
    4. 30" x 36"

57. What is stamped on construction documents after they have been reviewed by the building department?

    1. "Accepted for Code Compliance"
    2. "Reviewed for Code Compliance"
    3. "Processed for Code Compliance"
    4. "Approved for Code Compliance"

58. What is the MINIMUM size vertical attachment flange required for a weep screed used for an exterior plaster wall?

    1. 2.5"
    2. 3.0"
    3. 3.5"
    4. 4.0"

59. Cement and what two types of mortar are approved for filling the cellular spaces in isolated piers to support beams and girders?

　　1.　Type O or Type S
　　2.　Type N or Type O
　　3.　Type M or Type N
　　4.　Type M or Type S

60. A dwelling that contains two-family dwelling units shall have what type of wall separation between units?

　　1.　30-minute fire-resistance rating
　　2.　1-hour fire-resistance rating
　　3.　90-minute fire-resistance rating
　　4.　2-hour fire-resistance rating

61. What size corrosion-resistant mesh screen shall be used for protecting exterior air intakes supplying combustion air to a fireplace?

　　1.　1/16"
　　2.　1/8"
　　3.　1/4"
　　4.　3/8"

62. How long shall the building department maintain construction documents after the project is completed?

　　1.　90 days
　　2.　180 days
　　3.　240 days
　　4.　360 days

63. What is the MAXIMUM slope that can be used for the construction of residential ramps?

　　1.　1 unit vertical in 9 units horizontal
　　2.　1 unit vertical in 10 units horizontal
　　3.　1 unit vertical in 11 units horizontal
　　4.　1 unit vertical in 12 units horizontal

64. When a building foundation is built with wood, what MINIMUM size studs are used for the foundation walls?

　　1.　2" x 4"
　　2.　2" x 6"
　　3.　2" x 8"
　　4.　2" x 10"

65. Wood shingle roofs shall have an ice barrier that extends from the roof edge to what MINIMUM distance inside the exterior wall line?

    1. 18"
    2. 24"
    3. 30"
    4. 36"

66. In areas of the country where snow is a factor on concrete and clay roof tiles, what MINIMUM amount of fasteners are required on each tile?

    1. 1 fastener
    2. 2 fasteners
    3. 3 fasteners
    4. 4 fasteners

67. What is the MAXIMUM flame spread index allowed for fire-retardant-treated wood used for roof framing?

    1. 10
    2. 15
    3. 20
    4. 25

68. Each dwelling unit shall be provided with at least one egress door that has a MINIMUM clear height of

    1. 76" and shall not require a key to open.
    2. 78" and shall not require a key to open.
    3. 80" and shall not require a key to open.
    4. 82" and shall not require a key to open.

69. What is the MINIMUM height of a parapet from the point it intersects with the sloped roof's surface to the top of the parapet?

    1. 24"
    2. 30"
    3. 36"
    4. 42"

70. What is the MAXIMUM square footage of an accessory structure located on the same lot as a residence?

    1. 1,000 sq. feet
    2. 2,000 sq. feet
    3. 3,000 sq. feet
    4. 4,000 sq. feet

71. What MINIMUM distance above the top of the fireplace opening shall the ferrous metal damper be located on a masonry fireplace?

    1. 6"
    2. 8"
    3. 10"
    4. 12"

72. What is the MINIMUM amount of clearance required in front of a water closet in a residential home?

    1. 21"
    2. 22"
    3. 23"
    4. 24"

73. When installing a foundation on Soil Group I, Soil Classification SM, comprised of silty sands and sand-silt mixtures, what is the frost heave characteristic of this type of soil?

    1. Unsatisfactory
    2. Poor
    3. Good
    4. Medium

74. A truss design drawing must be submitted and approved before the trusses are installed. Who receives the truss design drawings?

    1. Building official
    2. Building contractor
    3. Testing agency
    4. Plans examiner

75. Precast wall panels shall have a MINIMUM of two ties per panel with a nominal tensile strength of

    1. 10,000 lbs. per tie.
    2. 15,000 lbs. per tie.
    3. 20,000 lbs. per tie.
    4. 25,000 lbs. per tie.

76. What is the MINIMUM thickness of slab-on-ground concrete floors supported directly on the ground?

    1. 3"
    2. 3.5"
    3. 4"
    4. 4.5"

77. What is the MAXIMUM thickness of stone veneer that is installed over a backing of wood or cold-formed steel?

    1. 4"
    2. 5"
    3. 6"
    4. 7"

78. What is the MINIMUM tread depth that can be used for a residential stairway?

    1. 8 inches
    2. 9 inches
    3. 10 inches
    4. 11 inches

79. All of the following cast-in-place construction activities are covered under the ACI 318 Structural Concrete Building Code EXCEPT

    1. footings.
    2. foundation walls.
    3. tanks.
    4. slabs-on-ground for dwellings.

80. Interior spaces intended for human occupancy shall have a heating system capable of maintaining what level of temperature measured 3 feet off the floor?

    1. 68°F
    2. 69°F
    3. 70°F
    4. 71°F

81. What MINIMUM amount of fasteners shall be used on a roofing strip shingle?

    1. 2 fasteners
    2. 3 fasteners
    3. 4 fasteners
    4. 5 fasteners

82. Openings in exterior masonry veneer shall have additional ties used around the openings when the size of the openings exceed

    1. 14" in either direction.
    2. 16" in either direction.
    3. 18" in either direction.
    4. 20" in either direction.

83. What size floor joist shall be used when joist spacing is 24" with #2 Hem-fir wood and a dead load of 20 psf to achieve a 12 foot span used for a residential living area?

    1. 2" x 6"
    2. 2" x 8"
    3. 2" x 10"
    4. 2" x 12"

84. Where shall the permit for a job be kept until the job is completed?

    1. In the contractor's office
    2. In the contractor's truck
    3. On the job site
    4. At city hall

85. What MINIMUM distance shall a wall tie be embedded in the mortar joints of solid masonry units?

    1. 3/4"
    2. 1-3/8"
    3. 1-1/2"
    4. 1-5/8"

86. Glass unit masonry panels shall be provided with expansion joints along the top, bottom and sides at all structural supports. What is the MINIMUM thickness of the expansion joints?

    1. 1/4"
    2. 3/8"
    3. 1/2"
    4. 5/8"

87. A cold formed 33 KSI steel floor joist with the designation of 1000S162-54 is being used for a building having a live load of 30 psf and a joist spacing of 24". What is the MAXIMUM distance the joist can span?

    1. 16' 8"
    2. 17' 3"
    3. 18' 6"
    4. 19' 9"

88. What type of separation is required between a garage and all habitable rooms located above the garage?

    1. 1/2" gypsum board or equivalent
    2. 1/2" Type X gypsum board or equivalent
    3. 5/8" gypsum board or equivalent
    4. 5/8" Type X gypsum board or equivalent

89. When admixtures are used in producing flowing concrete, they shall conform to which of the following Standards?

    1. ASTM C260
    2. ASTM C494
    3. ASTM C845
    4. ASTM C1017

90. Particle board used for floor underlayment shall conform to Type PBU and shall have a MINIMUM thickness of

    1. 1/4".
    2. 3/8".
    3. 1/2".
    4. 5/8".

91. How long before a permit becomes null and void if work is not started?

    1. 90 days
    2. 120 days
    3. 180 days
    4. 360 days

92. A double top plate shall have end joints offset at what MINIMUM distance?

    1. 18"
    2. 24"
    3. 30"
    4. 36"

93. Concrete used for basement walls that are exposed to moderate weather shall have what MINIMUM strength?

    1. 2,500 lbs.
    2. 2,800 lbs.
    3. 3,000 lbs.
    4. 3,200 lbs.

94. What is the MAXIMUM height for a riser on a residential stairway?

    1. 7"
    2. 7.25"
    3. 7.5"
    4. 7.75"

95. Concrete walls constructed with a thickness of more than 10" shall have reinforcement placed in 2 layers in both directions and also 2 bars. What size bars shall be used?

    1. No. 3 bars
    2. No. 4 bars
    3. No. 5 bars
    4. No. 6 bars

96. What MINIMUM amount of glazing is required to give a room natural light?

    1. 6% of the floor area of the room served
    2. 8% of the floor area of the room served
    3. 10% of the floor area of the room served
    4. 12% of the floor area of the room served

97. What is the MINIMUM lumber framing material recommended for structural insulated panel ("SIP") walls?

    1. No. 2 Southern pine
    2. No. 2 Hem-fir
    3. No. 2 Douglas-fir-larch
    4. No. 2 Spruce-pine-fir

98. The doubled cantilevered joists used for the cantilever of the first floor of a one story building shall extend what MINIMUM distance toward the inside of the building?

    1. 5 feet
    2. 6 feet
    3. 7 feet
    4. 8 feet

99. When installing glass unit masonry, what is the required thickness of the bed and head joints?

    1. 1/4"
    2. 3/8"
    3. 1/2"
    4. 5/8"

100. A kitchen is required in each dwelling unit. What is required to be installed in every kitchen?

    1. Stove
    2. Sink
    3. Range
    4. Refrigerator

101. Hallways in homes are used for egress. What is the MINIMUM allowed width of hallways?

    1. 34"
    2. 35"
    3. 36"
    4. 37"

102. When digging exterior footings, what is the MINIMUM distance a footing shall be placed below undisturbed soil?

    1. 12"
    2. 16"
    3. 20"
    4. 24"

103. When a crawl space is located under a floor that is not insulated, the crawl space walls shall be insulated from the floor down to the finished grade and an additional

    1. 20".
    2. 22".
    3. 24".
    4. 26".

104. When installing a foundation on Soil Group III, Soil Classification CH, comprised of inorganic clays of high plasticity or fat clays, what is the drainage characteristic of this type of soil?

    1. Unsatisfactory
    2. Poor
    3. Medium
    4. Good

105. What is the MAXIMUM amount of roof eave projection for a detached garage located within 2 feet of a lot line?

    1. 4"
    2. 6"
    3. 8"
    4. 10"

106. Exterior concrete that is exposed to the freezing-and-thawing cycle is listed as a Category F concrete. Which class of Category F concrete is exposed to the freezing-and-thawing cycles and in continuous contact with moisture?

    1. F0
    2. F1
    3. F2
    4. F3

107. All of the following steel roof framing members should be attached with No. 10 screws EXCEPT

    1. roof sheathing to rafters.
    2. truss to bearing wall.
    3. gable end truss to endwall top track.
    4. ceiling joist to top track of load-bearing wall.

108. Masonry chimneys shall have a cleanout located what distance from the base of each flue?

    1. 2"
    2. 4"
    3. 6"
    4. 8"

109. What is the MINIMUM clear width of a spiral stairway at and below the railing in a residential home?

    1. 25"
    2. 26"
    3. 27"
    4. 29"

110. All of the following masonry units can be used for load bearing construction EXCEPT

    1. clay.
    2. cement.
    3. solid.
    4. glass.

111. On what MINIMUM design roof slope can a liquid-applied roofing material be installed?

    1. One-eighth unit vertical in 12 units horizontal
    2. One-fourth unit vertical in 12 units horizontal
    3. One-third unit vertical in 12 units horizontal
    4. One-half unit vertical in 12 units horizontal

112. Wood foundations built in soil that is Class II, III and IV shall be equipped with a drainage system including a sump that is installed at least

  1. 24" below the bottom of the basement floor.
  2. 26" below the bottom of the basement floor.
  3. 28" below the bottom of the basement floor.
  4. 30" below the bottom of the basement floor.

113. In ceilings that do not have an attic space, what is the MINIMUM amount of insulation that will be required?

  1. R-26
  2. R-28
  3. R-30
  4. R-32

114. When a cold formed steel framed wall is being attached to a foundation by anchor bolts, the anchor bolts shall extend a MINIMUM of

  1. 12" into a masonry foundation.
  2. 13" into a masonry foundation.
  3. 14" into a masonry foundation.
  4. 15" into a masonry foundation.

115. What MINIMUM distance shall be maintained between adhered masonry veneer and a paved surface area?

  1. 1"
  2. 2"
  3. 3"
  4. 4"

116. Foam plastic insulation used for thermal insulating or acoustic purposes shall have a MINIMUM density of

  1. 10 pounds per cubic foot.
  2. 15 pounds per cubic foot.
  3. 20 pounds per cubic foot.
  4. 25 pounds per cubic foot.

117. What is the MAXIMUM cantilever span for a floor joist supporting an exterior balcony using 2" x 10" members with 16" spacing and a ground snow load of 50 psf?

    1. 39"
    2. 49"
    3. 54"
    4. 67"

118. Masonry fireplaces shall have the firebox lined with fire brick that has a MINIMUM thickness of

    1. 1-1/4".
    2. 1-1/2". ·
    3. 1-3/4".
    4. 2".

119. Structures built with an unvented under-the-floor crawl space shall have a Class 1 vapor barrier installed over the exposed earth. There is a second requirement for ventilation of the crawl space which can be a continuously operating mechanical exhaust system or a conditioned air supply. What rate of flow shall be needed to meet the ventilation requirement of exhaust or supply?

    1. 1 cubic foot per minute flow per 20 sq. ft. of floor area.
    2. 1 cubic foot per minute flow per 30 sq. ft. of floor area.
    3. 1 cubic foot per minute flow per 40 sq. ft. of floor area.
    4. 1 cubic foot per minute flow per 50 sq. ft. of floor area.

120. What is the MAXIMUM span of a 2" x 8" Hem-fir SS grade ceiling joist used for a residential living area and joist spacing of 16" with a live load of 40 psf and a dead load of 10 psf?

    1. 11' 11"
    2. 12' 0"
    3. 12' 10"
    4. 13' 4"

121. What shall be the MINIMUM fire separation distance for exterior walls with a 0 hour fire-resistance rating?

    1. $\geq$ 3 feet
    2. $\geq$ 4 feet
    3. $\geq$ 5 feet
    4. $\geq$ 6 feet

122. How long shall the records of concrete inspection be kept by the inspecting engineer or architect after the project is completed?

    1. 6 months
    2. 1 year
    3. 1.5 years
    4. 2 years

123. What MINIMUM clearance is required for all combustible materials including wood beams, joists and studs from the front faces and sides of masonry fireplaces?

    1. 2" clearance
    2. 3" clearance
    3. 4" clearance
    4. 5" clearance

124. The base flashings used against a vertical sidewall shall direct water away from the sidewall and be continuous or step design. What is the MINIMUM size of the flashing?

    1. 3" x 3"
    2. 4" x 4"
    3. 5" x 5"
    4. 6" x 6"

125. When a window greater than 16" in either dimension is located in a wall with a masonry veneer, the metal ties around the perimeter of the opening shall be placed within

    1. 12" of the wall opening.
    2. 14" of the wall opening.
    3. 16" of the wall opening.
    4. 18" of the wall opening.

126. In Seismic Design Categories D_0, D_1 and D_2, what size vertical reinforcement bar should be used for masonry stem walls?

    1. No. 3
    2. No. 4
    3. No. 5
    4. No. 6

127. How many and what type of fastener should be used to secure the following roof element: ceiling joists to plate?

    1. 3 - 6d common, toe nailed
    2. 3 - 8d common, toe nailed
    3. 3 - 10d common, toe nailed
    4. 3 - 16d common, toe nailed

128. Grade No. 2 wood shingles that are 24" length and installed on a 3:12 pitch roof shall have how much weather exposure?

    1. 4.5"
    2. 5.0"
    3. 5.5"
    4. 6.0"

129. What is the MINIMUM net clear opening square footage required for an emergency escape and rescue opening?

    1. 5.7 sq. feet
    2. 5.8 sq. feet
    3. 5.9 sq. feet
    4. 5.10 sq. feet

130. What size ceiling joist shall be used when rafter spacing is 16" on center and has a dead load of 10 psf with #1 Southern pine to achieve a span of 20 feet for uninhabitable attics without storage?

    1. 2" x 4"
    2. 2" x 6"
    3. 2" x 8"
    4. 2" x 10"

131. What is the MAXIMUM spacing between lateral ties used for reinforcement in a masonry column?

    1. 6"
    2. 8"
    3. 10"
    4. 12"

132. Every dwelling built shall have at least one habitable room with MINIMUM square footage of

    1. 100 sq. feet.
    2. 110 sq. feet.
    3. 120 sq. feet.
    4. 130 sq. feet.

133. Wood roof shakes that are preservative-treated taper sawn, made of No. 1 Southern Yellow Pine, and are 24" long shall have an exposure on a MINIMUM 4:12 roof of

1. 5-1/2".
2. 7-1/2".
3. 10".
4. 12".

134. All of the following information shall be included on the Certificate of Occupancy EXCEPT the

1. building permit number.
2. name of the building official.
3. address of the dwelling.
4. legal description of the property.

135. What is the MINIMUM thickness of aluminum used for valley lining material?

1. 0.0162"
2. 0.0179"
3. 0.024"
4. 0.027"

136. If a permit extension is granted to the permit holder, how long is each extension good for?

1. 30 days
2. 60 days
3. 90 days
4. 180 days

137. Exterior masonry veneer that is anchored with metal strand wire ties shall have an air space between the veneer and the sheathing. What is the MAXIMUM allowed amount of air space?

1. 3.0"
2. 3-1/2"
3. 4.0"
4. 4-1/2"

138. Fire-retardant-treated lumber used for roof framing shall use chemicals in a closed vessel pressure process with a MINIMUM of

1. 30 psig.
2. 40 psig.
3. 50 psig.
4. 60 psig.

139. Footings that are poured on piles shall be what MINIMUM depth above the bottom reinforcement?

    1. 6"
    2. 8"
    3. 10"
    4. 12"

140. A skylight on a roof sloped less than a 3:12 pitch shall be mounted on what MINIMUM height curb above the roof?

    1. 2"
    2. 4"
    3. 6"
    4. 8"

141. What is the MINIMUM length of a hearth extension on a fireplace with an opening of 6 square feet or larger?

    1. 16" in front of the fireplace
    2. 18" in front of the fireplace
    3. 20" in front of the fireplace
    4. 22" in front of the fireplace

142. What MINIMUM lap is required when installing horizontal fiber cement siding?

    1. 1"
    2. 1.25"
    3. 1.50"
    4. 1.75"

143. What is the MAXIMUM length of glass sections used in louvered windows or jalousies?

    1. 48"
    2. 52"
    3. 56"
    4. 60"

144. What is the MINIMUM square footage of a manufactured home when completely erected on site?

    1. 300 sq. feet
    2. 320 sq. feet
    3. 340 sq. feet
    4. 360 sq. feet

145. What is the MINIMUM nominal thickness for concrete wall members that are vertical or horizontal and made with a waffle-grid wall system?

    1. 4"
    2. 6"
    3. 8"
    4. 10"

146. A permanent wood foundation built for a crawl space shall have a base of gravel or crushed stone under the footing with a MINIMUM thickness of

    1. 3".
    2. 4".
    3. 5".
    4. 6".

147. What is the MINIMUM height that nonabsorbent walls shall extend above the floor of a shower?

    1. 5 feet
    2. 5.5 feet
    3. 6 feet
    4. 6.5 feet

148. What is the MAXIMUM length of an eave overhang on a residential home when measured horizontally?

    1. 20"
    2. 24"
    3. 28"
    4. 32"

149. What is the MINIMUM lap amount for horizontal lap siding that is rabbeted?

    1. 0.5"
    2. 0.75"
    3. 1.0"
    4. 1.5"

150. Metal shingle roofs shall have an ice barrier that consists of two layers of underlayment cemented together that extends from the roof edge to what MINIMUM distance inside the exterior wall line?

    1. 18"
    2. 20"
    3. 24"
    4. 30"

**The next section contains the Practice Exam
with Correct Answers and code reference locations**

CORRECT ANSWER KEYS

1. Key 1	39. Key 2	77. Key 2	115. Key 2
2. Key 3	40. Key 4	78. Key 3	116. Key 3
3. Key 1	41. Key 3	79. Key 3	117. Key 2
4. Key 1	42. Key 1	80. Key 1	118. Key 4
5. Key 3	43. Key 2	81. Key 3	119. Key 4
6. Key 3	44. Key 2	82. Key 2	120. Key 3
7. Key 1	45. Key 4	83. Key 4	121. Key 3
8. Key 2	46. Key 3	84. Key 3	122. Key 4
9. Key 4	47. Key 4	85. Key 3	123. Key 1
10. Key 2	48. Key 1	86. Key 2	124. Key 2
11. Key 3	49. Key 2	87. Key 3	125. Key 1
12. Key 4	50. Key 4	88. Key 4	126. Key 1
13. Key 2	51. Key 3	89. Key 3	127. Key 2
14. Key 4	52. Key 4	90. Key 1	128. Key 3
15. Key 2	53. Key 1	91. Key 3	129. Key 1
16. Key 2	54. Key 3	92. Key 2	130. Key 3
17. Key 4	55. Key 2	93. Key 3	131. Key 2
18. Key 1	56. Key 1	94. Key 4	132. Key 3
19. Key 3	57. Key 2	95. Key 3	133. Key 3
20. Key 4	58. Key 3	96. Key 2	134. Key 4
21. Key 3	59. Key 4	97. Key 4	135. Key 3
22. Key 2	60. Key 2	98. Key 2	136. Key 4
23. Key 2	61. Key 3	99. Key 1	137. Key 4
24. Key 1	62. Key 2	100. Key 2	138. Key 3
25. Key 4	63. Key 4	101. Key 3	139. Key 4
26. Key 2	64. Key 2	102. Key 1	140. Key 2
27. Key 2	65. Key 2	103. Key 3	141. Key 3
28. Key 3	66. Key 2	104. Key 2	142. Key 2
29. Key 1	67. Key 4	105. Key 1	143. Key 1
30. Key 4	68. Key 2	106. Key 3	144. Key 2
31. Key 3	69. Key 2	107. Key 1	145. Key 2
32. Key 1	70. Key 3	108. Key 3	146. Key 4
33. Key 3	71. Key 2	109. Key 2	147. Key 3
34. Key 1	72. Key 1	110. Key 4	148. Key 2
35. Key 2	73. Key 4	111. Key 2	149. Key 1
36. Key 2	74. Key 1	112. Key 1	150. Key 3
37. Key 1	75. Key 1	113. Key 3	
38. Key 1	76. Key 2	114. Key 4	

Practice Exam with
Correct Answers and Code Book Reference

1. Insulation materials used for wall assemblies, roof assemblies and crawl spaces shall have a MAXIMUM flame spread index of

    1. 25.
    2. 75.
    3. 200.
    4. 300.

Key 1   Ref-2012 IRC R302.10.1

2. A detached one- and two-family dwelling in Seismic Design Category D, E or F with a maximum height of 3 stories constructed with stud bearing walls can have plain concrete foundations and basement walls provided the MINIMUM thickness is

    1. 6.5".
    2. 7.0".
    3. 7.5".
    4. 8.0".

Key 3   Ref-2011 ACI 318 22.10.1(c)

3. What is the MINIMUM thickness of a solid masonry wall for a single story dwelling?

    1. 6"
    2. 8"
    3. 10"
    4. 12"

Key 1   Ref-2012 IRC R606.2.1

4. What MAXIMUM height off the finished floor can the sill of an emergency egress window be installed?

    1. 44"
    2. 45"
    3. 46"
    4. 47"

Key 1   Ref-2012 IRC R310.1

5. What is the MINIMUM thickness of foundation walls built with rubble stone?

    1. 12"
    2. 14"
    3. 16"
    4. 18"

Key 3   Ref-2012 IRC R404.1.8

6. What is the MINIMUM uniformly distributed live load for a sleeping room in a residential dwelling?

    1. 10 psf
    2. 20 psf
    3. 30 psf
    4. 40 psf

Key 3   Ref-2012 IRC Table R301.5

7. What MIMIMUM distance clearance shall be maintained from combustible materials around the outside surfaces of a masonry heater?

    1. 36"
    2. 40"
    3. 44"
    4. 48"

Key 1   Ref-2012 IRC R1002.5

8. A 6 mil vapor retarder shall be installed under which one of the following concrete floors?

    1. Garages
    2. Basement floors
    3. Utility buildings
    4. Accessory structures

Key 2   Ref-2012 IRC R506.2.3

9. Exterior insulation finishing systems ("EIFS") when installed on a home shall terminate what MINIMUM distance above the finished ground?

    1. 3"
    2. 4"
    3. 5"
    4. 6"

Key 4   Ref-2012 IRC R703.9.4.1

10. When admixtures are used for water reduction and setting time modification, they shall conform to which one of the following Standards?

    1. ASTM C260
    2. ASTM C494
    3. ASTM C845
    4. ASTM C1017

Key 2   Ref-2011 ACI 318   3.6.1

11. Foam plastic spray insulation applied to a sill plate and header shall have a MAXIMUM thickness of

    1. 2.75".
    2. 3.00".
    3. 3.25".
    4. 3.50".

Key 3   Ref-2012 IRC R316.5.11

12. When 29 gage steel siding is installed horizontally, what is the MAXIMUM fastener spacing?

    1. 12"
    2. 14"
    3. 16"
    4. Same as stud spacing

Key 4   Ref-2012 IRC Table R703.4

13. What is the MINIMUM width of the material used for lining an open valley on a residential roof?

    1. 18"
    2. 24"
    3. 30"
    4. 36"

Key 2   Ref-2012 IRC R905.2.8.2(1)

14. When handrails are being installed in a residential home, at what height shall the handrails be mounted?

    1. 30" to 34"
    2. 32" to 36"
    3. 33" to 37"
    4. 34" to 38"

Key 4   Ref-2012 IRC R311.7.8.1

15. When a permit application is submitted, what is the MINIMUM number of sets of construction documents required to accompany the application?

    1. 1 set
    2. 2 sets
    3. 3 sets
    4. 4 sets

Key 2   Ref-2012 IRC R106.1

16. What MINIMUM amount of under-floor space ventilation is required for the area between the floor joists and the earth below with no vapor barrier?

    1. 1 sq. foot for each 100 sq. feet of under-floor area
    2. 1 sq. foot for each 150 sq. feet of under-floor area
    3. 1 sq. foot for each 175 sq. feet of under-floor area
    4. 1 sq. foot for each 200 sq. feet of under-floor area

Key 2   Ref-2012 IRC R408.1

17. What shall be the MAXIMUM outside diameter of Type I round handrails installed in a dwelling?

    1. 1-1/4"
    2. 1-1/2"
    3. 1-3/4"
    4. 2"

Key 4   Ref-2012 IRC R311.7.8.3

18. What is the net cross-sectional area of a 12" x 16" rectangular flue in a masonry chimney?

    1. 131 sq. inches
    2. 173 sq. inches
    3. 181 sq. inches
    4. 222 sq. inches

Key 1   Ref-2012 IRC Table R1003.14(2)

19. Weepholes will be provided in the outside wythe of exterior masonry walls with a MAXIMUM spacing of

    1. 27" on center between holes.
    2. 30" on center between holes.
    3. 33" on center between holes.
    4. 36" on center between holes.

Key 3   Ref-2012 IRC R703.7.6

20. What MAXIMUM size floor joists can be used for a dwelling before they must be supported laterally with solid blocking or diagonal bridging?

    1. 2" x 6"
    2. 2" x 8"
    3. 2" x 10"
    4. 2" x 12"

Key 4   Ref-2012 IRC R502.7.1

21. Water-resistant gypsum board is being used for the ceiling in a shower with 16" on center framing spacing. What is the MINIMUM thickness of gypsum board required?

    1. 3/8"
    2. 1/2"
    3. 5/8"
    4. 3/4"

Key 3   Ref-2012 IRC R702.3.8

22. What is the MINIMUM distance that the foundation anchor bolts should be embedded into the concrete or grouted cells of the concrete masonry units?

    1. 6"
    2. 7"
    3. 8"
    4. 9"

Key 2   Ref-2012 IRC R403.1.6

23. What MINIMUM thickness roof sheathing should be used when rafters are spaced 24" apart?

    1. 1/2"
    2. 5/8"
    3. 3/4"
    4. 1"

Key 2   Ref-2012 IRC Table R803.1

24. What is the MINIMUM thickness of the concrete footings required for a masonry chimney?

    1. 12"
    2. 14"
    3. 16"
    4. 18"

Key 1   Ref-2012 IRC R1003.2

25. Fire escapes shall be designed to what MINIMUM amount uniformly distributed live load?

    1. 10 psf
    2. 20 psf
    3. 30 psf
    4. 40 psf

Key 4   Ref-2012 IRC Table R301.5

26. What MINIMUM distance above finished grade shall a concrete or masonry foundation extend at all points?

    1. 3"
    2. 4"
    3. 5"
    4. 6"

Key 2   Ref-2012 IRC R404.1.6

27. What is the MINIMUM nominal thickness in the least dimension for wood framing supporting gypsum board?

    1. 1"
    2. 2"
    3. 3"
    4. 4"

Key 2   Ref-2012 IRC R702.3.2

28. When glazing is used in walls, enclosures or fences of saunas, whirlpools and hot tubs, if the bottom of the exposed edge of the glazing is located less than what MINIMUM distance (measured vertically) above the standing surface, it shall be considered a hazardous location.

    1. 48"
    2. 54"
    3. 60"
    4. 66"

Key 3   Ref-2012 IRC R308.4.5

29. What is the MINIMUM nominal size wood column used for support in a residential house?

    1. 4" x 4"
    2. 4" x 6"
    3. 6" x 6"
    4. 6" x 8"

Key 1   Ref-2012 IRC R407.3

30. What is the MAXIMUM span of a 2" x 10" Southern pine #1 grade floor joist used for a residential sleeping area with joist spacing of 16" and a dead load of 20 psf?

    1. 14' 4"
    2. 15' 2"
    3. 16' 1"
    4. 17' 11"

Key 4   Ref-2012 IRC Table R502.3.1(1)

31. What is the MAXIMUM smoke-developed index for 6" thick foam plastic insulation?

    1. 350
    2. 400
    3. 450
    4. 500

Key 3   Ref-2012 IRC R316.3

32. What is the MINIMUM thickness of a masonry chimney wall built with solid masonry units or hollow units filled with grout?

    1. 4"
    2. 6"
    3. 8"
    4. 10"

Key 1   Ref-2012 IRC R1003.10

33. When drilling or notching a top plate more than 50% of its width, a galvanized metal tie shall be fastened across the opening and shall have a MINIMUM width of

    1. 1".
    2. 1-1/4".
    3. 1-1/2".
    4. 2".

Key 3   Ref-2012 IRC R602.6.1

34. Mechanical and gravity outdoor air intakes shall be located what MINIMUM distance from any hazardous or noxious contaminants?

    1. 10 feet
    2. 15 feet
    3. 20 feet
    4. 25 feet

Key 1   Ref-2012 IRC R303.5.1

35. All of the following information should be included in roof truss design drawings EXCEPT the

    1. location of all joints.
    2. name of designer and license number.
    3. required bearing widths.
    4. lumber size, species and grade for each member.

Key 2   Ref-2012 IRC R802.10.1

36. How many coats of exterior portland cement plaster shall be required when applied over metal lath?

    1. Not less than 2 coats
    2. Not less than 3 coats
    3. Not less than 4 coats
    4. Not less than 5 coats

Key 2   Ref-2012 IRC R703.6.2

37. A dwelling unit separation wall between townhouses that has no plumbing, mechanical, ducts or vents in the wall shall be a MINIMUM

    1. 1.0 hour fire-resistance rated wall.
    2. 1.5 hour fire-resistance rated wall.
    3. 2.0 hour fire-resistance rated wall.
    4. 2.5 hour fire-resistance rated wall.

Key 1   Ref-2012 IRC R302.2 Exception

38. What is the MINIMUM size access opening through a perimeter wall to the under-floor areas of a residential house?

    1. 16" x 24"
    2. 18" x 26"
    3. 20" x 30"
    4. 22" x 36"

Key 1   Ref-2012 IRC R408.4

39. What MINIMUM number of fasteners shall be used per wood shake when attached to the roof sheathing?

   1. 1 fastener
   2. 2 fasteners
   3. 3 fasteners
   4. 4 fasteners

Key 2   Ref-2012 IRC R905.8.6

40. In a building when making the truss to bearing wall connection, what number and size of screws should be used in each truss?

   1. 1 No. 8 screw
   2. 2 No. 8 screws
   3. 1 No. 10 screw
   4. 2 No. 10 screws

Key 4   Ref-2012 IRC Table R804.3

41. What is the MINIMUM thickness of standard unit glass masonry blocks for wall construction?

   1. 3"
   2. 3-1/8"
   3. 3-7/8"
   4. 4"

Key 3   Ref-2012 IRC R610.3.1

42. When an emergency situation requires the replacement or repair of equipment, how soon must the permit application be submitted to the building official?

   1. Within the next working day
   2. Within 2 working days
   3. Within 3 working days
   4. Within 4 working days

Key 1   Ref-2012 IRC R105.2.1

43. If ambient temperatures on a job are above or below the recommended temperature for placing and curing concrete, a record shall be kept of the protection used for the concrete. What is the temperature range?

    1. 35°F to 90°F
    2. 40°F to 95°F
    3. 45°F to 90°F
    4. 50°F to 95°F

Key 2   Ref-2011 ACI 318 1.3.3

44. What is the MAXIMUM spacing between screws on 1/2" gypsum used for wall board without adhesive and studs that are 24" on center?

    1. 10"
    2. 12"
    3. 14"
    4. 16"

Key 2   Ref-2012 IRC Table R702.3.5

45. Each end of a ceiling joist or rafter that is bearing on a concrete or masonry surface shall have what MINIMUM amount of bearing on that surface?

    1. 1-1/2"
    2. 2"
    3. 2-1/2"
    4. 3"

Key 4   Ref-2012 IRC R802.6

46. Wood foundation walls below grade shall have a moisture barrier installed. What thickness polyethylene film should be applied?

    1. 3 mil
    2. 4 mil
    3. 6 mil
    4. 8 mil

Key 3   Ref-2012 IRC R406.3.2

47. What type of valley lining material has a MINIMUM thickness of 0.027"?

   1. Aluminum
   2. Copper
   3. Lead
   4. Zinc alloy

Key 4   Ref-2012 IRC Table R905.2.8.2

48. Which one of the following building projects is required to have a permit?

   1. New deck, 300 square feet and 5 feet off the ground
   2. New one story accessory building, 180 square feet
   3. New privacy fence, 6 feet tall
   4. New retaining wall, 2.5 feet tall

Key 1   Ref-2012 IRC R105.2

49. What is the MINIMUM thickness lumber used for floor sheathing when joist or beam spacing is 16" and sheathing is installed diagonal to the joist?

   1. 1/2"
   2. 5/8"
   3. 3/4"
   4. 11/16"

Key 2   Ref-2012 IRC Table R503.1

50. Light-weight concrete shall contain aggregate that meets the density specifications determined by

   1. ASTM C33.
   2. ASTM C330.
   3. ASTM C496.
   4. ASTM C567.

Key 4   Ref-2011 ACI 318   2.2

51. What is the MINIMUM ceiling height for a bathroom in a residential home?

   1. 6' 6"
   2. 6' 7"
   3. 6' 8"
   4. 6' 9"

Key 3   Ref-2012 IRC R305.1 Exception 2

52. Which of the following jobs requires the contractor get a permit for the work?

    1. Fences less than 7 feet tall
    2. Retaining walls not over 4 feet tall
    3. One-story detached accessory buildings less than 200 sq. feet
    4. Installing a new shingle roof

Key 4   Ref-2012 IRC R105.2

53. What is the MAXIMUM allowed length of a building built with structural insulated panel ("SIP") construction?

    1. 60 feet
    2. 70 feet
    3. 80 feet
    4. 90 feet

Key 1   Ref-2012 IRC R613.2

54. What is the MINIMUM depth of a masonry or concrete fireplace firebox?

    1. 18"
    2. 19"
    3. 20"
    4. 21"

Key 3   Ref-2012 IRC R1001.6

55. A window well used for emergency escape and rescue shall have a permanently affixed ladder if the vertical depth is greater than

    1. 40".
    2. 44".
    3. 48".
    4. 52".

Key 2   Ref-2012 IRC R310.2.1

56. What is the MINIMUM size access opening to the attic of a dwelling with a combustible ceiling?

    1. 22" x 30"
    2. 24" x 30"
    3. 30" x 30"
    4. 30" x 36"

Key 1   Ref-2012 IRC R807.1

57. What is stamped on construction documents after they have been reviewed by the building department?

    1. "Accepted for Code Compliance"
    2. "Reviewed for Code Compliance"
    3. "Processed for Code Compliance"
    4. "Approved for Code Compliance"

Key 2   Ref-2012 IRC R106.3.1

58. What is the MINIMUM size vertical attachment flange required for a weep screed used for an exterior plaster wall?

    1. 2.5"
    2. 3.0"
    3. 3.5"
    4. 4.0"

Key 3   Ref-2012 IRC R703.6.2.1

59. Cement and what two types of mortar are approved for filling the cellular spaces in isolated piers to support beams and girders?

    1. Type O or Type S
    2. Type N or Type O
    3. Type M or Type N
    4. Type M or Type S

Key 4   Ref-2012 IRC R606.6

60. A dwelling that contains two-family dwelling units shall have what type of wall separation between units?

    1. 30-minute fire-resistance rating
    2. 1-hour fire-resistance rating
    3. 90-minute fire-resistance rating
    4. 2-hour fire-resistance rating

Key 2   Ref-2012 IRC R302.3

61. What size corrosion-resistant mesh screen shall be used for protecting exterior air intakes supplying combustion air to a fireplace?

    1. 1/16"
    2. 1/8"
    3. 1/4"
    4. 3/8"

Key 3   Ref-2012 IRC R1006.2

62. How long shall the building department maintain construction documents after the project is completed?

    1. 90 days
    2. 180 days
    3. 240 days
    4. 360 days

Key 2   Ref-2012 IRC R106.5

63. What is the MAXIMUM slope that can be used for the construction of residential ramps?

    1. 1 unit vertical in 9 units horizontal
    2. 1 unit vertical in 10 units horizontal
    3. 1 unit vertical in 11 units horizontal
    4. 1 unit vertical in 12 units horizontal

Key 4   Ref-2012 IRC R311.8.1

64. When a building foundation is built with wood, what MINIMUM size studs are used for the foundation walls?

    1. 2" x 4"
    2. 2" x 6"
    3. 2" x 8"
    4. 2" x 10"

Key 2   Ref-2012 IRC R404.2.2

65. Wood shingle roofs shall have an ice barrier that extends from the roof edge to what MINIMUM distance inside the exterior wall line?

    1. 18"
    2. 24"
    3. 30"
    4. 36"

Key 2   Ref-2012 IRC R905.7.3.1

66. In areas of the country where snow is a factor on concrete and clay roof tiles, what MINIMUM amount of fasteners are required on each tile?

    1. 1 fastener
    2. 2 fasteners
    3. 3 fasteners
    4. 4 fasteners

Key 2   Ref-2012 IRC R905.3.7

67. What is the MAXIMUM flame spread index allowed for fire-retardant-treated wood used for roof framing?

    1. 10
    2. 15
    3. 20
    4. 25

Key 4   Ref-2012 IRC R802.1.3

68. Each dwelling unit shall be provided with at least one egress door that has a MINIMUM clear height of

    1. 76" and shall not require a key to open.
    2. 78" and shall not require a key to open.
    3. 80" and shall not require a key to open.
    4. 82" and shall not require a key to open.

Key 2   Ref-2012 IRC R311.2

69. What is the MINIMUM height of a parapet from the point it intersects with the sloped roof's surface to the top of the parapet?

    1. 24"
    2. 30"
    3. 36"
    4. 42"

Key 2   Ref-2012 IRC R302.2.3

70. What is the MAXIMUM square footage of an accessory structure located on the same lot as a residence?

    1. 1,000 sq. feet
    2. 2,000 sq. feet
    3. 3,000 sq. feet
    4. 4,000 sq. feet

Key 3   Ref-2012 IRC R202

71. What MINIMUM distance above the top of the fireplace opening shall the ferrous metal damper be located on a masonry fireplace?

    1. 6"
    2. 8"
    3. 10"
    4. 12"

Key 2   Ref-2012 IRC R1001.7.1

72. What is the MINIMUM amount of clearance required in front of a water closet in a residential home?

    1. 21"
    2. 22"
    3. 23"
    4. 24"

Key 1   Ref-2012 IRC Figure R307.1

73. When installing a foundation on Soil Group I, Soil Classification SM, comprised of silty sands and sand-silt mixtures, what is the frost heave characteristic of this type of soil?

    1. Unsatisfactory
    2. Poor
    3. Good
    4. Medium

Key 4   Ref-2012 IRC Table R405.1

74. A truss design drawing must be submitted and approved before the trusses are installed. Who receives the truss design drawings?

    1. Building official
    2. Building contractor
    3. Testing agency
    4. Plans examiner

Key 1   Ref-2012 IRC R502.11.4

75. Precast wall panels shall have a MINIMUM of two ties per panel with a nominal tensile strength of

    1. 10,000 lbs. per tie.
    2. 15,000 lbs. per tie.
    3. 20,000 lbs. per tie.
    4. 25,000 lbs. per tie.

Key 1   Ref-2011 ACI 318 16.5.1.3(b)

76. What is the MINIMUM thickness of slab-on-ground concrete floors supported directly on the ground?

    1. 3"
    2. 3.5"
    3. 4"
    4. 4.5"

Key 2   Ref-2012 IRC R506.1

77. What is the MAXIMUM thickness of stone veneer that is installed over a backing of wood or cold-formed steel?

    1. 4"
    2. 5"
    3. 6"
    4. 7"

Key 2   Ref-2012 IRC R703.7

78. What is the MINIMUM tread depth that can be used for a residential stairway?

    1. 8 inches
    2. 9 inches
    3. 10 inches
    4. 11 inches

Key 3   Ref-2012 IRC R311.7.5.2

79. All of the following cast-in-place construction activities are covered under the ACI 318 Structural Concrete Building Code EXCEPT

    1. footings.
    2. foundation walls.
    3. tanks.
    4. slabs-on-ground for dwellings.

Key 3   Ref-2011 ACI 318   1.1.4 & 1.1.10

80. Interior spaces intended for human occupancy shall have a heating system capable of maintaining what level of temperature measured 3 feet off the floor?

    1. 68°F
    2. 69°F
    3. 70°F
    4. 71°F

Key 1   Ref-2012 IRC R303.9

81. What MINIMUM amount of fasteners shall be used on a roofing strip shingle?

    1. 2 fasteners
    2. 3 fasteners
    3. 4 fasteners
    4. 5 fasteners

Key 3   Ref-2012 IRC R905.2.6

82. Openings in exterior masonry veneer shall have additional ties used around the openings when the size of the openings exceed

    1. 14" in either direction.
    2. 16" in either direction.
    3. 18" in either direction.
    4. 20" in either direction.

Key 2   Ref-2012 IRC R703.7.4.1.1

83. What size floor joist shall be used when joist spacing is 24" with #2 Hem-fir wood and a dead load of 20 psf to achieve a 12 foot span used for a residential living area?

    1. 2" x 6"
    2. 2" x 8"
    3. 2" x 10"
    4. 2" x 12"

Key 4   Ref-2012 IRC Table R502.3.1(1)

84. Where shall the permit for a job be kept until the job is completed?

    1. In the contractor's office
    2. In the contractor's truck
    3. On the job site
    4. At city hall

Key 3   Ref-2012 IRC R105.7

85. What MINIMUM distance shall a wall tie be embedded in the mortar joints of solid masonry units?

    1. 3/4"
    2. 1-3/8"
    3. 1-1/2"
    4. 1-5/8"

Key 3   Ref-2012 IRC R607.3

86. Glass unit masonry panels shall be provided with expansion joints along the top, bottom and sides at all structural supports. What is the MINIMUM thickness of the expansion joints?

1. 1/4"
2. 3/8"
3. 1/2"
4. 5/8"

Key 2   Ref-2012 IRC R610.7

87. A cold formed 33 KSI steel floor joist with the designation of 1000S162-54 is being used for a building having a live load of 30 psf and a joist spacing of 24". What is the MAXIMUM distance the joist can span?

1. 16' 8"
2. 17' 3"
3. 18' 6"
4. 19' 9"

Key 3   Ref-2012 IRC Table R505.3.2(2)

88. What type of separation is required between a garage and all habitable rooms located above the garage?

1. 1/2" gypsum board or equivalent
2. 1/2" Type X gypsum board or equivalent
3. 5/8" gypsum board or equivalent
4. 5/8" Type X gypsum board or equivalent

Key 4   Ref-2012 IRC Table R302.6

89. When admixtures are used in producing flowing concrete, they shall conform to which of the following Standards?

1. ASTM C260
2. ASTM C494
3. ASTM C845
4. ASTM C1017

Key 3   Ref-2011 ACI 318   3.6.1

90. Particle board used for floor underlayment shall conform to Type PBU and shall have a MINIMUM thickness of

    1. 1/4".
    2. 3/8".
    3. 1/2".
    4. 5/8".

Key 1   Ref-2012 IRC R503.3.2

91. How long before a permit becomes null and void if work is not started?

    1. 90 days
    2. 120 days
    3. 180 days
    4. 360 days

Key 3   Ref-2012 IRC R105.5

92. A double top plate shall have end joints offset at what MINIMUM distance?

    1. 18"
    2. 24"
    3. 30"
    4. 36"

Key 2   Ref-2012 IRC R602.3.2

93. Concrete used for basement walls that are exposed to moderate weather shall have what MINIMUM strength?

    1. 2,500 lbs.
    2. 2,800 lbs.
    3. 3,000 lbs.
    4. 3,200 lbs.

Key 3   Ref-2012 IRC Table R402.2

94. What is the MAXIMUM height for a riser on a residential stairway?

    1. 7"
    2. 7.25"
    3. 7.5"
    4. 7.75"

Key 4   Ref-2012 IRC R311.7.5.1

95. Concrete walls constructed with a thickness of more than 10" shall have reinforcement placed in 2 layers in both directions and also 2 bars. What size bars shall be used?

    1. No. 3 bars
    2. No. 4 bars
    3. No. 5 bars
    4. No. 6 bars

Key 3   Ref-2011 ACI 318   14.3.4 & 14.3.7

96. What MINIMUM amount of glazing is required to give a room natural light?

    1. 6% of the floor area of the room served
    2. 8% of the floor area of the room served
    3. 10% of the floor area of the room served
    4. 12% of the floor area of the room served

Key 2   Ref-2012 IRC R303.1

97. What is the MINIMUM lumber framing material recommended for structural insulated panel ("SIP") walls?

    1. No. 2 Southern pine
    2. No. 2 Hem-fir
    3. No. 2 Douglas-fir-larch
    4. No. 2 Spruce-pine-fir

Key 4   Ref-2012 IRC R613.3.4

98. The doubled cantilevered joists used for the cantilever of the first floor of a one story building shall extend what MINIMUM distance toward the inside of the building?

    1. 5 feet
    2. 6 feet
    3. 7 feet
    4. 8 feet

Key 2   Ref-2012 IRC R505.3.6

99. When installing glass unit masonry, what is the required thickness of the bed and head joints?

1. 1/4"
2. 3/8"
3. 1/2"
4. 5/8"

Key 1   Ref-2012 IRC R610.10

100. A kitchen is required in each dwelling unit. What is required to be installed in every kitchen?

1. Stove
2. Sink
3. Range
4. Refrigerator

Key 2   Ref-2012 IRC R306.2

101. Hallways in homes are used for egress. What is the MINIMUM allowed width of hallways?

1. 34"
2. 35"
3. 36"
4. 37"

Key 3   Ref-2012 IRC R311.6

102. When digging exterior footings, what is the MINIMUM distance a footing shall be placed below undisturbed soil?

1. 12"
2. 16"
3. 20"
4. 24"

Key 1   Ref-2012 IRC R403.1.4

103. When a crawl space is located under a floor that is not insulated, the crawl space walls shall be insulated from the floor down to the finished grade and an additional

1. 20".
2. 22".
3. 24".
4. 26".

Key 3   Ref-2012 IRC N1102.2.10

104. When installing a foundation on Soil Group III, Soil Classification CH, comprised of inorganic clays of high plasticity or fat clays, what is the drainage characteristic of this type of soil?

1. Unsatisfactory
2. Poor
3. Medium
4. Good

Key 2   Ref-2012 IRC Table R405.1

105. What is the MAXIMUM amount of roof eave projection for a detached garage located within 2 feet of a lot line?

1. 4"
2. 6"
3. 8"
4. 10"

Key 1   Ref-2012 IRC R302.1 Exception 4

106. Exterior concrete that is exposed to the freezing-and-thawing cycle is listed as a Category F concrete. Which class of Category F concrete is exposed to the freezing-and-thawing cycles and in continuous contact with moisture?

1. F0
2. F1
3. F2
4. F3

Key 3   Ref-2011 ACI 318 Table 4.2.1

107. All of the following steel roof framing members should be attached with No. 10 screws EXCEPT

1. roof sheathing to rafters.
2. truss to bearing wall.
3. gable end truss to endwall top track.
4. ceiling joist to top track of load-bearing wall.

Key 1   Ref-2012 IRC Table R804.3

108. Masonry chimneys shall have a cleanout located what distance from the base of each flue?

    1. 2"
    2. 4"
    3. 6"
    4. 8"

Key 3   Ref-2012 IRC R1003.17

109. What is the MINIMUM clear width of a spiral stairway at and below the railing in a residential home?

    1. 25"
    2. 26"
    3. 27"
    4. 29"

Key 2   Ref-2012 IRC R311.7.10.1

110. All of the following masonry units can be used for load bearing construction EXCEPT

    1. clay.
    2. cement.
    3. solid.
    4. glass.

Key 4   Ref-2012 IRC R202

111. On what MINIMUM design roof slope can a liquid-applied roofing material be installed?

    1. One-eighth unit vertical in 12 units horizontal
    2. One-fourth unit vertical in 12 units horizontal
    3. One-third unit vertical in 12 units horizontal
    4. One-half unit vertical in 12 units horizontal

Key 2   Ref-2012 IRC R905.15.1

112. Wood foundations built in soil that is Class II, III and IV shall be equipped with a drainage system including a sump that is installed at least

    1. 24" below the bottom of the basement floor.
    2. 26" below the bottom of the basement floor.
    3. 28" below the bottom of the basement floor.
    4. 30" below the bottom of the basement floor.

Key 1   Ref-2012 IRC R405.2.3

113. In ceilings that do not have an attic space, what is the MINIMUM amount of insulation that will be required?

    1. R-26
    2. R-28
    3. R-30
    4. R-32

Key 3   Ref-2012 IRC N1102.2.2

114. When a cold formed steel framed wall is being attached to a foundation by anchor bolts, the anchor bolts shall extend a MINIMUM of

    1. 12" into a masonry foundation.
    2. 13" into a masonry foundation.
    3. 14" into a masonry foundation.
    4. 15" into a masonry foundation.

Key 4   Ref-2012 IRC R603.3.1

115. What MINIMUM distance shall be maintained between adhered masonry veneer and a paved surface area?

    1. 1"
    2. 2"
    3. 3"
    4. 4"

Key 2   Ref-2012 IRC R703.12.1(2)

116. Foam plastic insulation used for thermal insulating or acoustic purposes shall have a MINIMUM density of

    1. 10 pounds per cubic foot.
    2. 15 pounds per cubic foot.
    3. 20 pounds per cubic foot.
    4. 25 pounds per cubic foot.

Key 3   Ref-2012 IRC R202

117. What is the MAXIMUM cantilever span for a floor joist supporting an exterior balcony using 2" x 10" members with 16" spacing and a ground snow load of 50 psf?

   1. 39"
   2. 49"
   3. 54"
   4. 67"

Key 2   Ref-2012 IRC Table R502.3.3(2)

118. Masonry fireplaces shall have the firebox lined with fire brick that has a MINIMUM thickness of

   1. 1-1/4".
   2. 1-1/2".
   3. 1-3/4".
   4. 2".

Key 4   Ref-2012 IRC R1001.5

119. Structures built with an unvented under-the-floor crawl space shall have a Class 1 vapor barrier installed over the exposed earth. There is a second requirement for ventilation of the crawl space which can be a continuously operating mechanical exhaust system or a conditioned air supply. What rate of flow shall be needed to meet the ventilation requirement of exhaust or supply?

   1. 1 cubic foot per minute flow per 20 sq. ft. of floor area.
   2. 1 cubic foot per minute flow per 30 sq. ft. of floor area.
   3. 1 cubic foot per minute flow per 40 sq. ft. of floor area.
   4. 1 cubic foot per minute flow per 50 sq. ft. of floor area.

Key 4   Ref-2012 IRC R408.3   1&2

120. What is the MAXIMUM span of a 2" x 8" Hem-fir SS grade ceiling joist used for a residential living area and joist spacing of 16" with a live load of 40 psf and a dead load of 10 psf?

   1. 11' 11"
   2. 12' 0"
   3. 12' 10"
   4. 13' 4"

Key 3   Ref-2012 IRC Table R502.3.1(2)

121. What shall be the MINIMUM fire separation distance for exterior walls with a 0 hour fire-resistance rating?

    1. $\geq$ 3 feet
    2. $\geq$ 4 feet
    3. $\geq$ 5 feet
    4. $\geq$ 6 feet

Key 3   Ref-2012 IRC Table R302.1(1)

122. How long shall the records of concrete inspection be kept by the inspecting engineer or architect after the project is completed?

    1. 6 months
    2. 1 year
    3. 1.5 years
    4. 2 years

Key 4   Ref-2011 ACI 318   1.3.4

123. What MINIMUM clearance is required for all combustible materials including wood beams, joists and studs from the front faces and sides of masonry fireplaces?

    1. 2" clearance
    2. 3" clearance
    3. 4" clearance
    4. 5" clearance

Key 1   Ref-2012 IRC R1001.11

124. The base flashings used against a vertical sidewall shall direct water away from the sidewall and be continuous or step design. What is the MINIMUM size of the flashing?

    1. 3" x 3"
    2. 4" x 4"
    3. 5" x 5"
    4. 6" x 6"

Key 2 Ref-2012 IRC R905.2.8.3

125. When a window greater than 16" in either dimension is located in a wall with a masonry veneer, the metal ties around the perimeter of the opening shall be placed within

    1.   12" of the wall opening.
    2.   14" of the wall opening.
    3.   16" of the wall opening.
    4.   18" of the wall opening.

Key 1   Ref-2012 IRC R703.7.4.1.1

126. In Seismic Design Categories D_0, D_1 and D_2, what size vertical reinforcement bar should be used for masonry stem walls?

    1.   No. 3
    2.   No. 4
    3.   No. 5
    4.   No. 6

Key 1   Ref-2012 IRC R404.1.4.1(4)

127. How many and what type of fastener should be used to secure the following roof element: ceiling joists to plate?

    1.   3 - 6d common, toe nailed
    2.   3 - 8d common, toe nailed
    3.   3 - 10d common, toe nailed
    4.   3 - 16d common, toe nailed

Key 2   Ref-2012 IRC Table R602.3(1)

128. Grade No. 2 wood shingles that are 24" length and installed on a 3:12 pitch roof shall have how much weather exposure?

    1.   4.5"
    2.   5.0"
    3.   5.5"
    4.   6.0"

Key 3   Ref-2012 IRC Table R905.7.5

129. What is the MINIMUM net clear opening square footage required for an emergency escape and rescue opening?

    1. 5.7 sq. feet
    2. 5.8 sq. feet
    3. 5.9 sq. feet
    4. 5.10 sq. feet

Key 1   Ref-2012 IRC R310.1.1

130. What size ceiling joist shall be used when rafter spacing is 16" on center and has a dead load of 10 psf with #1 Southern pine to achieve a span of 20 feet for uninhabitable attics without storage?

    1. 2" x 4"
    2. 2" x 6"
    3. 2" x 8"
    4. 2" x 10"

Key 3   Ref-2012 IRC Table R802.4(1)

131. What is the MAXIMUM spacing between lateral ties used for reinforcement in a masonry column?

    1. 6"
    2. 8"
    3. 10"
    4. 12"

Key 2   Ref-2012 IRC R606.12.3.3

132. Every dwelling built shall have at least one habitable room with MINIMUM square footage of

    1. 100 sq. feet.
    2. 110 sq. feet.
    3. 120 sq. feet.
    4. 130 sq. feet.

Key 3   Ref-2012 IRC R304.1

133. Wood roof shakes that are preservative-treated taper sawn, made of No. 1 Southern Yellow Pine, and are 24" long shall have an exposure on a MINIMUM 4:12 roof of

    1. 5-1/2".
    2. 7-1/2".
    3. 10".
    4. 12".

Key 3   Ref-2012 IRC Table R905.8.6

134. All of the following information shall be included on the Certificate of Occupancy EXCEPT the

    1. building permit number.
    2. name of the building official.
    3. address of the dwelling.
    4. legal description of the property.

Key 4   Ref-2012 IRC R110.3

135. What is the MINIMUM thickness of aluminum used for valley lining material?

    1. 0.0162"
    2. 0.0179"
    3. 0.024"
    4. 0.027"

Key 3   Ref-2012 IRC Table R905.2.8.2

136. If a permit extension is granted to the permit holder, how long is each extension good for?

    1. 30 days
    2. 60 days
    3. 90 days
    4. 180 days

Key 4   Ref-2012 IRC R105.5

137. Exterior masonry veneer that is anchored with metal strand wire ties shall have an air space between the veneer and the sheathing. What is the MAXIMUM allowed amount of air space?

    1. 3.0"
    2. 3-1/2"
    3. 4.0"
    4. 4-1/2"

Key 4   Ref-2012 IRC Table R703.7.4

138. Fire-retardant-treated lumber used for roof framing shall use chemicals in a closed vessel pressure process with a MINIMUM of

    1. 30 psig.
    2. 40 psig.
    3. 50 psig.
    4. 60 psig.

Key 3   Ref-2012 IRC R802.1.3.1

139. Footings that are poured on piles shall be what MINIMUM depth above the bottom reinforcement?

    1. 6"
    2. 8"
    3. 10"
    4. 12"

Key 4   Ref-2011 ACI 318 15.7

140. A skylight on a roof sloped less than a 3:12 pitch shall be mounted on what MINIMUM height curb above the roof?

    1. 2"
    2. 4"
    3. 6"
    4. 8"

Key 2   Ref-2012 IRC R308.6.8

141. What is the MINIMUM length of a hearth extension on a fireplace with an opening of 6 square feet or larger?

    1. 16" in front of the fireplace
    2. 18" in front of the fireplace
    3. 20" in front of the fireplace
    4. 22" in front of the fireplace

Key 3   Ref-2012 IRC R1001.10

142. What MINIMUM lap is required when installing horizontal fiber cement siding?

    1. 1"
    2. 1.25"
    3. 1.50"
    4. 1.75"

Key 2   Ref-2012 IRC R703.10.2

143. What is the MAXIMUM length of glass sections used in louvered windows or jalousies?

    1. 48"
    2. 52"
    3. 56"
    4. 60"

Key 1   Ref-2012 IRC R308.2

144. What is the MINIMUM square footage of a manufactured home when completely erected on site?

    1. 300 sq. feet
    2. 320 sq. feet
    3. 340 sq. feet
    4. 360 sq. feet

Key 2   Ref-2012 IRC R202

145. What is the MINIMUM nominal thickness for concrete wall members that are vertical or horizontal and made with a waffle-grid wall system?

    1. 4"
    2. 6"
    3. 8"
    4. 10"

Key 2   Ref-2012 IRC R611.3.2

146. A permanent wood foundation built for a crawl space shall have a base of gravel or crushed stone under the footing with a MINIMUM thickness of

    1. 3".
    2. 4".
    3. 5".
    4. 6".

Key 4   Ref-2012 IRC Figure R403.1(3)

147. What is the MINIMUM height that nonabsorbent walls shall extend above the floor of a shower?

1. 5 feet
2. 5.5 feet
3. 6 feet
4. 6.5 feet

Key 3 Ref-2012 IRC R307.2

148. What is the MAXIMUM length of an eave overhang on a residential home when measured horizontally?

1. 20"
2. 24"
3. 28"
4. 32"

Key 2 Ref-2012 IRC R804.3.2.1.1

149. What is the MINIMUM lap amount for horizontal lap siding that is rabbeted?

1. 0.5"
2. 0.75"
3. 1.0"
4. 1.5"

Key 1 Ref-2012 IRC R703.3.2

150. Metal shingle roofs shall have an ice barrier that consists of two layers of underlayment cemented together that extends from the roof edge to what MINIMUM distance inside the exterior wall line?

1. 18"
2. 20"
3. 24"
4. 30"

Key 3 Ref-2012 IRC R905.4.3.1

International Residential Code, 2018
Chapters 1 and 44 Administration and Referenced Standards
Questions and Answers

1. The *International Residential Code* is applicable to single-family dwellings a maximum of
_____ stories in above-grade-plane height.

A. One
B. Two
C. Three
D. Four

2. If there is a conflict in the code between a general requirement and a specific requirement, the
_____ requirement shall apply.

A. General
B. Specific
C. Least restrictive
D. Most restrictive

3. Provisions of the appendices do not apply unless _____ .

A. Specified in the code
B. Applicable to unique conditions
C. Specifically adopted
D. Relevant to fire or life safety

4. _____ is the term used in the IRC to describe the individual in charge of the department of
building safety.

A. Building official
B. Code official
C. Code administrator
D. Chief building inspector

5. The building official has the authority to _____ the provisions of the code.

A. Ignore
B. Waive
C. Violate
D. Interpret

6. Used materials may be utilized under which one of the following conditions?

A. They meet the requirements for new materials
B. When approved by the building official
C. Used materials may never be used in new construction
D. A representative sampling is tested for compliance

7. The building official has the authority to grant modifications to the code _____ .

A. For only those issues not affecting life safety or fire safety
B. For individual cases where the strict letter of the code is impractical
C. Where the intent and purpose of the code cannot be met
D. Related only to administrative functions

8. Unless supporting a surcharge, retaining walls having a maximum height of _____ inches, measured from the bottom of the footing to the top of the wall, do not require a permit.

A. 30
B. 36
C. 48
D. 60

9. Tests performed by _____ may be required by the building official where there is insufficient evidence of code compliance.

A. The owner
B. The contractor
C. An approved agency
D. A design professional

10. A permit is not required for the construction of a one-story detached accessory structure when it has a maximum floor area of _____ square feet.

A. 100
B. 120
C. 150
D. 200

11. Prefabricated swimming pools are subject to a building permit where they have a minimum depth of

_____ .

A. 12 inches
B. 24 inches
C. 30 inches
D. 36 inches

12. Unless an extension is authorized, a permit becomes invalid when work does not commence within _____ after permit issuance.

A. 90 days
B. 180 days
C. One year
D. Two years

13. The building permit, or a copy of the permit, shall be kept _____ until completion of the project.

A. At the job site
B. By the permit applicant
C. By the contractor
D. By the owner

14. When a building permit is issued, the construction documents shall be approved_____.

A. In writing or by stamp
B. And two sets returned to the applicant
C. And stamped as "accepted as reviewed"
D. Pending payment of the plan review fee

15. Unless otherwise mandated by state or local laws, the approved construction documents shall be retained by the building official for a minimum of _____ from the date of completion of the permitted work.

A. 90 days
B. 180 days
C. One year
D. Two years

16. Where applicable, which one of the following inspections is not specifically identified by the *International Residential Code* as a required inspection?

A. Foundation inspection
B. Frame inspection
C. Fire-resistance-construction inspection
D. Energy efficiency inspection

17. Whose duty is it to provide access to work in need of inspection?

A. The permit holder or agent
B. The owner or owner's agent
C. The contractor
D. The person requesting the inspection

18. The certificate of occupancy shall contain all of the following information except:

A. The name and address of the owner or owner's agent
B. The name of the building official
C. The edition of the code under which the permit was issued
D. The maximum occupant load

19. A temporary certificate of occupancy is valid for what period of time?

A. 30 days
B. 60 days
C. 180 days
D. A period set by the building official

20. The board of appeals is not authorized to rule on an appeal based on a claim that_____.

A. The provisions of the code do not fully apply
B. A code requirement should be waived
C. The rules have been incorrectly interpreted
D. A better form of construction is provided

21. The membership of the board of appeals _____

A. Shall include a jurisdictional member
B. Must consist of at least five members
C. Shall be knowledgeable of building construction
D. Must include an engineer or an architect

22. A permit is not required for construction of a fence with a maximum height of_____feet.

A. 5
B. 6
C. 7
D. 8

23. When a stop work order is issued, it shall be given to any of the following individuals except for the _____.

A. Owner
B. Owner's agent
C. Permit applicant
D. Person doing the work

24. Which of the following standards is applicable for factory-built fireplaces?

A. Ansi z21.42-2014
B. Cpsc 16 cfr part 1404
C. Nfpa 259-13
D. Ul 127–2011

25. ACI 318-14 is a reference standard addressing _____.

A. Structural concrete
B. Wood construction
C. Structural steel buildings
D. Gypsum board

26. All of the following issues are specifically identified for achieving the purpose of the *International Residential Code*, except for _____ .

A. Affordability
B. Structural strength
C. Energy conservation
D. Usability and accessibility

27. A permit is not required for the installation of a window awning provided the awning projects a maximum of _____ inches from the exterior wall and does not require additional support.

A. 30
B. 36
C. 48
D. 54

28. Where a self-contained refrigeration system contains a maximum of _____ pound(s) of refrigerant, a permit is not required.

A. 1
B. 2
C. 5
D. 10

29. It is the duty of the _____ or their agent to notify the building official that work is ready for inspection.

A. Permit holder
B. Owner
C. Contractor
D. Design professional

30. What is the role of the building official in relationship to the board of appeals?

A. Advisor only
B. Ex officio member
C. Full voting member
D. Procedural reviewer

31. Where the enforcement of a code provision would violate the conditions of an appliance's listing, the conditions of the listing _____ .

A. Are no longer valid
B. May be disregarded
C. Shall apply
D. Are optional

32. Inspection reports shall be retained in the official records for what minimum period?

A. Until after the certificate of occupancy is issued
B. 180 days after the report is issued
C. The time required for the retention of public records
D. 180 days after the certificate of occupancy is issued

33. Which of the following reasons is not specifically identified by the code as authority to suspend or revoke a permit?

A. The permit was issued in error
B. Required inspections have not been performed
C. It was issued in violation of a jurisdictional ordinance
D. Inaccurate information was provided at the time of issuance

34. A permit for a temporary structure is limited as to time of service, but shall not be allowed for more than _____ days.

A. 30
B. 60
C. 90
D. 180

35. The issuance of a certificate of occupancy is not required for what maximum size of accessory building?

A. 120 square feet
B. 150 square feet
C. 180 square feet
D. All accessory buildings are exempt

International Residential Code, 2018
Chapters 1 and 44 Administration and Referenced Standards
Answer Key

No.	Answer	Sec.
1.	C	R101.2
2.	B	R102.1
3.	C	R102.5
4.	A	R103.1
5.	D	R104.1
6.	B	R104.9.1
7.	B	R104.10
8.	C	R105.2, #B3
9.	C	R104.11.1
10.	D	R105.2, #B1
11.	B	R105.2, #B7
12.	B	R105.5
13.	A	R105.7
14.	A	R106.3.1
15.	B	R106.5
16.	D	R109.1
17.	D	R109.3
18.	D	R110.3
19.	D	R110.4
20.	B	R112.2
21.	C	R112.3
22.	C	R105.2, #B2
23.	C	R114.1
24.	D	Chapter 44
25.	A	Chapter 44
26.	D	R101.3
27.	D	R105.2, #B9
28.	D	R105.2, #M7
29.	A	R109.3
30.	B	R112.1
31.	C	R102.4, Exception
32.	C	R104.7
33.	B	R105.6
34.	D	R107.1
35.	D	R110.1, Exception 2

International Residential Code, 2018
Sections R301 and R302 - Questions and Answers

1. What is the weathering potential for all dwelling sites located in the state of South Dakota?

    A. severe
    B. moderate
    C. negligible
    D. none

2. The ultimate wind speed to be used for a majority of the United States is_____.

    A. 85 mph
    B. 90 mph
    C. 110 mph
    D. 115 mph

3. Based on Figure R301.2 (6), what is the ground snow load for most of western Colorado?

    A. 30 psf
    B. 40 psf
    C. 50 psf
    D. site-specific due to extreme local variations

4. Unless local conditions warrant otherwise, what is the probability for termite infestation for dwellings constructed in most of Idaho?

    A. very heavy
    B. moderate to heavy
    C. slight to moderate
    D. none to slight

5. For the purpose of determining the component and cladding loads on the roof surface of a building, the area at the ridge of a gable roof sloped at 20 degrees shall be considered as Pressure Zone _____ at other than the eaves.

    A. 0
    B. 1
    C. 2
    D. 3

6. Where wood structural panels are used to protect windows in buildings located in windborne debris regions, #8 wood screws shall be located at a maximum of _____ on center to fasten those panels that span 8 feet.

   A. 8 inches
   B. 9 inches
   C. 12 inches
   D. 16 inches

7. Where a referenced document is based upon nominal design wind speeds and no conversion between ultimate design wind speeds and nominal design wind speeds is provided, an ultimate design wind speed of 115 mph shall be converted to a nominal design wind speed of _____ mph.

   A. 85
   B. 89
   C. 93
   D. 101

8. What wind exposure category is appropriate for a dwelling located in a residential development in a suburban area?

   A. Exposure A
   B. Exposure B
   C. Exposure C
   D. Exposure D

9. The seismic design category for a site having a calculated S_{DS} of 0.63g is _____.

   A. B
   B. D_0
   C. D_1
   D. E

10. Habitable attics shall be designed with a minimum uniformly distributed live load of _____ psf.

    A. 10
    B. 20
    C. 30
    D. 40

11. For a dwelling assigned to Seismic Design Category D₂ and constructed under the conventional provisions of the IRC, what is the maximum dead load permitted for 8-inch-thick masonry walls?

   A. 40 psf
   B. 65 psf
   C. 80 psf
   D. 85 psf

12. A portion of a building is considered irregular for seismic purposes when a floor opening, such as for a stairway, exceeds the lesser of 12 feet or _____ of the least floor dimension.

   A. 15 percent
   B. 25 percent
   C. 33 1/3 percent
   D. 50 percent

13. Buildings constructed in regions where the ground snow load exceeds a minimum of _____ must be designed in accordance with accepted engineering practice.

   A. 30 psf
   B. 50 psf
   C. 70 psf
   D. 90 psf

14. For rooms other than sleeping rooms, what is the minimum uniformly distributed live load that is to be used for the design of the floor system?

   A. 20 psf
   B. 30 psf
   C. 40 psf
   D. 50 psf

15. A minimum uniformly distributed live load of 10 psf is to be used for the design of uninhabitable attic areas having a maximum clear height of _____ inches.

   A. 30
   B. 36
   C. 42
   D. 60

16. A minimum uniformly distributed live load of _____ shall be used for the design of sleeping rooms.

   A. 10 psf
   B. 20 psf
   C. 30 psf
   D. 40 psf

17. Where no snow load is present, what is the minimum roof design live load for a 240 square foot tributary-loaded roof area having a slope of 8:12?

   A. 20 psf
   B. 16 psf
   C. 14 psf
   D. 12 psf

18. What is the maximum allowable deflection for floor joists?

   A. L/120
   B. L/180
   C. L/240
   D. L/360

19. The maximum allowable deflection permitted for 7:12-sloped rafters with no finished ceiling attached to the rafters is _____.

   A. L/120
   B. L/180
   C. L/240
   D. L/360

20. A fire-resistance rating is not required for exterior walls of nonsprinklered dwellings having a minimum fire separation distance of _____.

   A. 3 feet
   B. 4 feet
   C. 5 feet
   D. 10 feet

21. A roof projection on a dwelling shall be located a minimum of _____ from an interior lot line.

   A. 0 feet (it may extend to the lot line)
   B. 12 inches
   C. 2 feet
   D. 4 feet

22. Tool and storage sheds, playhouses and similar accessory structures having a maximum floor area of _____ are not required to have exterior wall protection based on location on the lot.

    A. 100 square feet
    B. 120 square feet
    C. 150 square feet
    D. 200 square feet

23. Walls and ceiling finishes shall have a maximum flame spread index of _____.

    A. 25
    B. 75
    C. 200
    D. 450

24. Where located in an exterior wall having a minimum required fire-resistance rating of one hour, through penetrations protected with an approved penetration firestop system shall have a minimum fire-resistance rating of _____.

    A. 20 minutes
    B. 30 minutes
    C. 45 minutes
    D. 1 hour

25. Where a detached garage is located within 2 feet of a lot line, the maximum eave projection is limited to _____ inches.

    A. 4
    B. 6
    C. 8
    D. 12

26. For wind design purposes, a building located along the shoreline in the Great Lakes region is categorized as Exposure _____ where exposed to wind coming from over the water.

    A. A
    B. B
    C. C
    D. D

27. Which of the following buildings is exempt from the seismic requirements of the code?

   A. a townhouse in Seismic Design Category C
   B. a one-family dwelling in Seismic Design Category C
   C. a townhouse in Seismic Design Category D_0
   D. a two-family dwelling in Seismic Design Category D_1

28. Where a solid wood door is installed as a permitted opening between a garage and a residence, the minimum thickness of the door shall be_____inches.

   A. 1 3/8
   B. 1 ½
   C. 1 5/8
   D. 1 ¾

29. When a common wall is used to separate townhouses provided with fire sprinkler protection, it shall have a minimum _____ fire-resistance rating.

   A. 1-hour
   B. 2-hour
   C. 3-hour
   D. 4-hour

30. An in-fill panel for a guard shall be designed to withstand a minimum load of _____ applied horizontally on an area of 1 square foot.

   A. 50 pounds
   B. 80 pounds
   C. 100 pounds
   D. 200 pounds

31. Where structural wood panels are used to provide windborne debris protection for glazed openings, the fasteners shall be long enough to penetrate through the sheathing and into wood wall framing a minimum of _____ inch(es).

   A. 1
   B. 1 ½
   C. 2
   D. 2 ½

32. In the determination of the allowable deflection for cantilevered structural members, "L" shall be taken as _____ length of the cantilever.

    A. the actual
    B. 1 ½ times the
    C. twice the
    D. 3 times the

33. Attic spaces served by a fixed stair shall be designed to support a minimum live load of _____.

    A. 10
    B. 20
    C. 30
    D. 40

34. Unless listed for lesser clearances, combustible insulation shall be separated a minimum of _____ inch(es) from recessed luminaires, fan motors and other heat-producing devices.

    A. 1
    B. 3
    C. 4
    D. 6

35. The aggregate area of openings in an exterior wall of a nonsprinklered dwelling located with a fire separation distance of four feet is limited to a maximum of _____ percent of the exterior wall area.

    A. 10
    B. 25
    C. 50
    D. 100

1.	A	Figure R301.2(4)
2.	D	Figure R301.2(5)A
3.	D	Figure R301.2(6)
4.	C	Figure R301.2(7)
5.	C	Figure R301.2(8)
6.	A	Table R301.2.1.2
7.	B	Table R301.2.1.3
8.	B	Sec. R301.2.1.4, #1
9.	B	Table R301.2.2.1.1
10.	C	Table 301.5
11.	C	Sec. R301.2.2.2.1, #5
12.	D	Sec. R301.2.2.2.6, #4
13.	C	Sec. R301.2.3
14.	C	Table R301.5
15.	C	Table R301.5, Note b
16.	C	Table R301.5
17.	C	Table R301.6
18.	D	Table R301.7
19.	B	Table R301.7
20.	C	Table R302.1(1)
21.	C	Tables R302.1(1), R302.1(2)
22.	D	Sec. R302.1, Exception 3; R105.2, #Bl
23.	C	Sec. R302.9.1
24.	D	Sec. R302.4.1.2
25.	A	Sec. R302.1, Exception 4
26.	D	Sec. R301.2.1.4, #3
27.	B	Sec. R301.2.2, #2
28.	A	Sec. R302.5.1
29.	A	Sec. R302.2, Item 1
30.	A	Table R301.5, Note f
31.	C	Table R301.2.1.2, Note c
32.	C	Table R301.7, Note b
33.	C	Table R301.5
34.	B	Table R302.14
35.	B	Table R302.1(1)

International Residential Code, 2018
Sections R303 - R310 - Questions and Answers

1. When natural light is used to satisfy the minimum light requirements for habitable rooms, the aggregate glazing area shall be a minimum of _____ of the floor area.

   A. 4 percent
   B. 5 percent
   C. 8 percent
   D. 10 percent

2. When natural ventilation is used to satisfy the minimum ventilation requirements for habitable rooms, the aggregate open area to the outdoors shall be a minimum of _____ of the floor area.

   A. 4 percent
   B. 5 percent
   C. 8 percent
   D. 10 percent

3. Garage sprinklers, when required, shall be residential sprinklers or quick-response sprinklers, designed to provide a density of _____ gpm/sf.

   A. 0.05
   B. 0.10
   C. 0.15
   D. 0.25

4. Where applicable escape and rescue openings are provided and a whole-house mechanical ventilation system is installed, glazing is not required for natural light purposes if artificial light is provided capable of producing an average illumination of _____ footcandle(s) over the area of the room at a height of 30 inches above the floor level.

   A. 1
   B. 5
   C. 6
   D. 10

5. Habitable rooms other than kitchens shall have a minimum floor area of _____ square feet.

   A. 70
   B. 100
   C. 120
   D. 150

6. The floor area beneath a furred ceiling can be considered to be contributing to the minimum required habitable area for the room where it has a minimum height of _____ above the floor.

   A. 5 feet
   B. 6 feet, 4 inches
   C. 6 feet, 8 inches
   D. 7 feet

7. Other than in a kitchen, what is the minimum permitted horizontal dimension of any habitable room?

   A. 6 feet
   B. 7 feet
   C. 8 feet
   D. 9 feet

8. In general, the minimum required ceiling height of all habitable rooms is _____.

   A. 6 feet, 8 inches
   B. 7 feet, 0 inches
   C. 7 feet, 6 inches
   D. 8 feet, 0 inches

9. Ceilings in portions of basements without habitable spaces shall have a minimum ceiling height of _____ from the finished floor to beams, ducts, or other obstructions.

   A. 6 feet, 4 inches
   B. 6 feet, 6 inches
   C. 6 feet, 8 inches
   D. 7 feet, 0 inches

10. A minimum clearance of _____ shall be provided in front of a water closet.

   A. 21 inches
   B. 24 inches
   C. 30 inches
   D. 32 inches

11. The minimum distance between the centerline of a water closet and a side wall shall be _____.

    A. 15 inches
    B. 16 inches
    C. 18 inches
    D. 21 inches

12. Within a shower compartment, the walls shall be finished with a nonabsorbent surface to a minimum height of _____.

    A. 70 inches
    B. 72 inches
    C. 78 inches
    D. 84 inches

13. Complying heating facilities are not required in dwelling units where the winter design temperature of the locale is a minimum of _____ .

    A. 60°F
    B. 64°F
    C. 68°F
    D. 70°F

14. Where located less than 5 feet above the walking surface, glazing in a wall enclosing an outdoor hot tub shall be considered to be installed in a hazardous location unless the glazing is a minimum of _____ horizontally from the water's edge.

    A. 3 feet
    B. 4 feet
    C. 5 feet
    D. 10 feet

15. A skylight is defined by the IRC as glass or other glazing material installed at a minimum slope of _____.

    A. 15 degrees from the vertical
    B. 30 degrees from the vertical
    C. 15 degrees from the horizontal
    D. 30 degrees from the horizontal

16. Curbs are not required for skylights installed on roofs having a minimum slope of _____.

    A.   2:12
    B.   3:12
    C.   4:12
    D.   5:12

17. A screen used to protect an air exhaust opening that terminates outdoors shall have a minimum opening size of inch and a maximum opening size of _____ inch and a maximum opening size of _____ inch.

    A. 1/8, ¼
    B. ¼, 3/8
    C. ¼, ½
    D. ½, ¾

18. A minimum clearance of _____ inches shall be provided in front of the opening to a shower.

    A. 24
    B. 30
    C. 32
    D. 36

19. Regular glass used in a louvered window shall be a minimum of _____ inch in nominal thickness.

    A. 3/32
    B. 1/8
    C. 5/32
    D. 3/16

20. Emergency escape and rescue openings shall have a maximum sill height of _____ above the floor.

    A. 40 inches
    B. 42 inches
    C. 44 inches
    D. 48 inches

21. Emergency escape and rescue openings, when considered as grade floor openings, shall have a minimum net clear opening of _____.

    A. 4.0 square feet
    B. 4.4 square feet
    C. 5.0 square feet
    D. 5.7 square feet

22. For an emergency escape and rescue opening, the minimum clear opening height shall be _____ , and the minimum clear opening width shall be _____ .

    A. 24 inches, 20 inches
    B. 24 inches, 28 inches
    C. 28 inches, 22 inches
    D. 28 inches, 24 inches

23. Where a window well is required in conjunction with an escape and rescue opening, the window well shall have a minimum net clear area of _____ square feet with a minimum horizontal dimension of _____ .

    A. 5.7, 20 inches
    B. 5.7, 24 inches
    C. 9.0, 30 inches
    D. 9.0, 36 inches

24. An asphalt surface is permitted as the floor surface of a carport provided the surface is _____ .

    A. limited to 400 square feet
    B. located at ground level
    C. sealed with an approved material
    D. sloped a minimum of 1:48

25. A 6-square-foot skylight of laminated glass shall have a minimum _____ polyvinyl butyral interlayer where located 14 feet above the walking surface.

    A. 0.015-inch
    B. 0.030-inch
    C. 0.024-inch
    D. 0.044-inch

26. Unless located at least 3 feet below the contaminant source, a mechanical outside air intake opening shall be located a minimum of _____ feet from a plumbing vent.

    A. 3
    B. 5
    C. 10
    D. 12

27. The illumination source for interior stairs shall be capable of illuminating the treads and landings to a minimum level of _____ foot-candle(s).

    A. 1
    B. 5
    C. 8
    D. 10

28. A shower shall have a minimum ceiling height of _____ above an area of not less than 30 inches by 30 inches at the showerhead.

   A. 6 feet, 6 inches
   B. 6 feet, 8 inches
   C. 6 feet, 10 inches
   D. 7 feet, 0 inches

29. Glazing adjacent to a door to a storage closet is not required to be safety glazing provided the closet is a maximum of _____ in depth.

   A. 24 inches
   B. 30 inches
   C. 36 inches
   D. 42 inches

30. Glazing in a door shall be safety glazing where the opening allows the passage of a minimum _____ sphere.

   A. 3-inch
   B. 3 ½-inch
   C. 4-inch
   D. 6-inch

31. Where window wells are provided for escape and rescue openings, window well drainage is not required where the building foundation is supported by Group _____ soils.

   A. I
   B. I or II
   C. I, II, or III
   D. IV

32. Where lighting outlets are installed in interior stairways, a wall switch shall be provided at each floor level to control the light outlet where the stairway has a minimum of _____ risers.

   A. two
   B. three
   C. four
   D. six

33. A 4-square-foot glazed panel installed in an entry door shall have a minimum glazing category classification of CPSC 16 CFR 1201 Category _____.

   A. I
   B. II
   C. III
   D. IV

34. Except for storm shelters and those basements with a maximum floor area of _____ square feet used only to house mechanical equipment, all basements shall be provided with at least one operable emergency escape and rescue opening.

   A. 120
   B. 150
   C. 200
   D. 400

35. An emergency escape window may be installed under a deck or porch, provided a minimum height of _____ inches is maintained to a yard or court.

   A. 24
   B. 36
   C. 44
   D. 48

International Residential Code, 2018
Sections R303 – R310 - Answers

1.	C	Sec. R303.1
2.	A	Sec. R303.1
3.	A	Sec. R309.5
4.	C	Sec. R303.1, Exception 2
5.	A	Sec. R304.1
6.	D	Sec. R304.3
7.	B	Sec. R304.2
8.	B	Sec. R305.1
9.	A	Sec. R305.1.1, Exception
10.	A	Figure R307.1 (also found in P2705 #5)
11.	A	Figure R307.1 (also found in P2705 #5)
12.	B	Sec. R307.2
13.	A	Sec. R303.10
14.	C	Sec. R308.4.5
15.	A	Secs. R308.6.1, R202
16.	B	Sec. R308.6.8
17.	C	Sec. R303.6
18.	A	Figure R307.1
19.	D	Sec. R308.2
20.	C	Sec. R310.2.2
21.	C	Sec. R310.2.1, Exception
22.	A	Sec. R310.2.1
23.	D	Sec. R310.2.3
24.	B	Sec. R309.2, Exception
25.	C	Sec. R308.6.2, #1
26.	C	Sec. R303.5.1, Exception 1
27	A	Sec. R303.7
28.	B	Sec. R305.1, Exception 2
29.	C	Sec. R308.4.2, Exception 3
30.	A	Sec. R308.4.1, Exception 1
31.	A	Sec. R310.2.3.2, Exception
32.	D	Sec. R303.7.1
33.	A	Table R308.3.l(l)
34.	C	Sec. R310.1, Exception
35.	B	Sec. R310.2.4

International Residential Code, 2018
Sections R311 - R323 - Questions and Answers

1. The minimum width of a hallway shall be _____.

   A. 32 inches
   B. 36 inches
   C. 42 inches
   D. 44 inches

2. Where the stairway has a straight run, a stairway landing shall have a minimum depth of _____ measured in the direction of travel.

   A. 30 inches
   B. 32 inches
   C. 36 inches
   D. 42 inches

3. Unless technically infeasible due to site constraints, the maximum slope of a ramp serving the required egress door shall be one unit vertical in _____ units horizontal.

   A. five
   B. eight
   C. ten
   D. twelve

4. Handrails are not required on ramps having a maximum slope of _____.

   A. 1:5
   B. 1:8
   C. 1:12
   D. 1:15

5. Where a ramp changes direction, the width of the landing perpendicular to the ramp slope shall be a minimum of _____ inches.

   A. 36
   B. 42
   C. 48
   D. 60

6. Stairways shall be a minimum _____ wide at all points above the permitted handrail height and below the required headroom height.

   A. 30 inches
   B. 34 inches
   C. 36 inches
   D. 38 inches

7. Where a handrail is provided on one side of a stairway, what is the minimum required clear width at and below the handrail height?

   A. 27 inches
   B. 29 inches
   C. 31 1/2 inches
   D. 36 inches

8. Stairways shall have a maximum riser height of _____ and a minimum tread run of _____.

   A. 8 1/4 inches, 9 inches
   B. 8 inches, 9 inches
   C. 7 3/4 inches, 10 inches
   D. 7 1/2 inches, 10 inches

9. The maximum variation between the greatest riser height and the smallest riser height within any flight of stairs shall be _____.

   A. 1 /4 inch
   B. 3/8 inch
   C. 1/2 inch
   D. 5/8 inch

10. Unless a minimum tread depth of _____ is provided, a minimum 3/4-inch nosing is required at the leading edge of all treads.

   A. 9 ½ inches
   B. 10 inches
   C. 11 inches
   D. 12 inches

11. Unless the stair has a total rise of no more than 30 inches, the opening between treads at open risers shall be such that a minimum _____ sphere shall not pass through.

   A. 3-inch
   B. 4-inch
   C. 6-inch
   D. no limitation is mandated

12. In the identification of flood hazard areas, areas that have been determined to be subject to maximum wave heights of _____ are not required to be designated coastal high-hazard areas feet unless subject to high-velocity wave action or wave-induced erosion.

    A. 3
    B. 4
    C. 5
    D. 6

13. What is the maximum riser height permitted for spiral stairways?

    A. 7 ¾ inches
    B. 8 inches
    C. 8 ¼ inches
    D. 9 ½ inches

14. Stairway handrail height shall be, measured vertically from the nosing of the treads, a minimum of _____ and a maximum of _____.

    A. 30 inches, 34 inches
    B. 30 inches, 38 inches
    C. 34 inches, 38 inches
    D. 34 inches, 42 inches

15. Where a stairway handrail is located adjacent to a wall, a minimum clearance of _____ shall be provided between the wall and the handrail.

    A. 1 ¼ inches
    B. 1 ½ inches
    C. 2 inches
    D. 3 ½ inches

16. A Type I handrail having a circular cross section shall have a minimum outside diameter of _____ and a maximum outside diameter of _____.

    A. 1 1/4 inches, 2 inches
    B. 1 ¼ inches, 2 5/8 inches
    C. 1 ½ inches, 2 inches
    D. 1 ½ inches, 2 5/8 inches

17. A porch, balcony or similar raised floor surface more than 30 inches above the floor or grade below shall be provided with a guard having a minimum height of _____.

    A. 32 inches
    B. 34 inches
    C. 36 inches
    D. 42 inches

18. Required guards on open sides of raised floor areas shall be provided with intermediate rails or ornamental closures such that a minimum _____ sphere cannot pass through.

    A. 3-inch
    B. 4-inch
    C. 6-inch
    D. 9-inch

19. Which one of the following areas in a dwelling unit does not specifically require the installation of a smoke alarm?

    A. basement
    B. kitchen
    C. habitable attic
    D. sleeping room

20. Where gypsum wallboard is used to separate foam plastic from the interior of the dwelling, the separation shall be minimum _____ gypsum board.

    A. ½-inch
    B. ½-inch Type X
    C. 5/8-inch
    D. 5/85-inch Type X

21. When carbon monoxide alarms are required in new construction, they shall be installed _____.

    A. within every bedroom
    B. on all floor levels of multistory units
    C. outside of each separate sleeping area
    D. in the garage

22. An automatic residential fire sprinkler system shall be provided in all buildings containing _____ or more townhouses.

    A. 3 (all townhouses require a sprinkler system)
    B. 8
    C. 16
    D. sprinkler systems are not required in townhouses

155

23. In new construction, carbon monoxide alarms are required in dwelling units _____.

    A. where fuel-fired appliances are installed
    B. that have attached garages with an opening to the dwelling
    C. with habitable space below grade
    D. either a or b

24. Unless they are made of pressure preservatively treated or naturally durable wood, wood framing members that rest on masonry or concrete exterior foundation walls shall be located a minimum of _____ from exposed ground.

    A. 6 inches
    B. 8 inches
    C. 12 inches
    D. 18 inches

25. In the establishment of a design flood elevation, the depth of peak elevation of flooding for a _____ flood is used.

    A. 10-year
    B. 20-year
    C. 50-year
    D. 100-year

26. Where stair risers are not vertical, they shall be sloped under the tread above at a maximum angle of _____ from the vertical.

    A.   10°
    B.   15°
    C.   22°
    D.   30°

27. Where foam plastic is spray applied to a sill plate without a thermal barrier, it shall have a maximum density of _____ pcf.

    A. 1.0
    B. 1.5
    C. 2.0
    D. 3.0

28. The maximum width above the recess of a Type II handrail shall be_____ inches.

    A. 1 ½
    B. 2
    C. 2 5/8
    D. 2 ¾

29. Handrails shall be provided on at least one side of a stairway having a minimum of _____ risers.

    A. 2
    B. 3
    C. 4
    D. 5

30. What is the minimum required clear opening for an egress door from a dwelling unit?

    A. 32 inches by 78 inches
    B. 32 inches by 80 inches
    C. 36 inches by 78 inches
    D. 36 inches by 80 inches

31. Where the door does not swing over the landing, the exterior landing at a required egress door shall be located a maximum of _____ inches below the top of the threshold.

    A. 7
    B. 7 ½
    C. 7 ¾
    D. 8

32. Where nosings are required on a stairway with solid risers, the nosings shall extend a minimum of _____ inch(es) and a maximum of _____ inch(es) beyond the risers.

    A. 1/2, 1
    B. ¾, 1 ¼
    C. 1, 1 ½
    D. 1 1/4, 2

33. Address numbers used for building identification shall have a minimum height of _____inches.

    A. 4
    B. 6
    C. 8
    D. 9

34. Openings for required guards on the sides of stair treads shall be provided with intermediate rails or ornamental closures such that a minimum _____ sphere cannot pass through.

    A. 3 ½
    B. 4
    C. 4 3/8
    D. 6

35. Where a safe room is constructed as a storm shelter in order to provide safe refuge from high winds, the room shall be constructed in accordance with _____.

    A. ICC/NSSA-500
    B. CPSC 16 CFR, Part 1201
    C. DOC PS 1-07
    D. FEMA TB-2-93

International Residential Code, 2018
Sections R311 – R323 - Answers

1.	B	Sec. R311.6
2.	C	Sec. R311.7.6
3.	D	Sec. R311.8.1
4.	C	Sec. R311.8.3
5.	A	Sec. R311.8.2
6.	C	Sec. R311.7.1
7.	C	Sec. R311.7.1
8.	C	Sec. R311.7.5.1, R311.7.5.2
9.	B	Sec. R311.7.5.1
10.	C	Sec. R311.7.5.3, Exception
11.	B	Sec. R311.7.5.1
12.	A	Sec. R322.3
13.	D	Sec. R311.7.10.1
14.	C	Sec. R311.7.8.1
15.	B	Sec. R311.7.8.3
16.	A	Sec. R311.7.8.5, #1
17.	C	Sec. R312.1.2
18.	B	Sec. R312.1.3
19.	B	Sec. R314.3
20.	A	Sec. R316.4
21.	C	Sec. R315.3
22.	A	Sec. R313.1
23.	D	Sec. R315.2.1
24.	B	Sec. R317.1, #2
25.	D	Sec. R322.1.4, #1
26.	D	Sec. R311.7.5.1
27.	C	Sec. R316.5.11, #2
28.	D	Sec. R311.7.8.5, #2
29.	C	Sec. R311.7.8
30.	A	Sec. R311.2
31.	C	Sec. R311.3.1, Exception
32.	B	Sec. R311.7.5.3
33.	A	Sec. R319.1
34.	C	Sec. R312.1.3, Exception 2
35.	A	Sec. R323.1

International Residential Code, 2018
Chapter 4 - Questions and Answers

1. Unless grading is prohibited by physical barriers, lots shall be graded away from the foundation with a minimum fall of _____ within the first _____.

   A. 6 inches, 5 feet
   B. 6 inches, 10 feet
   C. 12 inches, 5 feet
   D. 12 inches, 10 feet

2. In the absence of a complete geotechnical evaluation to determine the soil's characteristics, clayey sand material shall be assumed to have a presumptive load-bearing value of _____.

   A. 1,500 psf
   B. 2,000 psf
   C. 3,000 psf
   D. 4,000 psf

3. Concrete used in a basement slab shall have a minimum compressive strength of _____ where a severe weathering potential exists.

   A. 2,000 psi
   B. 2,500 psi
   C. 3,000 psi
   D. 3,500 psi

4. Air entrainment for concrete subjected to weathering, when required for locations other than garage floors with a steel troweled finish, shall have a total air content of _____ minimum and _____ maximum.

   A. 4 percent, 7 percent
   B. 4 percent, 8 percent
   C. 5 percent, 7 percent
   D. 5 percent, 8 percent

5. What is the minimum required width and thickness for concrete footings supporting light-frame construction for a two-story 32-foot-wide house with a crawl space, in a locale with a 30 psf snow load and soil with a load-bearing value of 2000?

    A. 12 inches by 6 inches
    B. 13 inches by 6 inches
    C. 19 inches by 6 inches
    D. 24 inches by 7 inches

6. Where there is evidence that the groundwater table can rise to within _____ inch(es) of the finished floor at the building perimeter, the grade in the under-floor space shall be as high as the outside finished grade unless an approved drainage system is provided.

    A. 1
    B. 2
    C. 4
    D. 6

7. What are the minimum and maximum required footing projections for a concrete footing having a thickness of 8 inches?

    A. 2 inches, 4 inches
    B. 2 inches, 8 inches
    C. 4 inches, 8 inches
    D. 8 inches, 12 inches

8. Where a permanent wood foundation basement wall system is used, the wall shall be supported by a minimum _____ footing plate resting on gravel or crushed stone fill a minimum of _____ in width.

    A. 2-inch-by-6-inch, 12 inches
    B. 2-inch-by-8-inch, 16 inches
    C. 2-inch-by-12-inch, 16 inches
    D. 2-inch-by-12-inch, 24 inches

9. For concrete foundation systems constructed in Seismic Design Category D2, foundations with stem walls shall be provided with a minimum of _ bar(s) at the top of the wall and ____ bar(s) near the bottom of the footing.

    A. one #4, one #4
    B. one #5, one #5
    C. one #5, two #4
    D. two #4, two #5

10. All exterior footings shall be placed a minimum of _____ below the undisturbed ground surface.

    A. 6 inches
    B. 8 inches
    C. 9 inches
    D. 12 inches

11. The maximum permitted slope for the bottom surface of footings shall be _____.

    A. 1:8
    B. 1:10
    C. 1:12
    D. 1:20

12. For a two-story dwelling assigned to Seismic Design Category B, anchor bolts used to attach wood sill plates to foundation walls shall be spaced a maximum of _____ on center.

    A. 4 feet
    B. 5 feet
    C. 6 feet
    D. 7 feet

13. Anchor bolts used to attach a wood sole plate to a concrete foundation shall be a minimum of _____ .in diameter and extend a minimum of _____ into the concrete.

    A. 1/2 inch, 7 inches
    B. 1/2 inch, 15 inches
    C. 5/8 inch, 7 inches
    D. 5/8 inch, 15 inches

14. Soil described as a "sandy clay" has a Unified Soil Classification System Symbol of _____ and is considered to be in Soil Group _____.

    A. SC, I
    B. CL, II
    C. SM, III
    D. CH, IV

15. In order to use frost protected shallow foundations, the monthly mean temperature of the building must be maintained at a minimum of _____.

   A. 60°F
   B. 64°F
   C. 68°F
   D. 70°F

16. A dwelling located in an area with an air freezing index of 3,500 is constructed with a frost-protected shallow foundation. What is the minimum required horizontal insulation R-value at the corners of the foundation?

   A. 8.0
   B. 8.6
   C. 11.2
   D. 13.1

17. A 9-foot-high plain masonry foundation wall is subjected to 7 feet of unbalanced backfill. If the soil class is GC, what is the minimum required nominal wall thickness?

   A. 8 inches solid
   B. 10 inches grout
   C. 12 inches solid
   D. 12 inches grout

18. An 8-foot-high, flat concrete foundation wall of nominal 10-inch thickness is subjected to 6 feet of unbalanced backfill. If the soil class is GP, what minimum vertical reinforcement is required?

   A. #4 at 38 inches on center
   B. #5 at 47 inches on center
   C. #6 at 43 inches on center
   D. no vertical reinforcement required

19. Where masonry veneer is used, concrete and masonry foundations shall extend a minimum of _____ above adjacent finished grade.

   A. 4 inches
   B. 6 inches
   C. 8 inches
   D. 12 inches

20. Where the foundation wall supports a minimum of _____ of unbalanced backfill, backfill shall not be placed against the wall until the wall has sufficient strength and has been anchored to the floor above or has been sufficiently braced.

    A. 2 feet
    B. 4 feet
    C. 6 feet
    D. 8 feet

21. Where wood studs having an Fb value of 1320 are used in a wood foundation wall, the minimum stud size shall be _____ and the maximum stud spacing shall be _____ on center.

    A. 2 inches by 4 inches, 24 inches
    B. 2 inches by 4 inches, 16 inches
    C. 2 inches by 6 inches, 24 inches
    D. 2 inches by 6 inches, 16 inches

22. What is the maximum height of backfill permitted against a wood foundation wall not designed by AF&PA Report # 7?

    A. 3 feet
    B. 4 feet
    C. 6 feet
    D. 7 feet

23. Required foundation drains of gravel or crushed stone shall extend a minimum of _____ beyond the outside edge of the footing and _____ above the top of the footing.

    A. 6 inches, 4 inches
    B. 6 inches, 6 inches
    C. 12 inches, 4 inches
    D. 12 inches, 6 inches

24. As a general rule, the under-floor space between the bottom of floor joists and the earth shall be provided with ventilation openings sized for a minimum net area of 1 square foot for each _____ square feet of under-floor area.

    A. 100
    B. 120
    C. 150
    D. 200

25. Access to an under-floor space through a perimeter wall shall be provided by a minimum _____ access opening.

    A. 16-inch-by-20-inch
    B. 16-inch-by-24-inch
    C. 18-inch-by-24-inch
    D. 18-inch-by-30-inch

26. Frost protection is not required for a foundation that supports a freestanding accessory structure of light-framed construction that has a maximum floor area of _____ square feet and a maximum eave height of _____ feet.

    A.   200, 10
    B.   400, 10
    C.   400, 12
    D.   600, 10

27. Gravel used as a footing material for a wood foundation shall be washed, well graded and have a maximum stone size of _____ inch.

    A. ¼
    B. ½
    C. ¾
    D. 1

28. Horizontal insulation used in a frost protected shallow foundation system shall be protected against damage if it is located less than _____ inches below the ground surface.

    A. 12
    B. 15
    C. 18
    D. 24

29. Where waterproofing of a masonry foundation wall is necessary due to the presence of a high water table, a minimum membrane thickness of _____ is required if the waterproofing material is polymer-modified asphalt.

    A. 6-mil
    B. 30-mil
    C. 40-mil
    D. 60-mil

30. Ventilating openings providing under-floor ventilation shall be located so that at least one such opening is installed a maximum of ____ .feet from each corner of the building.

   A. 2
   B. 3
   C. 5
   D. 6

31. A minimum of _____ anchor bolt(s) located _____ of the plate section is required to anchor maximum 24-inch-long walls connecting offset braced wall panels.

   A. 1, within the middle third
   B. 1, within the middle one-half
   C. 2, in the outer one-fourths
   D. 2, within 6 inches of each end

32. Unless specifically approved, what is the maximum slump permitted for concrete placed in removable foundation wall forms?

   A. 4 inches
   B. 4 ½
   C. 5 inches
   D. 6 inches

33. Where one coat of complying surface-bonding cement is used as the required dampproofing over the parging of a masonry foundation wall, the cement coating must be a minimum of _____ inch thick.

   A. 1/8
   B. 3/16
   C. ¼
   D. 3/8

34. Steel columns used as a part of a foundation system shall be a minimum of _____ inches in diameter standard pipe size or approved equivalent.

   A. 3
   B. 3 ½
   C. 4
   D. 5

35. The continuous vapor barrier required in an unvented crawl space shall extend a minimum of _____ inches up the stem wall.

    A. 3
    B. 4
    C. 6
    D. 8

International Residential Code, 2018
Chapter 4 - Answers

1.	B	Sec. R401.3
2.	B	Table R401.4.1
3.	B	Table R402.2
4.	C	Table R402.2, Note d
5.	B	Table R403.1(1)
6.	D	Sec. R408.6
7.	B	Sec. R403.1.1
8.	B	Figure R403.1(2)
9.	A	Sec. R403.1.3.1
10.	D	Sec. R403.1.4
11.	B	Sec. R403.1.5
12.	C	Sec. R403.1.6
13.	A	Sec. R403.1.6
14.	B	Table R405.1
15.	B	Sec. R403.3
16.	C	Table R403.3(1)
17.	B	Table R404.1.l(l)
18.	D	Table R404.1.2(4)
19.	A	Sec. R404.1.6
20.	B	Sec. R404.1.7, Exception
21.	D	Sec. R404.2.2
22.	B	Sec. R404.2.3
23.	D	Sec. R405.1
24.	C	Sec. R408.1
25.	B	Sec. R408.4
26.	D	Sec. R403.1.4.1, Exception 1
27.	C	Sec. R403.2
28.	A	Sec. R403.3.2
29.	C	Sec. R406.2, #5
30.	B	Sec. R408.2
31.	A	Sec. R403.1.6, Exception 1
32.	D	Sec. R404.1.3.3.4
33.	A	Sec. R406.1, #3
34.	A	Sec. R407.3
35.	C	Sec. R408.3, #1

International Residential Code, 2018
Chapter 5 - Questions and Answers

1. A minimum design live load of _____ shall be used for the determination of the maximum allowable floor joist spans in attics that are accessed by a fixed stairway.

   A. 10 psf
   B. 20 psf
   C. 30 psf
   D. 40 psf

2. Where 2-inch by 10-inch floor joists of #2 hem-fir are spaced at 16 inches on center, what is the maximum allowable span where such joists support a sleeping room and a dead load of 10 psf?

   A. 16 feet, 0 inches
   B. 16 feet, 10 inches
   C. 17 feet, 8 inches
   D. 19 feet, 8 inches

3. Where 2-inch by 10-inch floor joists of #1 spruce-pine-fir are spaced at 16 inches on center, what is the maximum allowable span where such joists support a living room and a dead load of 20 psf?

   A. 14 feet, 1 inch
   B. 15 feet, 5 inches
   C. 16 feet, 0 inches
   D. 16 feet, 9 inches

4. Where the ground snow load is 30 psf, what is the maximum allowable span of a built-up spruce-pine-fir girder consisting of three 2 by 12s when it is located at an exterior bearing wall and supports a roof, a ceiling and one center-bearing floor in a building having a width of 28 feet?

   A. 5 feet, 2 inches
   B. 7 feet, 8 inches
   C. 8 feet, 0 inches
   D. 8 feet, 11 inches

5. Where a built-up girder of three Southern pine 2 by 10s is used for an exterior bearing wall, what is the minimum number of jack studs required to support a girder that carries a roof, ceiling and one clear span floor in a building having a width of 20 feet?

   A. 1
   B. 2
   C. 3
   D. 4

6. What is the maximum allowable girder span for an interior bearing wall using a built-up girder consisting of three hem fir 2 by 10s and supporting one floor in a building having a width of 36 feet?

   A. 5 feet, 5 inches
   B. 6 feet, 9 inches
   C. 7 feet, 7 inches
   D. 8 feet, 10 inches

7. Doubled joists under parallel bearing partitions that are separated to permit the installation of piping or vents shall be blocked at maximum intervals of _____ on center.

   A. 16 inches
   B. 32 inches
   C. 48 inches
   D. 60 inches

8. The ends of floor joists shall bear a minimum of _____ on wood or metal.

   A. 1 inch
   B. 1 ½ inches
   C. 2 ½ inches
   D. 3 inches

9. Where floor joists frame from opposite sides across the top of a wood girder and are lapped, the minimum lap shall be _____.

   A. 3 inches
   B. 4 inches
   C. 6 inches
   D. 8 inches

10. Bridging shall be provided to support floor joists laterally where the minimum 2xjoist depth exceeds _____ nominal size.

   A. 6 inches
   B. 8 inches
   C. 10 inches
   D. 12 inches

11. What is the maximum permitted length of a notch in a floor joist?

   A. 2 inches
   B. twice the notch depth
   C. 1/3 the depth of the joist
   D. 1/6 the depth of the joist

12. A hole bored through a floor joist shall have a maximum diameter of _____.

   A. 2 inches
   B. 1/6 the depth of the joist
   C. 1/4 the depth of the joist
   D. 1/3 the depth of the joist

13. Where a solid lumber floor joist is both notched and bored, a minimum of _____ inch(es) shall be provided between the notch and the bored hole.

   A. 1
   B. 1 ½
   C. 2
   D. 4

14. Where a ceiling is suspended below the floor framing, draftstops shall be installed so that the maximum area of any concealed space is _____ square feet.

   A. 100
   B. 400
   C. 1,000
   D. 1,500

15. Where wood structural panels are used for required draftstops in concealed floor/ceiling assemblies, what is the minimum thickness mandated?

   A. 5/16 inch
   B. 3/8 inch
   C. 15/32 inch
   D. 23/32 inch

16. Wood structural panels 15/32-inch thick are to be used as subfloor sheathing and are to be covered with 3/4-inch wood finish flooring installed at right angles to the joists. What is the maximum allowable span of the wood structural panels if the span rating of the panels is 32/16?

   A. 0 inches; the panels may not be used as subfloor sheathing
   B. 16 inches
   C. 20 inches
   D. 24 inches

17. Where Species Group 2 sanded plywood is used as combination subfloor underlayment, what is the minimum required plywood thickness where the joists are spaced at 16 inches on center?

   A. ½ inch
   B. 5/8 inch
   C. ¾ inch
   D. 7/8 inch

18. Steel floor framing constructed in accordance with the prescriptive provisions of the IRC is limited to buildings a maximum of _____ stories above grade plane with each story having a maximum length perpendicular to the joist span of _____ feet.

   A. 2, 40
   B. 2, 60
   C. 3, 40
   D. 3, 60

19. Screws attaching floor sheathing to cold-formed steel joists shall be installed with a minimum edge distance of _____ inch.

   A. ¼
   B. 3/8
   C. ½
   D. 5/8

20. In a steel floor framing system, No. 8 screws spaced at a maximum of _____ on center on the edges and _____ on center at the intermediate supports shall be used to fasten the subfloor to the floor joists.

   A. 6 inches, 10 inches
   B. 6 inches, 12 inches
   C. 8 inches, 12 inches
   D. 8 inches, 14 inches

21. Cold-formed 33 ksi steel joists are installed as single spans at 16 inches on center in the floor framing system for a dwelling. If the nominal joist size is 800S162-43, the maximum span for a 40 psf live load is _____.

   A. 10 feet, 5 inches
   B. 12 feet, 3 inches
   C. 14 feet, 1 inch
   D. 15 feet, 6 inches

22. Where a wood beam does not bear directly on a masonry wall, a 2-inch-thick sill plate must be provided under the beam with a minimum nominal bearing area of _____ square inches.

   A. 32
   B. 48
   C. 60
   D. 64

23. The maximum fill depth when preparing a site for construction of a concrete slab-on-ground floor_____ is for earth and _____ for clean sand or gravel.

   A. 6 inches, 12 inches
   B. 8 inches, 16 inches
   C. 8 inches, 24 inches
   D. 12 inches, 24 inches

24. A base course is not required for the prepared subgrade for a concrete floor slab below grade where the soil is classified as _____.

   A. GM
   B. SC
   C. CH
   D. OH

25. Where a vapor retarder is required between a concrete floor slab and the prepared subgrade, the joints of the vapor retarder shall be lapped a minimum of

   A. 2 inches
   B. 4 inches
   C. 6 inches
   D. 8 inches

26. Where supporting only a light-frame exterior bearing wall and roof, what is the maximum cantilever span for 2 by 10 floor joists spaced at 16 inches on center, provided the roof has a width of 32 feet and the ground snow load is 30 psf?

   A. 18 inches
   B. 21 inches
   C. 22 inches
   D. 26 inches

27. Where supporting an exterior balcony in an area having a ground snow load of 50 psf, what is the maximum cantilever span for 2 by 12 floor joists spaced at 16 inches on center?

   A. 49 inches
   B. 57 inches
   C. 67 inches
   D. 72 inches

28. Unless the joists are of sufficient size to carry the load, bearing partitions perpendicular to floor joists shall be offset a maximum of _____ from supporting girders, walls or partitions.

   A. 6 inches
   B. 12 inches
   C. the depth of the floor sheathing
   D. the depth of the floor joists

29. Where an opening in floor framing is framed with a single header joist the same size as the floor joist, the maximum header joist span shall be _____ feet.

   A. 3
   B. 4
   C. 6
   D. 12

30. If a base course is required for a concrete floor slab installed below grade, the minimum thickness of the base course shall be _____ inches.

   A. 3
   B. 4
   C. 6
   D. 8

31. Unless supported by other approved means, the ends of each joist, beam or girder shall have a minimum of _____ inches of bearing on masonry or concrete.

   A. 1 ½
   B. 2
   C. 3
   D. 4

32. Notches at the ends of solid lumber joists, rafters and beams shall have a maximum depth of _____.

   A. 2 inches
   B. 3 inches
   C. one-half the depth of the member
   D. one-fourth the depth of the member

33. Holes bored into solid lumber joists, rafter and beams shall be located a minimum of _____ from the top or bottom of the member.

   A. 1 inch
   B. 2 inches
   C. one-sixth the member depth
   D. one-third the member depth

34. Deck joists for wood-framed exterior decks are permitted to cantilever a maximum of _____ of the actual, adjacent joist span.

   A. 1/6
   B. ¼
   C. 1/3
   D. ½

35. Where reinforcement is provided in concrete slab-on-ground floors, the reinforcement shall be supported to remain within what section of the slab during the concrete placement?

   A. the middle one-third
   B. the middle one-half
   C. the center to the upper one-third
   D. the center to the upper one-fourth

International Residential Code, 2018
Chapter 5 - Answers

1.	C	Sec. R502.3.1
2.	B	Table R502.3.1(1)
3.	A	Table R502.3.1(2)
4.	D	Sec. R502.5, Table R602.7(1)
5.	B	Sec. R502.5, Table R602.7(1)
6.	B	Sec. R502.5, Table R602.7(2)
7.	C	Sec. R502.4
8.	B	Sec. R502.6
9.	A	Sec. R502.6.1
10.	D	Sec. R502.7.1
11.	C	Sec. R502.8.1
12.	D	Sec. R502.8.1
13.	C	Sec. R502.8.1
14.	C	Secs. R502.12, R302.12
15.	B	Secs. R502.12, R302.12.1
16.	D	Table R503.2.1.1(1), Note h
17.	B	Table R503.2.1.1(2)
18.	D	Sec. R505.1.1
19.	B	Sec. R505.2.5
20.	B	Table R505.3.1(2)
21.	C	Table R505.3.2
22.	B	Sec. R502.6
23.	C	Sec. R506.2.1
24.	A	Sec. R506.2.2, Exception; Table R405.1
25.	C	Sec. R506.2.3
26.	A	Table R502.3.3(1)
27.	C	Table R502.3.3(2)
28.	D	Sec. R502.4
29.	B	Sec. R502.10
30.	B	Sec. R506.2.2
31.	C	Sec. R502.6
32.	D	Sec. R502.8.1
33.	B	Sec. R502.8.1
34.	B	Sec. R507.6
35.	C	Sec. R506.2.4

International Residential Code, 2018
Chapter 6 and 7 - Questions and Answers

1. What is the maximum center-to-center stud spacing permitted for a 2-inch by 6-inch, 8-foot-high wood stud bearing wall supporting two floors, roof and ceiling?

   A. 8 inches
   B. 12 inches
   C. 16 inches
   D. 24 inches

2. In wood wall framing where top and bottom plates are attached to the studs, which of the following fastening methods is acceptable?

   A. three 8d box, toe nailed
   B. three 8d common, end nailed
   C. three 10d box, toe nailed
   D. three 10d box, end nailed

3. The minimum offset for end joints in a double top plate shall be_____.

   A. 24 inches
   B. 36 inches
   C. 48 inches
   D. 60 inches

4. A single top plate is permitted in a wood stud bearing wall where the rafters or joists are located within _____ of the center of the studs.

   A. 0 inches; no tolerance is permitted
   B. 1 inch
   C. 1 ½ inches
   D. 5 inches

5. Where the wall sheathing is used to resist wind pressures, what is the maximum stud spacing permitted for 3/8-inch wood structural panel wall sheathing with a span rating of 24/0.

   A. 12 inches o.c.
   B. 16 inches o.c.
   C. 20 inches o.c.
   D. 24 inches o.c.

6. In a nonbearing partition, a wood stud may be notched a maximum of _____ inch

   A. 5/8 inch
   B. 1 3/8 inches
   C. 40 percent of the stud width
   D. 60 percent of the stud width

7. A bored hole shall be located a minimum of _____ from the edge of a wood stud.

   A. 3/8 inch
   B. ½ inch
   C. 5/8 inch
   D. 1 inch

8. In a nonbearing interior partition, what is the maximum diameter permitted for a bored hole in a wood stud?

   A. 1 ½ inches
   B. 25 percent of the stud depth
   C. 40 percent of the stud depth
   D. 60 percent of the stud depth

9. A 15-inch-deep box header in an exterior wall is constructed with wood structural panels on both sides. What is the maximum allowable header span for a condition where the header supports a clear-span roof truss with a span of 26 feet?

   A. 4 feet
   B. 5 feet
   C. 7 feet
   D. 8 feet

10. Which of the following materials is not specifically identified by the IRC as a fireblocking material?

    A. 1/4-inch cement-based millboard
    B. 1/2-inch gypsum board
    C. 15/32-inch wood structural panel
    D. 3/4-inch particleboard

11. Where unfaced fiberglass batt insulation is used as a freeblocking material in the wall cavity of a wood stud wall system, the insulation shall be installed with a minimum vertical height of _____.

    A. 16 inches
    B. 3 feet
    C. 4 feet
    D. the entire stud space

12. A foundation cripple wall shall be considered an additional story for stud sizing requirements where the wall height exceeds _____.

   A. 14 inches
   B. 30 inches
   C. 36 inches
   D. 48 inches

13. The distance between adjacent edges of braced wall panels along a braced wall line must be a maximum of _____ feet.

   A. 16
   B. 20
   C. 25
   D. 35

14. Where located in Seismic Design Category B, braced wall panels shall begin a maximum of _____ from each end of a braced wall line.

   A. 4 feet
   B. 8 feet
   C. 10 feet
   D. 12 feet, 6 inches

15. In steel-framed wall construction, rafters may be offset a maximum of _____ from the centerline of the load-bearing steel studs.

   A. 0 inches; no tolerance is permitted
   B. 3/4 inch
   C. 1 inch
   D. 5 inches

16. Web holes in load-bearing steel wall framing members shall have a minimum distance of _____ between the edge of the bearing surface and the edge of the hole.

   A. 1 1/2 inches
   B. 3 inches
   C. 4 inches
   D. 10 inches

17. Exterior walls parallel to a braced wall line are permitted to be offset a maximum of _____ feet from the designated braced wall line location.

 A. 2
 B. 4
 C. 5
 D. 6

18. Where ledgers are used at the connection between a masonry wall and a wood floor system having floor joists spanning 16 feet, 1 / 2-inch ledger bolts shall be located at a maximum of _____ on center, provided the building is in Seismic Design Category A, B or C and the wind loads are less than 30 psf.

 A. 1 foot, 0 inches
 B. 1 foot, 3 inches
 C. 1 foot, 9 inches
 D. 2 feet, 0 inches

19. When 1/2-inch gypsum board is used as an interior wall covering and installed perpendicular to framing members at 16 inches on center, the maximum spacing of nails is _____ on center where adhesive is used.

 A. 7 inches
 B. 8 inches
 C. 12 inches
 D. 16 inches

20. Screws for attaching gypsum board to wood framing shall penetrate the wood a minimum of _____.

 A. ¼ inch
 B. 3/8 inch
 C. ½ inch
 D. 5/8 inch

21. Water-resistant gypsum board shall not be installed over which of the following classifications of vapor retarders when located in a tub or shower compartment?

 A. I or II
 B. II or III
 C. I, II or III
 D. III only

22. Where 3/8-inch particleboard is used as an exterior wall covering, what type of fasteners are required if the particleboard is attached directly to the studs?

   A. 0.120 nail, 2 inches long
   B. 6d box nail
   C. 8d box nail
   D. direct attachment to the studs is prohibited

23. In Seismic Design Category D1, metal ties for anchoring masonry veneer to a supporting wall shall support a maximum of _____ of wall area.

   A. 2 square feet
   B. 2 2/3 square feet
   C. 3 1/2 square feet
   D. 4 1/2 square feet

24. An Exterior Insulation Finish System (EIFS) shall terminate a minimum of _____ above the finished ground level.

   A. 1 inch
   B. 2 inches
   C. 6 inches
   D. 8 inches

25. What is the minimum required size of a steel angle spanning 8 feet used as a lintel supporting one story of masonry veneer above?

   A. 3 x 3 x ¼
   B. 4 x 3 x ¼
   C. 5 x 3 ½ x 5/16
   D. 6 x 3 ½ x 5/16

26. Utility grade studs, where used in loadbearing walls supporting only a roof and a ceiling, shall have a maximum height of _____ feet.

   A. 8
   B. 10
   C. 12
   D. 14

27. Asphalt felt applied as a portion of the exterior wall envelope shall be applied horizontally, with the upper layer lapped over the lower layer a minimum of _____ inch(es).

   A. 1
   B. 2
   C. 4
   D. 6

28. 15 /3 2-inch wood structural panels attached to wall framing with 15 gage staples shall be fastened at a maximum of _____ inches at the panel edges and inches at the intermediate supports.

   A. 3, 6
   B. 4, 8
   C. 5, 10
   D. 6, 12

29. Where the top plate of an interior load-bearing wall is notched by more than _____ of its width to accommodate piping, a complying metal tie shall be installed.

   A. 25 percent
   B. 33 1/3 percent
   C. 40 percent
   D. 50 percent

30. A weep screed installed on exterior stud walls in an exterior plaster application must be placed a minimum of _____ inch(es) above paved areas.

   A. 1
   B. 2
   C. 4
   D. 6

31. Where an exterior wall top plate is notched to the extent that a metal tie is required across the opening, the tie shall be fastened to the plate at each side of the opening with a minimum of _____ 10d nails at each side, or equivalent.

   A. two
   B. four
   C. six
   D. eight

32. For a building located in Seismic Design Category Do, plate washers used in the connection of braced wall line sills to a concrete foundation shall be a minimum of _____ in size.

   A. 0.188 inch by 2 inches by 2 inches
   B. 0.229 inch by 2 inches by 2 inches
   C. 0.229 inch by 3 inches by 3 inches
   D. 0.375 inch by 3 inches by 3 inches

33. Fasteners for hardboard panel and lap siding shall penetrate a minimum of _____ inch(es) into framing.

   A. ¾
   B. 7/8
   C. 1 ¼
   D. 1 ½

34. End-jointed lumber used in an assembly required by the IRC to have a fire resistance rating must have the designation _____ included in its grade mark.

   A. Fire Assembly Certified (FAC)
   B. Fire Resistant Rated (FRR)
   C. Heat and Fire Resistant (HFR)
   D. Heat Resistant Adhesive (HRA)

35. The water-resistive vapor permeable barrier required to be applied over wood-based wall sheathing shall have a performance level equivalent to that of _____ layer(s) of Grade _____ paper.

   A. one, A
   B. one, B
   C. two, C
   D. two, D

International Residential Code, 2018
Chapter 6 and 7 - Answers

1.	C	Table R602.3(5)
2.	D	Table R602.3(1), #16
3.	A	Sec. R602.3.2
4.	B	Sec. R602.3.2, Exception, #2
5.	B	Table R602.3(3)
6.	C	Sec. R602.6, #1
7.	C	Sec. R602.6, #2
8.	D	Sec. R602.6, #2
9.	D	Table R602.7.3
10.	C	Sec. R602.8, R302.11.1
11.	A	Sec. R602.8, R302.11.1.2
12.	D	Sec. R602.9
13.	B	Sec. R602.10.2.2
14.	C	Sec. R602.10.2.2
15.	B	Sec. R603.1.2, #1
16.	D	Sec. R603.2.6.1, #6
17.	B	Sec. R602.10.1.2
18.	A	Figure R606.11(l)
19.	D	Table R702.3.5
20.	D	Sec. R702.3.5.1
21.	A	Sec. R702.3.7
22.	D	Table R703.3(1)
23.	A	Sec. R703.8.4.1, Exception
24.	C	Sec. R703.9.1, #5
25.	C	Table R703.8.3.1
26.	A	Sec. R602.3.1, Exception 1
27.	B	Sec. R703.2
28.	B	Table R602.3(2)
29.	D	Sec. R602.6.1
30.	B	Sec. R703.7.2.1
31.	D	Sec. R602.6.1
32.	C	Sec. R602.11.1
33.	D	Sec. R703.3.4, #2
34.	D	Sec. R602.1.2
35.	D	Sec. R703.7.3

International Residential Code, 2018
Chapter 8 and 9 - Questions and Answers

1. On a site having expansive soil, roof drainage water shall discharge a minimum of _____ from the foundation walls or to an approved drainage system.

   A. 2 feet
   B. 5 feet
   C. 4 feet
   D. 10 feet

2. Where the roof pitch is less than _____, the structural members that support rafters and ceiling joists (such as ridge beams, hips and valleys) shall be designed as beams.

   A. 3:12
   B. 4:12
   C. 5:12
   D. 6:12

3. The maximum spacing of collar ties shall be _____ on center.

   A. 16 inches
   B. 4 feet
   C. 5 feet
   D. 8 feet

4. Ends of ceiling joists shall be lapped a minimum of _____ unless butted and toenailed to the supporting member.

   A. 1 1/2 inches
   B. 3 inches
   C. 4 inches
   D. 6 inches

5. Where SPF #2 ceiling joists create an uninhabitable attic without storage and are spaced 24 inches on center, what is the maximum allowable span when 2-inch by 6-inch members are used?
   A. 11 feet, 2 inches
   B. 14 feet, 5 inches
   C. 14 feet, 9 inches
   D. 15 feet, 11 inches

6. A roof system is subjected to a 50 psf ground snow load and creates a dead load of 20 psf. The ceiling is not attached to the rafters. Assuming that rafter ties are provided at the top plate line, what is the maximum span of 2-inch by 8-inch Hem-Fir#1 rafters spaced at 24 inches on center?

   A. 9 feet, 10 inches
   B. 10 feet, 6 inches
   C. 11 feet, 6 inches
   D. 11 feet, 10 inches

7. Purlins shall be supported by braces having a maximum unbraced length of _____ and spaced at a maximum of _____ on center.

   A. 8 feet, 4 feet
   B. 8 feet, 6 feet
   C. 12 feet, 4 feet
   D. 12 feet, 6 feet

8. The ends of a ceiling joist shall have a minimum of _____ bearing on wood and a minimum of _____ on metal.

   A. 1 1/2 inches, 1 1/2 inches
   B. 1 1/2 inches, 3 inches
   C. 3 inches, 1 1/2 inches
   D. 3 inches, 3 inches

9. Notches in solid sawn lumber ceiling joists shall not be located in the middle _____ of the span and are limited in depth to _____ the depth of the joist.

   A. one-fourth, one-sixth
   B. one-fourth, one-third
   C. one-third, one-sixth
   D. one-third, one-third

10. An opening in a wood framed roof system may be framed with a single header and single trimmer joists provided the header joist is located a maximum of _____ from the trimmer joist bearing.

   A. 3 feet
   B. 4 feet
   C. 6 feet
   D. 12 feet

11. Where 15/32-inch wood structural panels having a span rating of 32/16 are used as roof sheathing, what is the maximum span without edge support?

   A. 16 inches
   B. 24 inches
   C. 28 inches
   D. 32 inches

12. A dwelling is located in an area having a 115 mph wind speed and Exposure B. The ground snow load is 20 psf. What is the maximum allowable rafter span for 800S162-43 50 ksi steel rafters installed at 24 inches on center with a roof slope of 12:12?

   A. 7 feet, 11 inches
   B. 9 feet, 9 inches
   C. 10 feet, 10 inches
   D. 13 feet, 4 inches

13. In a steel-framed roof system, eave overhangs shall not exceed _____ in horizontal projection.

   A. 12 inches
   B. 18 inches
   C. 24 inches
   D. 30 inches

14. Openings provided for roof ventilation, where covered with corrosion-resistant wire cloth screening, shall have openings a minimum of _____ and a maximum of _____.

   A. 1/16 inch, 1/4 inch
   B. 1/8 inch, ¼ inch
   C. ¼ inch, 3/8 inch
   D. ¼ inch, 1/2 inch

15. A required attic access opening shall have a minimum rough opening size of _____.

   A. 18 inches by 24 inches
   B. 18 inches by 30 inches
   C. 22 inches by 30 inches
   D. 24 inches by 36 inches

16. A net free cross-ventilating area of 1/300 is permitted for roof ventilation in buildings in Climate Zones 6, 7 and 8, provided a minimum _____ vapor barrier is installed on the warm-in-winter side of the ceiling.

    A. Class I only
    B. Class II only
    C. Class III only
    D. Class I or II

17. Fire-retardant-treated wood, when used in roof construction, shall have a maximum listed flame spread index of _____.

    A. 25
    B. 75
    C. 100
    D. 200

18. In the attachment of asphalt shingles, special methods of fastening as established by the manufacturer are required where the roof slope of _____ is exceeded.

    A. 12 units vertical in 12 units horizontal
    B. 15 units vertical in 12 units horizontal
    C. 18 units vertical in 12 units horizontal
    D. 21 units vertical in 12 units horizontal

19. Double underlayment is required for an asphalt shingle application where the roof has a slope of up to _____.

    A. 2:12
    B. 2 ½:12
    C. 3:12
    D. 4:12

20. In an asphalt shingle roof application, step flashing on a sidewall shall be a minimum of _____ inches high and _____ inches wide.

    A. 3, 6
    B. 4, 4
    C. 6, 6
    D. 6, 8

21. Nails used to attach concrete roof tiles to the roof deck shall penetrate the deck a minimum of _____ or through the thickness of the deck, whichever is less.

    A. 1/2 inch
    B. 5/8 inch
    C. ¾ inch
    D. 7/8 inch

22. Where the cantilevered portion of a rafter is notched, a minimum of _____ inches of the member depth must remain.

    A. 3
    B. 3 ½
    C. 4
    D. 5

23. Where No. 2 wood shingles of naturally durable wood are installed on a roof having a 5:12 pitch, the maximum weather exposure for 16-inch shingles shall be _____.

    A. 3 1 /2 inches
    B. 4 inches
    C. 5 1/2 inches
    D. 6 ½ inches

24. For preservative-treated tapersawn shakes installed on a roof, the spacing between wood shakes shall be a minimum of _____ and a maximum of _____.

    A. 1/8 inch, 3/8 inch
    B. 1/8 inch, 5/8 inch
    C. 1/4 inch, 3/8 inch
    D. 3/8 inch, 5/8 inch

25. For a wood shake roof system, sheet metal roof valley flashing shall extend a minimum of _____ from the centerline of the valley in each direction.

    A. 4 inches
    B. 7 inches
    C. 11 inches
    D. 12 inches

26. A notch located in the end of a solid lumber ceiling joist shall have a maximum depth of
_____.

   A. 1 inch
   B. 2 inches
   C. one-third the joist depth
   D. one-fourth the joist depth

27. In the framing of an opening in ceiling construction, approved hangers are not required for the header joist to trimmer joist connections where the header joist span is a maximum of _____ feet.

   A. 4
   B. 6
   C. 8
   D. 12

28. Where eave or cornice vents are installed, a minimum _____ air space shall be provided between the insulation and the roof sheathing at the vent location.

   A. ½-inch
   B. 1-inch
   C. 2-inch
   D. 3-inch

29. Where the attic height is 30 inches or greater, an access opening is not required in attics of combustible construction where the attic space is a maximum of _____ square feet in area.

   A. 30
   B. 50
   C. 100
   D. 120

30. Overflow scuppers utilized for secondary roof drainage shall have a minimum size _____ of the roof drain.

   A. equal to that
   B. twice the size
   C. three times the size
   D. four times the size

31. A ridge board shall be a minimum of _____ -inch in nominal thickness and have a minimum depth equal to _____ .

    A. 1, the cut end of the rafter
    B. 1, the nominal depth of the rafter
    C. 2, the actual depth of the rafter
    D. 2, the cut end of the rafter

32. What is the minimum total net free ventilating area required for a 1,500-square-foot attic space where 75 percent of the required ventilation area is provided by ventilators located in the upper portion of the attic space?

    A. 5 square feet
    B. 7.5 square feet
    C. 10 square feet
    D. 15 square feet

33. Where an unvented conditioned attic assembly is utilized for a residence, the use of wood shakes on the roof would require a minimum continuous _____ -inch vented air space between the shakes and the roofing felt.

    A. ¼
    B. ½
    C. ¾
    D. 1

34. Where required on an asphalt-shingled roof of 5:12 slope, an ice barrier shall extend from the lowest edges of the roof surfaces to a minimum of _____ inches inside the exterior wall line of the building.

    A. 8
    B. 12
    C. 16
    D. 24

35. Drip edges provided at eaves and gables of asphalt shingle roofs shall extend a minimum of _____ inch below the roof sheathing.

    A. ¼
    B. ½
    C. ¾
    D. 1

International Residential Code, 2018
Chapter 8 and 9 - Answers

1.	B	Sec. R801.3
2.	A	Sec. R802.4.4
3.	B	Sec. R802.4.6
4.	B	Sec. R802.5.2.1
5.	C	Table R802.5.1(1)
6.	A	Table R802.4.1(5)
7.	A	Sec. R802.4.5
8.	A	Sec. R802.6
9.	C	Sec. R802.7.1, R502.8.1
10.	A	Sec. R802.9
11.	C	Sec. R803.2.2, Table R503.2.1.1(1)
12.	C	Tables R804.3.2.1(2), R804.3.2.1(1)
13.	C	Sec. R804.3.2.1.1
14.	A	Sec. R806.1
15.	C	Sec. R807.1
16.	D	Sec. R806.2, Exception, #1
17.	A	Sec. R802.1.5
18.	D	Sec. R905.2.6
19.	D	Sec. R905.2.3, Table R905.1.1(2)
20.	B	Sec. R905.2.8.3
21.	C	Sec. R905.3.6
22.	B	Sec. R802.7.1.1
23.	B	Table R905.7.5(1)
24.	D	Sec. R905.8.6
25.	C	Sec. R905.8.8
26.	D	Secs. R802.7.1, R502.8.1
27.	B	Sec. R802.9
28.	B	Sec. R806.3
29.	A	Sec. R807.1
30.	C	Sec. R903.4.1
31.	A	Sec. R802.3
32.	C	Sec. R806.2
33.	A	Sec. R806.5, #3
34.	D	Sec. R905.2.7, R905.1.2
35.	A	Sec. R905.2.8.5

International Residential Code, 2018
Chapter 10 and 11 - Questions and Answers

1. The footing for a masonry fireplace and chimney shall be a minimum of _____ thick.

    A. 6 inches
    B. 8 inches
    C. 10 inches
    D. 12 inches

2. A masonry chimney wall shall not change size or shape for a minimum of _____ above or below where the chimney passes through floor, ceiling or roof components.

    A. 6 inches
    B. 12 inches
    C. 24 inches
    D. 30 inches

3. In all cases, a masonry chimney shall extend a minimum of _____ above the highest point where the chimney passes through the roof.

    A. 12 inches
    B. 18 inches
    C. 24 inches
    D. 36 inches

4. A clay flue liner for a masonry chimney shall be carried vertically, with a maximum permitted slope of _____ from the vertical.

    A. 15 degrees
    B. 22 1/2 degrees
    C. 30 degrees
    D. 45 degrees

5. When two or more flues are located in the same masonry chimney, they shall be separated by masonry wythes having a minimum thickness of _____.

    A. 2 inches
    B. 4 inches
    C. 6 inches
    D. 8 inches

6. Unless cleaning is possible through the fireplace opening, a cleanout opening shall be provided within _____ of the base of a flue in a masonry chimney.

   A. 6 inches
   B. 8 inches
   C. 12 inches
   D. 18 inches

7. Where a masonry chimney is constructed totally outside the exterior walls of a dwelling, a minimum air space clearance to combustibles of _____ is required.

   A. 0 inches; no clearance is required
   B. 1/2 inch
   C. 1 inch
   D. 2 inches

8. Foundations for masonry fireplaces and their chimneys shall extend a minimum of _____ beyond the face of the fireplace or support walls on all sides.

   A. 4 inches
   B. 6 inches
   C. 8 inches
   D. 12 inches

9. Where a 60-inch-wide masonry chimney and fireplace are located in Seismic Design Category D1, the chimney shall be reinforced with _____ No. 4 continuous vertical reinforcing bars.

   A. 0; no reinforcement is required
   B. 2
   C. 4
   D. 6

10. What is the minimum required thickness of the back and side walls of a masonry firebox constructed of solid masonry without a firebrick lining?

   A. 6 inches
   B. 8 inches
   C. 10 inches
   D. 12 inches

11. Where firebricks are used as lining for a masonry fireplace, the maximum joint spacing shall be
    _____ between firebricks.

    A. 1/8 inch
    B. ¼ inch
    C. 3/8 inch
    D. ½ inch

12. The damper or throat for a masonry fireplace shall be located a minimum of _____ above the
    lintel supporting masonry over the fireplace opening.

    A. 4 inches
    B. 6 inches
    C. 8 inches
    D. 12 inches

13. What is the minimum required thickness for the hearth of a masonry fireplace?

    A. 3/8 inch
    B. ¾ inch
    C. 2 inches
    D. 4 inches

14. What is the minimum required size of a hearth extension for a masonry fireplace having a 30-inch-high
    by 42-inch-wide fireplace opening?

    A. 16 inches by 42 inches
    B. 16 inches by 58 inches
    C. 20 inches by 58 inches
    D. 20 inches by 66 inches

15. A minimum 3/8-inch-thick noncombustible hearth extension is permitted for a masonry fireplace where
    the bottom of the firebox opening is a minimum of _____ inches above the top of the hearth
    extension.

    A. 6
    B. 8
    C. 12
    D. 15

16. Wood studs shall have a minimum clearance of _____ from the back face of a masonry fireplace.

    A. 0 inches; no clearance is required
    B. 1 inch
    C. 2 inches
    D. 4 inches

17. When masonry chimneys are constructed as part of masonry walls, combustible materials in contact with the masonry wall must be located a minimum of _____ inches from the inside surface of the nearest flue lining.

   A. 4
   B. 6
   C. 12
   D. 30

18. Combustible trim projecting a distance of 1 inch beyond the fireplace opening of a masonry fireplace shall be located a minimum of _____ from the opening.

   A. 2 inches
   B. 6 inches
   C. 8 inches
   D. 12 inches

19. Factory-built fireplaces shall be tested in accordance with _____.

   A. ASTM C 199
   B. ASTM C 315
   C. UL 103
   D. UL 127

20. Unless the room is mechanically ventilated and controlled so that the indoor pressure is neutral or positive, a combustion air passageway having a minimum size of _____ square inches and a maximum size of _____ square inches shall be provided as an exterior air supply for a factory-built or masonry fireplace.

   A. 6, 25
   B. 6, 55
   C. 25, 55
   D. 25, 75

21. Unless a certification is provided by the insulation installers, an R-value identification mark shall be applied by the manufacturer to each piece of building thermal envelope insulation that is a minimum of inches wide.

   A. 12
   B. 15
   C. 18
   D. 22

22. Exposed insulation applied to the exterior of basement walls shall be protected with a covering that extends a minimum of _____ inches below grade.

   A. 6
   B. 12
   C. 18
   D. 24

23. In Climate Zone 2, what is the minimum R-value required for a wood-frame exterior wall when using the prescriptive method for the building thermal envelope?

   A. 11
   B. 13
   C. 15
   D. 19

24. Other than site-built elements, windows, skylights and sliding glass doors shall have a maximum air infiltration rate of _____ cfm per square foot.

   A. 0.05
   B. 0.1
   C. 0.3
   D. 1.0

25. Unless located completely inside the building thermal envelope, 3-inch supply ducts in attics shall be insulated to a minimum of _____ when using the prescriptive method.

   A. R-6
   B. R-8
   C. R-11
   D. R-13

26. Concrete foundations for masonry chimneys shall extend a minimum _____ of inches beyond each side of the exterior dimensions of the chimney.

   A. 3
   B. 6
   C. 8
   D. 12

27. The net free area of a spark arrester for a masonry chimney shall be a minimum of _____ time(s) the net free area of the outlet of the chimney flue it serves.

   A. one
   B. two
   C. three
   D. four

28. Where a 54-inch-wide masonry chimney is constructed above a roof having a slope of 8:12, a required cricket shall have a minimum height of _____ inches.

   A. 9
   B. 13 ½
   C. 18
   D. 27

29. Except for Rumford fireplaces, the firebox of a masonry fireplace shall have a minimum depth of _____ inches.

   A. 12
   B. 18
   C. 20
   D. 24

30. In general, a minimum clearance of _____ inches is required between the outside surface of a masonry heater and combustible materials.

   A. 6
   B. 12
   C. 18
   D. 36

31. Where a steel fireplace unit incorporating a steel firebox lining is installed with solid masonry to form a masonry fireplace, it shall be constructed with minimum _____ -inch steel.

   A. 1/8
   B. 3/16
   C. ¼
   D. 5/16

32. A Rumsford fireplace shall have a minimum fireplace depth of _____ inches where the fireplace opening is 42 inches in width.

   A. 12
   B. 14
   C. 15
   D. 20

33. Where the hearth extension for a masonry fireplace is located at the same level as the bottom of the firebox opening, the minimum required thickness of the hearth extension is _____ inches.

   A. 1 ½
   B. 2
   C. 3
   D. 4

34. Unlisted combustion air ducts installed to serve a factory-built or masonry fireplace shall be installed with a minimum _____ -inch clearance to combustibles for those portions of the duct within feet of the duct outlet.

   A. 1, 5
   B. 1, 10
   C. 2, 5
   D. 2, 10

35. The thickness of blown-in cellulose roof/ceiling insulation shall be provided on markers installed throughout the attic space at a maximum rate of one marker for every _____ square feet maximum.

   A. 100
   B. 200
   C. 300
   D. 500

1.	D	Sec. R1001.2
2.	A	Sec. R1003.6
3.	D	Sec. R1003.9
4.	C	Sec. R1003.12
5.	B	Sec. R1003.13
6.	A	Sec. R1003.17
7.	C	Sec. R1003.18
8.	B	Sec. R1001.2
9.	D	Sec. R1001.3.1
10.	C	Sec. R1001.5
11.	B	Sec. R1001.5
12.	C	Sec. R1001.7
13.	D	Sec. R1001.9.1
14.	D	Sec. R1001.10
15.	B	Sec. R1001.9.2, Exception
16.	D	Sec. R1001.11
17.	C	Sec. R1003.18, Exception 2
18.	B	Sec. R1001.11, Exception 4
19.	D	Sec. R1004.1
20.	B	Sec. R1006.4
21.	A	Sec. N1101.10.1
22.	A	Sec. N1101.11.1
23.	B	Table N1102.1.2
24.	C	Sec. N1102.4.3
25.	B	Sec. N1103.3.1
26.	B	Sec. R1003.2
27.	D	Sec. R1003.9.2, #1
28.	C	Table R1003.20
29.	C	Sec. R1001.6
30.	D	Sec. R1002.5
31.	C	Sec. R1001.5.1
32.	B	Sec. R1001.6, Exception
33.	B	Sec. R1001.9.2
34.	A	Sec. R1006.3
35.	C	Sec. N1101.10.1.1

International Residential Code, 2018
Chapter 13 and 14 - Questions and Answers

1. In order for someone to service an appliance other than a room heater, a minimum working space of
_____ inches deep by 30 inches wide shall be provided in front of the control side of the
appliance.

    A. 24
    B. 30
    C. 36
    D. 48

2. Where an appliance is located in the attic, a level service space a minimum of _____ in size is
required along all sides of the appliance where access is required.

    A. 20 inches by 30 inches
    B. 22 inches by 30 inches
    C. 30 inches by 30 inches
    D. 30 inches by 34 inches

3. The clear access opening to an attic containing an appliance shall have a minimum clear opening size of
_____and be large enough to allow the removal of the largest appliance.

    A. 20 inches by 30 inches
    B. 22 inches by 30 inches
    C. 30 inches by 30 inches
    D. 30 inches by 34 inches

4. Where an appliance is installed in a compartment accessed by a passageway, the passageway shall have
a minimum unobstructed width of _____, but not less than necessary to allow removal of the
largest appliance in the space.

    A. 24 inches
    B. 30 inches
    C. 36 inches
    D. 42 inches

5. Where an appliance is installed in an attic, the clear access opening shall be a minimum of _____, but in no case less than necessary to allow removal of the largest appliance.

    A. 20-inches by 30-inches
    B. 22-inches by 30-inches
    C. 30-inches by 30-inches
    D. 36-inches by 36-inches

6. Appliances suspended from the floor shall have a minimum clearance of _____ from the ground.

    A. 3 inches
    B. 4 inches
    C. 6 inches
    D. 8 inches

7. Excavations for appliance installations shall extend a minimum depth of _____ below the appliance with a minimum clearance of _____ on all sides except the control side.

    A. 3 inches, 6 inches
    B. 6 inches, 6 inches
    C. 6 inches, 12 inches
    D. 12 inches, 12 inches

8. Where ventilated air space is used to reduce the required clearance between an appliance and unprotected combustible materials, what is the minimum air space that is typically required?

    A. 1/2 inch
    B. 1 inch
    C. 2 inches
    D. 3 inches

9. An appliance requires a minimum clearance without protection of 12 inches above the appliance to combustible material. If 1/2-inch-thick insulation board with a ventilated air space is used as protection, the minimum clearance may be reduced to _____.

    A. 4 inches
    B. 6 inches
    C. 9 inches
    D. 12 inches

10. A solid-fuel-burning appliance requires a minimum clearance without protection of 18 inches from the sides and back to combustible material. If 24 gage sheet metal with a ventilated air space is used as protection, the minimum clearance may be reduced to _____.

   A. 4 inches
   B. 6 inches
   C. 9 inches
   D. 12 inches

11. Where an appliance with an ignition source is located in the garage, the source of ignition shall be located a minimum of _____ above the garage floor.

   A. 12 inches
   B. 18 inches
   C. 36 inches
   D. 48 inches

12. A combustion air opening for a central furnace shall be unobstructed for a minimum distance of_____ in front of the opening.

   A. 3 inches
   B. 6 inches
   C. 12 inches
   D. 30 inches

13. Piping conveying condensate from cooling coils and evaporators from the drain pan outlet to an approved location shall maintain a minimum horizontal slope in the direction of discharge of _____ unit vertical in 12 units horizontal.

   A. 1/8
   B. ¼
   C. ½
   D. 1

14. Refrigerant piping installed a minimum of _____ inch(es) of the underside of roof decks need not be protected from damage caused by nails and other fasteners.

   A. 7/8
   B. 1
   C. 1 ½
   D. 2

15. Radiant heating panels installed on wood framing shall be fastened a minimum of _____ inch from an element.

   A. ¼
   B. ½
   C. ¾
   D. 1

16. Unless listed and labeled for closer installation, a duct heater shall be located a minimum of _____ from a heat pump or air conditioner.

   A. 18 inches
   B. 24 inches
   C. 36 inches
   D. 48 inches

17. The furnace register of a vented floor furnace shall be located a minimum of _____ inches from doors in any position, draperies and other similar combustible objects.

   A. 3
   B. 6
   C. 12
   D. 60

18. The access opening through the foundation wall to a vented floor furnace shall have a minimum size of _____.

   A. 18-inches by 24-inches
   B. 20-inches by 30-inches
   C. 22-inches by 30-inches
   D. 30-inches by 30-inches

19. Where the lower 6 inches of a vented floor furnace is sealed to prevent water entry, a minimum _____ clearance shall be provided between the furnace and the ground.

   A. 2-inch
   B. 3-inch
   C. 4-inch
   D. 6-inch

20. A minimum clearance of _____ shall be provided between the inlet or outlet of a vented wall furnace and a door at any point in its swing, measured at a right angle to the opening.

   A. 6 inches
   B. 12 inches
   C. 18 inches
   D. 36 inches

21. Unless listed and labeled for such use, cooling coils of refrigeration cooling equipment shall not be located _____ of heat exchangers.

   A. within 12 inches
   B. within 36 inches
   C. upstream
   D. downstream

22. Condensate drain lines from all cooling coils or evaporators shall be a minimum of _____ inch(es) nominal diameter.

   A. ½
   B. ¾
   C. 1
   D. 1 ¼

23. Where an auxiliary drain pan with a separate drain is installed under the cooling coils where condensate will occur, the minimum depth of the pan shall be _____.

   A. 1 inch
   B. 1 ½ inches
   C. 2 inches
   D. 3 inches

24. Evaporative coolers shall be installed on a level platform or base located a minimum of _____ above the adjoining ground.

   A. 3 inches
   B. 4 inches
   C. 6 inches
   D. 12 inches

25. The supporting structure for a hearth extension for a fireplace stove shall be located _____ the supporting structure for the fireplace unit.

   A. at least 6 inches below
   B. at least 3 inches below
   C. at the same level as
   D. at least 3 inches above

26. Where an appliance is located in an underfloor space, a minimum _____ level service space shall be provided at the front or service side of the appliance.

A. 30-inch by 30-inch
B. 36-inch by 30-inch
C. 36-inch by 36-inch
D. 42-inch by 36-inch

27. The required lower strapping for a water heater in Seismic Design Categories Do, D1 and D2 shall be located a minimum of _____ inches above the controls.

A. 3
B. 4
C. 6
D. 8

28. A private garage containing a hydrogen-generating appliance shall be limited to a maximum of _____ square feet in area.

A. 720
B. 800
C. 850
D. 1,000

29. Where piping other than cast-iron or galvanized steel is installed through bored holes of studs within a concealed wall space, steel shield plates are not required where the holes are a minimum of _____ inch(es) from the nearest edge of the stud.

A. ¾
B. 1 ¼
C. 1 3/8
D. 1 ½

30. Unless listed for use on combustible floors without floor protection, a floor-mounted vented room heater shall be located so that noncombustible flooring materials extend a minimum of _____ inches beyond the appliance on all sides.

A. 12
B. 18
C. 24
D. 36

31. Where access to an appliance located in an attic is provided by an unobstructed passageway at least 6 feet high and 22 inches wide, the passageway shall have a maximum length of _____.

    A. 10 feet
    B. 20 feet
    C. 50 feet
    D. an unlimited distance

32. The two permanent outdoor openings required to be provided in a private garage containing a hydrogen-generating appliance shall have a minimum free area of _____ per 1,000 cubic feet of garage volume.

    A. 1/2 square foot
    B. 1 square foot
    C. 2 square feet
    D. 5 square feet

33. The piping and fittings for the refrigerant vapor (suction) lines of cooling equipment shall be insulated with insulation having a minimum thermal resistivity of _____.

    A. R-4
    B. R-5
    C. R-8
    D. R-11

34. The register of a vented floor furnace shall be located a minimum of _____ below any projecting combustible materials.

    A. 12 inches
    B. 2 feet
    C. 3feet
    D. 5 feet

35. Secondary drain piping from a cooling coil or evaporator shall maintain a minimum horizontal slope in the direction of discharge of _____ unit vertical in 12 units horizontal.

    A. 1/12
    B. 1/8
    C. ¼
    D. ½

International Residential Code, 2018
Chapter 13 and 14 - Answers

1.	B	Sec. M1305.1
2.	C	Sec. M1305.1.2
3.	A	Sec. M1305.1.2
4.	A	Sec. M1305.1.1
5.	B	Sec. M1305.1.2
6.	C	Sec. M1305.1.3.1
7.	C	Sec. M1305.1.3.2
8.	B	Sec. M1306.2.2
9.	B	Table M1306.2
10.	D	Sec. M1306.2.3, Table M1306.2
11.	B	Sec. M1307.3
12.	B	Sec. M1402.3
13.	A	Sec. M1411.3
14.	C	Sec. M1411.7
15.	A	Sec. M1406.3, #2
16.	D	Sec. M1407.3
17.	C	Sec. M1408.3, #3
18.	A	Sec. M1408.4
19.	A	Sec. M1408.5, #3
20.	B	Sec. M1409.2, #2
21.	C	Sec. M1411.2
22.	B	Sec. M1411.3.2
23.	B	Sec. Ml411.3.1, #1
24.	A	Sec. M1413.1, #2, M1305.1.3.1
25.	C	Sec. M1414.2
26.	A	Sec. M1305.1.3
27.	B	Sec. M1307.2 #1
28.	C	Sec. M1307.4.1
29.	D	Sec. M1308.2.1
30.	B	Sec. M1410.2
31.	C	Sec. M1305.1.2, Exception 2
32.	A	Sec. M1307.4.1.1
33.	A	Sec. M1411.6
34.	D	Sec. M1408.3, #4
35.	B	Sec. M1411.3.1

International Residential Code, 2018
Chapter 15, 16 and 19 - Questions and Answers

1. Screws that join clothes dryer exhaust ducts may protrude a maximum of _____ inch into the inside of the duct.

   A. 0, the use of screws is prohibited
   B. 1/8
   C. 3/16
   D. 1/4

2. Unless modified by the manufacturer's installation instructions, what is the maximum permitted length of a clothes dryer exhaust duct when measured from the dryer location to the outlet termination?

   A. 18 feet
   B. 25 feet
   C. 30 feet
   D. 35 feet

3. Unless modified by the manufacturer's installation instructions or determined by engineering calculation, what is the maximum permitted length of a clothes dryer exhaust duct that has one 6-inch-radius smooth 90-degree elbow and two 6-inch-radius smooth 45-degree elbows?

   A. 25 feet, 0 inches
   B. 28 feet, 6 inches
   C. 31 feet, 3 inches
   D. 35 feet, 0 inches

4. Which of the following requirements is not applicable to a duct serving a range hood?

   A. It shall have a smooth interior surface.
   B. It shall be airtight.
   C. It shall be equipped with a backdraft damper.
   D. It may terminate in an attic space.

5. When serving a domestic kitchen cooking appliance equipped with a down-draft exhaust system, a schedule 40 PVC exhaust duct shall extend a maximum of _____ above grade outside the building.

   A. 1 inch
   B. 6 inches
   C. 12 inches
   D. 36 inches

6. A domestic open-top broiler unit shall be provided with a minimum clearance of _____ between the hood and the underside of combustible material or cabinets.

   A. 0 inches; no clearance is required
   B. 1/4 inch
   C. ½ inch
   D. 1 inch

7. For a domestic open-top boiler unit, a minimum of _____ shall be maintained between the cooking surface and combustible material or cabinet.

   A. 24 inches
   B. 28 inches
   C. 30 inches
   D. 32 inches

8. Heating equipment connected to an above-ground duct system shall be designed to limit discharge air temperature to a maximum of _____.

   A. 125°F
   B. 200°F
   C. 225°F
   D. 250°F

9. Where ductwrap is installed as a duct insulation material, the installed thickness used to determine its R-value shall be assumed to be _____ percent of nominal thickness.

   A. 50
   B. 75
   C. 90
   D. 100

10. Return air for heating, ventilation and air conditioning systems shall not be taken from a kitchen unless the openings serve only the kitchen and are located a minimum of _____ feet from any cooking appliances.

    A. 5
    B. 6
    C. 10
    D. 12

11. Gypsum board may be used in the construction of a return air plenum in an above-ground duct system, provided the maximum air temperature is _____ and the exposed surfaces are not subject to condensation.

   A. 125°F
   B. 150°F
   C. 180°F
   D. 210°F

12. What is the maximum flame spread index permitted for materials used to construct above-ground duct systems?

   A. 25
   B. 75
   C. 200
   D. 450

13. Where used in an underground duct system, the maximum permitted duct temperature for plastic ducts shall be _____.

   A. 125°F
   B. 150°F
   C. 180°F
   D. 210°F

14. When protected by concrete, metal ducts installed in an underground duct system shall be encased with a minimum thickness of _____.

   A. 1 inch
   B. 2 inches
   C. 3 inches
   D. 4 inches

15. As a general rule, duct coverings and linings shall have a maximum flame spread index of _____ and a maximum smoke-developed index of _____.

   A. 25, 50
   B. 25, 200
   C. 50, 200
   D. 50,450

16. External reflective duct insulation shall be identified at maximum intervals of _____ with the name of the manufacturer, the thermal resistance R-value, the flame spread index and the smoke-developed index.

   A. 3 feet
   B. 5 feet
   C. 6 feet
   D. 10 feet

17. Where vibration isolators are installed between mechanical equipment and metal ducts, they shall have a maximum length of _____.

   A. 6 inches
   B. 10 inches
   C. 12 inches
   D. 24 inches

18. Clothes dryer exhaust ducts shall be _____ inches nominal in diameter.

   A. 3
   B. 3 ½
   C. 4
   D. 5

19. In an existing structure, an under-floor space used as a supply plenum shall be formed by materials having a maximum flame spread rating of _____.

   A. 25
   B. 50
   C. 75
   D. 200

20. Where the under-floor space is permitted to be used as a supply plenum, a duct shall extend from the furnace supply outlet to a minimum of _____ inch(es) below the combustible framing.

   A. 1
   B. 3
   C. 6
   D. 8

21. Unless in compliance with the manufacturer's design criteria or verified by the installer or a third party, the maximum length of a 4-inch smooth-wall exhaust duct shall be _____ where the fan airflow rating is 100 cfm.

   A. unlimited
   B. 42 feet
   C. 10 feet
   D. 0 feet (prohibited)

22. Range hood exhaust systems capable of exhausting more than _____ cubic feet per minute shall be mechanically or naturally provided with makeup air at a rate approximately equal to the exhaust air rate.

   A. 100
   B. 200
   C. 300
   D. 400

23. Air exhaust openings shall terminate a minimum of_____ feet from property lines.

   A. 3
   B. 5
   C. 8
   D. 10

24. Built-in or freestanding ranges shall have a minimum vertical clearance of _____ above the cooking top to an unprotected combustible construction.

   A. 24 inches
   B. 30 inches
   C. 32 inches
   D. 36 inches

25. Sauna heaters shall be equipped with a thermostat that will limit room temperature to a maximum of _____.

   A. 120°F
   B. 140°F
   C. 172°F
   D. 194°F

26. A mechanically ventilated kitchen area shall be provided with a minimum ventilation rate of
_____ cfm where continuous ventilation is utilized.

    A. 20
    B. 25
    C. 50
    D. 100

27. A bathroom ventilated by an intermittent mechanical means shall have a minimum mechanical exhaust
capacity of _____ cfm.

    A. 20
    B. 25
    C. 50
    D. 100

28. The access through the floor to an under-floor plenum shall provide a minimum opening size of
_____.

    A. 18 inches by 24 inches
    B. 20 inches by 24 inches
    C. 22 inches by 30 inches
    D. 24 inches by 30 inches

29. Where an under-floor space is used as a supply plenum in an existing structure, the furnace shall be
equipped with an approved automatic control that limits the outlet air temperature to a maximum of
_____ °F.

    A. 150
    B. 200
    C. 225
    D. 250

30. Where the thermostat used to limit sauna room temperature is not an integral part of the sauna heater,
the heat-sensing element shall be located a maximum of _____ inches below the ceiling.

    A. 3
    B. 4
    C. 6
    D. 8

31. Unless modified by the manufacturer's installation instructions, a clothes dryer exhaust duct shall terminate outside of the building a minimum of _____ feet in any direction from openings into the building.

    A. 2
    B. 3
    C. 5
    D. 10

32. A transition duct for a clothes dryer exhaust system is limited to a maximum length of _____ feet.

    A. 3
    B. 5
    C. 6
    D. 8

33. Where aluminum foil is installed on the exterior of insulation on cooling supply ducts that pass through unconditioned space conducive to condensation, a minimum foil thickness of _____ mil(s) is required.

    A. 1
    B. 2
    C. 3
    D. 4

34. Crimp joints for round metal ducts shall have a minimum contact lap of _____ inch(es).

    A. ¾
    B. 1
    C. 1 ½
    D. 2

35. Unless in conformance with the criteria for underground duct systems, ducts shall be installed with a minimum of _____ inches separation from earth.

    A. 3
    B. 4
    C. 6
    D. 12

International Residential Code, 2018
Chapter 15, 16 and 19 - Answers

1.	B	Sec. M1502.4.2
2.	D	Sec. M1502.4.5.1
3.	C	Table M1502.4.5.1
4.	D	Sec. M1503.3
5.	A	Sec. M1503.4, Exception, #4
6.	B	Sec. M1503.2.1
7.	A	Sec. M1503.2.1
8.	D	Sec. M1601.1.1, #1
9.	B	Sec. M1601.3, #4.2
10.	C	Sec. M1602.2, #4, Exception 1
11.	A	Sec. M1601.1.1, #5
12.	C	Sec. M1601.1.1, #6
13.	B	Sec. M1601.1.2
14.	B	Sec. M1601.1.2
15.	A	Sec. M1601.3, #1
16.	A	Sec. M1601.3, #3
17.	B	Sec. M1601.2
18.	C	Sec. M1502.4.1
19.	D	Sec. M1601.5.2
20.	C	Sec. M1601.5.3
21.	C	Table M1504.2
22.	D	Sec. M1503.6
23.	A	Sec. M1504.3, #1
24.	B	Sec. M1901.1
25.	D	Sec. M1902.4
26.	B	Table M1505.4.4
27.	C	Table M1505.4.4
28.	A	Sec. M1601.5.4
29.	B	Sec. M1601.5.5
30.	C	Sec. M1902.4
31.	B	Sec. M1502.3
32.	D	Sec. M1502.4.3
33.	B	Sec. M1601.4.6, #1
34.	B	Sec. M1601.4.2
35.	B	Sec. M1601.4.8

International Residential Code, 2018
Chapter 17, 18 20, 21, 22 and 23 - Questions and Answers

1. Which of the following types of appliances is required to be provided with combustion air in accordance with NFPA 31?

    A. solid-fuel burning
    B. oil-fired
    C. direct-vent
    D. gas-fired

2. Manually-operated dampers shall not be installed in vents except in connectors or chimneys serving _____ appliances.

    A. solid-fuel-burning
    B. oil-fired
    C. direct vent
    D. gas-fired

3. Where a single-wall metal pipe vent connector serving an oil-fired appliance listed for a Type L vent passes through a wall, the pipe shall be guarded by a ventilated metal thimble with a minimum diameter of _____ inches larger than the vent connector.

    A. 3
    B. 4
    C. 6
    D. 8

4. The bottom of the vent terminal for a mechanical draft system shall be located a minimum of _____ inches above finished ground level.

    A. 3
    B. 4
    C. 6
    D. 12

5. Unless an integral part of a listed and labeled appliance, an individual Type L vent for a single appliance shall have a minimum cross-sectional area of _____ inches.

   A. 5
   B. 6
   C. 7
   D. 8

6. A chimney connector shall enter a masonry chimney a minimum of _____ inches above the bottom of the chimney.

   A. 6
   B. 8
   C. 9
   D. 12

7. Nonpressurized expansion tanks shall be supported to carry _____ times the weight of the tank filled with water.

   A. 1 ½
   B. 2
   C. 2 ½
   D. 3

8. In a hydronic piping system, solder joints in a metal pipe shall occur a minimum of _____ inches from the transition from such metal pipe to PR-RT pipe or tubing.

   A. 6
   B. 8
   C. 12
   D. 18

9. A pipe in the ground-source heat pump hydronic piping system having an exterior surface temperature exceeding 250 F shall have a minimum clearance of _____ inch(es) from the combustible material.

   A. 1
   B. 1 ½
   C. 2
   D. 3

10. A ground source heat pump loop system shall be pressure tested with water at _____ psi for _____ minutes with no observed leaks prior to the backfilling of the connection trenches.

   A. 60, 30
   B. 80, 15
   C. 80, 30
   D. 100, 15

11. Oil supply tanks used within a building with a capacity of more than 10 gallons shall be placed a minimum of _____ feet from any fire or flame within a fuel-burning appliance.

   A. 5
   B. 10
   C. 12
   D. 15

12. The horizontal run of an uninsulated connector to a natural draft chimney shall be a maximum of _____ percent of the height of the vertical portion of the chimney above the connector.

   A. 50
   B. 75
   C. 100
   D. 125

13. For other than direct vent appliances, the vent termination for a mechanical draft system shall be mounted a minimum of _____ feet horizontally from an oil tank or gas meter.

   A. 3
   B. 4
   C. 15
   D. 10

14. Vent piping for an oil tank shall terminate a minimum of _____ feet, measured vertically or horizontally, from any building opening.

   A. 2
   B. 3
   C. 5
   D. 10

15. In low temperature hydronic piping, solder joints in a metal pipe shall occur a minimum of _____ inches from any transition from the metal pipe to PE-AL-PE pressure pipe.

    A. 12
    B. 18
    C. 24
    D. 36

16. Unless specified otherwise in the manufacturer's installation instructions, the cross-sectional area of a chimney flue connected to a solid-fuel-burning appliance shall be a maximum of _____ times the area of the flue collar.

    A. 1 ½
    B. 2
    C. 3
    D. 4

17. Vent and chimney connectors shall have a minimum slope of _____ rise per foot of run.

    A. 1/8 inch
    B. ¼ inch
    C. 3/8 inch
    D. ½ inch

18. The horizontal run of a listed vent connector to a natural draft chimney shall be a maximum of _____ of the height of the vertical portion of the chimney above the connector.

    A. 50 percent
    B. 75 percent
    C. 100 percent
    D. 125 percent

19. Unless modified by Table M1306.2, what is the minimum required clearance between an unlisted Type L vent piping connector serving a solid fuel appliance and any combustible materials?

    A. 3 inches
    B. 6 inches
    C. 9 inches
    D. 18 inches

20. A natural draft gas vent serving a wall furnace shall terminate a minimum height of _____ above the bottom of the furnace.

   A. 5 feet
   B. 8 feet
   C. 10 feet
   D. 12 feet

21. Chimney flues connected to more than one appliance shall be sized based on the area of the largest connector plus _____ of the areas of additional chimney connectors.

   A. 50 percent
   B. 75 percent
   C. 100 percent
   D. 125 percent

22. The pressurized expansion tank for a boiler shall be capable of withstanding a minimum hydrostatic test pressure _____ the allowable working pressure of the system.

   A. equal to
   B. twice
   C. two and one-half times
   D. three times

23. Hydronic piping to be embedded in concrete shall be tested by applying a minimum hydrostatic pressure of _____ for a minimum time period of _____.

   A. 50 psi, 15 minutes
   B. 50 psi, 30 minutes
   C. 100 psi, 15 minutes
   D. 100 psi, 30 minutes

24. Fill piping for oil tanks shall terminate outside of a building a minimum distance of _____ from any building opening at the same or lower level.

   A. 12 inches
   B. 2 feet
   C. 5 feet
   D. 10 feet

25. Solar energy systems shall be equipped with means to limit the maximum water temperature of the system fluid entering or exchanging heat with any pressurized vessel inside the dwelling to a maximum of _____.

   A. 120°F
   B. 150°F
   C. 180°F
   D. 210°F

26. Fuel-fired water heaters shall not be installed in a _____.

   A. bathroom
   B. bedroom
   C. kitchen
   D. storage closet

27. PEX tubing used for hydronic piping shall be supported at maximum intervals of _____ when installed in a horizontal position.

   A. 2 feet, 8 inches
   B. 4 feet
   C. 6 feet, 6 inches
   D. 8 feet

28. Hydronic piping shall be tested hydrostatically at a minimum pressure of _____ the maximum system design pressure, but not less than _____ psi.

   A. one time, 75
   B. one and one-half times, 100
   C. two times, 125
   D. two and one-half times, 125

29. Unless intended for the storage of fuel oil used for space or water heating, fuel oil storage tank installed inside of a building shall have a maximum capacity of _____ gallons.

   A. 330
   B. 660
   C. 1,000
   D. 2,000

30. Pressure at the fuel oil supply inlet to an appliance shall be a maximum of _____ psi.

   A. 3
   B. 5
   C. 10
   D. 15

31. A nonpressurized expansion tank for a hot water boiler shall have a minimum capacity of _____ gallons where the system volume of the forced hot-water system is 50 gallons.

   A. 3.0
   B. 6.0
   C. 7.5
   D. 12.0

32. Vents for natural draft appliances shall terminate a minimum of _____ feet above the highest connected appliance outlet.

   A. 3
   B. 5
   C. 10
   D. 12

33. Discharge piping beyond the pressure relief valve of a boiler shall terminate a maximum of _____ inch(es) above the floor or to an open receptor.

   A. 1
   B. 6
   C. 12
   D. 18

34. Fuel oil tanks installed outside above ground shall be located a minimum of _____ feet from an adjoining property line.

   A. 5
   B. 10
   C. 15
   D. 20

35. Vent piping for a fuel oil tank shall have a minimum pipe size of _____ inch/es.

    A. ¾
    B. 1
    C. 1 ¼
    D. 1 ½

International Residential Code, 2018
Chapter 17, 18 20, 21, 22 and 23 - Answers

1.	B	Sec. M 1701.1
2.	A	Sec. M1802.2.1
3.	B	Sec. M1803.3.1, #2
4.	D	Sec. M1804.2.6, #4
5.	C	Sec. M1804.3.1
6.	A	Sec. M1805.2
7.	B	Sec. M2003.1
8.	D	Sec. M2105.13.2
9.	A	Sec. M2105.20
10.	D	Sec. M2105.28
11.	A	Sec. M2201.2.1
12.	B	Sec. M1803.3.2
13.	A	Sec. M1804.2.6, #5
14.	A	Sec. M2203.5
15.	B	Sec. M2104.4.2
16.	C	Sec. M1805.3.1
17.	B	Sec. M1803.3
18.	C	Sec. M1803.3.2
19.	C	Table M1803.3.4
20.	D	Sec. M1804.2.3
21.	A	Sec. M1805.3
22.	C	Sec. M2003.1.1
23.	D	Sec. M2103.4
24.	B	Sec. M2203.3
25.	C	Sec. M2301.2.12
26.	D	Sec. M2005.2
27.	B	Table M2101.9
28.	B	Sec. M2101.10
29.	B	Sec. M2201.2
30.	A	Sec. M2204.3
31.	C	Table M2003.2
32.	B	Sec. M1804.2.3
33.	D	Sec. M2002.4
34.	A	Sec. M2201.2.2
35.	C	Sec. M2203.4

International Residential Code, 2018
Chapter 24 - Questions and Answers

1. In general, fuel-fired appliances are permitted to be located in which one of the following spaces?

   A. sleeping rooms
   B. storage closets
   C. bathrooms
   D. garages

2. Where located in a hazardous location, fuel-gas equipment and appliances having an ignition source shall be elevated such that the ignition source is located a minimum of _____ above the floor.

   A. 6 inches
   B. 12 inches
   C. 18 inches
   D. 30 inches

3. Unless protected from motor vehicle damage, fuel-gas appliances located in private garages shall be installed with a minimum clearance of _____ above the floor.

   A. 60 inches
   B. 72 inches
   C. 80 inches
   D. 84 inches

4. Assume that a fuel-gas appliance requires a minimum clearance without protection of 36 inches above the appliance to combustible material. If 1/2-inch thick insulation board over 1-inch glass fiber batts is used as protection, the minimum clearance may be reduced to _____.

   A. 9 inches
   B. 12 inches
   C. 18 inches
   D. 24 inches

5. Assume that a fuel-gas appliance requires a minimum clearance without protection of 9 inches from the sides and back to combustible material. If 0.024 sheet metal with a ventilated air space is used as protection, the minimum clearance may be reduced to _____.

   A. 2 inches
   B. 3 inches
   C. 4 inches
   D. 6 inches

6. For other than steel pipe, exposed gas piping shall be identified by a yellow label marked "Gas" spaced at maximum intervals of _____ unless in the same room as the appliance served.

    A. 5 feet
    B. 6 feet
    C. 8 feet
    D. 10 feet

7. Unless special conditions are met, the maximum design operating pressure for gas piping systems located inside buildings shall be _____.

    A. 5 psig
    B. 10 psig
    C. 15 psig
    D. 20 psig

8. LP-gas systems designed to operate below _____ shall be designed to either accommodate liquid LP-gas or prevent LP-gas vapor from condensing into a liquid.

    A. -5°F
    B. 0°F
    C. 20°F
    D. 32°F

9. Copper tubing to be used with gases shall comply with standard _____ of ASTM B 88 or ASTM B 280.

    A. Type K only
    B. Type L only
    C. Type K or Type L
    D. Type L or Type M

10. For the field threading of 1-inch metallic pipe, a length of _____ (approximate) shall be provided for the threaded portion.

    A. ¾ inch
    B. 7/8 inch
    C. 1 inch
    D. 1 1/8 inch

11. In which of the following locations is the installation of gas piping not specifically prohibited?

    A. in a supply air duct
    B. through a clothes chute
    C. in an elevator shaft
    D. adjacent to an exterior stairway

12. For gas piping, other than black or galvanized steel, installed in a concealed location, a shield plate need not be provided for protection against physical damage where a bored hole is located a minimum of _____ from the edge of the wood member.

   A. 5/8 inch
   B. 1 inch
   C. 1 ¼
   D. 1 ½

13. In general, underground gas piping shall be installed a minimum depth of _____ below grade.

   A. 6 inches
   B. 12 inches
   C. 18 inches
   D. 24 inches

14. The unthreaded portion of gas p1pmg outlets shall extend a minimum of _____ through finished ceilings and walls.

   A. 1 inch
   B. 2 inches
   C. 3 inches
   D. 4 inches

15. The tracer wire required adjacent to underground nonmetallic gas piping shall be a minimum of _____ wire size.

   A. 14AWG
   B. 16AWG
   C. 18AWG
   D. 20AWG

16. The inside radius of a bend in a metallic gas pipe shall be a minimum of _____ the outside diameter of the pipe.

   A. six times
   B. eight times
   C. twelve times
   D. twenty-five times

17. Gas piping shall be tested at a minimum pressure _____ the proposed maximum working pressure, but not less than 3 psig.
   A. equal to
   B. of one and one-half times
   C. of twice
   D. of two and one-halftimes

18. Where outdoor combustion air is provided for gas-fired appliances through openings to the outdoors, the minimum dimension of such air openings shall be _____ inches.

   A. 3
   B. 4
   C. 10
   D. 12

19. Gas piping for other than dry gas conditions shall be sloped a minimum _____ of to prevent traps.

   A. 1/8 inch in 10 feet
   B. 1/8 inch in 15 feet
   C. 1/4 inch in 10 feet
   D. 1/4 inch in 15 feet

20. Unless located at the manifold, a gas shutoff valve for an appliance shall be provided within a maximum distance of _____ between the valve and the appliance.

   A. 3 feet
   B. 4 feet
   C. 6 feet
   D. 10 feet

21. In general, appliance fuel connectors shall have a maximum overall length of _____.

   A. 3 feet
   B. 5 feet
   C. 6 feet
   D. 10 feet

22. The radius of the inner curve of plastic gas pipe bends shall be a minimum of _____ times the inside diameter of the pipe.

   A. 12
   B. 16
   C. 20
   D. 25

23. Gas appliance connectors, where connected to a masonry chimney, shall connect at a point a minimum of _____ above the lowest portion of the interior of the chimney flue.

   A. 12 inches
   B. 18 inches
   C. 30 inches
   D. 36 inches

24. A sauna room provided with a gas-fired sauna heater shall be provided with a minimum _____ ventilation opening located near the top of the door into the sauna room.

   A. 4-inch by 8-inch
   B. 4-inch by 12-inch
   C. 8-inch by 8-inch
   D. 8-inch by 12-inch

25. Unvented gas room heaters shall be limited to a maximum input rating of _____.

   A. 35,000 Btu/h
   B. 40,000 Btu/h
   C. 50,000 Btu/h
   D. 65,000 Btu/h

26. Gas-fired equipment and appliances, where suspended above grade level, shall be provided with a minimum clearance of _____ inches from adjoining grade.

   A. 2
   B. 4
   C. 6
   D. 8

27. Fuel gas piping installed across a roof surface shall be elevated above the roof a minimum of _____ inches.

   A. 1 ½
   B. 2
   C. 3 ½
   D. 6

28. Which of the following test mediums shall not be used in the testing of a fuel gas piping system?

   A. Air
   B. nitrogen
   C. carbon dioxide
   D. oxygen

29. One-inch O.D. smooth-wall tubing used as fuel gas piping shall be supported horizontally at maximum intervals of _____ feet.

   A. 4
   B. 6
   C. 8
   D. 10

30. Where a post-mounted illuminating gas appliance is installed on a steel pipe post having a height of 30 inches, what is the minimum size Schedule 40 steel pipe required?

    A. ¾-inch
    B. 1-inch
    C. 1 ½-inch
    D. 2 ½-inch

31. An MP pressure regulator, when installed in a gas piping system and connected to rigid piping, shall be provided with a union installed within _____ inches of either side of the regulator.

    A. 12
    B. 18
    C. 24
    D. 36

32. The unthreaded portion of a gas piping outlet passing up through an outdoor patio shall extend a minimum of _____ inch(es) above the patio.

    A. 1
    B. 2
    C. 4
    D. 6

33. Where approved and not susceptible to physical damage, an individual gas line to an outdoor barbeque grill shall be installed a minimum of_____ inches below finished grade.

    A. 6
    B. 8
    C. 12
    D. 18

34. The union fitting required for gas-fired appliances connected by rigid metallic pipe shall be accessible and located a maximum of _____ feet from the appliance.

    A. 3
    B. 5
    C. 6
    D. 10

35. Suspended-type gas-fired unit heaters shall have a minimum clearance to combustible materials of _____ inches on the sides.

A. 6
B. 12
C. 15
D. 18

1.	D	Sec. G2406.2
2.	C	Sec. G2408.2
3.	B	Sec. G2408.3
4.	D	Table G2409.2
5.	B	Table G2409.2
6.	A	Sec. G2412.5
7.	A	Sec. G2413.7
8.	A	Sec. G2413.7.1
9.	C	Sec. G2414.5.3
10.	B	Table G2414.9.2
11.	D	Sec. G2415.3
12.	D	Sec. G2415.7.1
13.	B	Sec. G2415.12
14.	A	Sec. G2415.16
15.	C	Sec. G2415.17.3
16.	A	Sec. G2416.2, #5
17.	B	Sec. G2417.4.1
18.	A	Sec. G2407.6
19.	D	Sec. G2419.1
20.	C	Sec. G2420.5, G2420.5.1
21.	C	Sec. G2422.1.2.1
22.	D	Sec. G2416.3, #3
23.	A	Sec. G2425.9
24.	A	Sec. G2440.7
25.	B	Sec. G2445.3
26.	C	Sec. G2408.4
27.	C	Sec. G2415.9
28.	D	Sec. G2417.2
29.	C	Table G2424.1
30.	A	Sec. G2450.3
31.	A	Sec. G2421.2, #7
32.	B	Sec. G2415.16
33.	B	Sec. G2415.12.1
34.	C	Sec. G2422.1.4
35.	D	Sec. G2444.4

International Residential Code, 2018
Chapter 25, 26, and 27 - Questions and Answers

1. Testing of the building sewer may be accomplished with a minimum _____ head of water with the ability to maintain such pressure for a minimum of _____.

   A. 8-foot, 10 minutes
   B. 8-foot, 15 minutes
   C. 10-foot, 10 minutes
   D. 10-foot, 15 minutes

2. When tested by air, the DWV system shall be tested at _____ or 10 inches of mercury column with the ability to maintain such pressure for a minimum of _____.

   A. 5 psi, 10 minutes
   B. 5 psi, 15 minutes
   C. 10 psi, 10 minutes
   D. 10 psi, 15 minutes

3. The water-supply system shall be proved tight under a water pressure not less than the working pressure of the system, or by a minimum _____ air test for other than plastic piping.

   A. 5 psi
   B. 10 psi
   C. 20 psi
   D. 50 psi

4. Where copper piping is to pass through holes bored in wood studs, the pipe shall be protected by shield plates except for those holes that are a minimum of _____ from the nearest edge.

   A. 5/8 inch
   B. ¾ inch
   C. 1 ¼ inches
   D. 1 ½ inches

5. Shield plates required to protect piping installed through notches or bored holes in framing members shall extend a minimum of _____ above sole plates and below top plates.

   A. ½ inch
   B. 1 inch
   C. 2 inches
   D. 3 inches

6. Unless provided with a relieving arch, a building drain passing through a foundation wall shall pass through a pipe sleeve sized _____ greater than the pipe passing through.

    A. 1 inch
    B. 2 inches
    C. one pipe size
    D. two pipe sizes

7. Where buried, water service pipe shall be installed a minimum of _____ deep.

    A. 6 inches
    B. 12 inches
    C. 24 inches
    D. 30 inches

8. Where a frost line is established at 30 inches, water service pipe shall be installed a minimum of _____ below the frost line.

    A. 30 inches
    B. 36 inches
    C. 32 inches
    D. 42 inches

9. Where unstable soil conditions exist in an area to be trenched for a piping installation, the trench shall be over excavated by a minimum of _____.

    A. 4 inches
    B. 6 inches
    C. one pipe diameter
    D. two pipe diameters

10. The backfilling of a trench where piping is installed shall be done in maximum _____ layers when using loose earth.

    A. 4-inch
    B. 6-inch
    C. 8-inch
    D. 12-inch

11. One-half-inch copper water pipe installed horizontally shall be supported at maximum intervals of _____.

    A. 3 feet
    B. 4 feet
    C. 6 feet
    D. 12 feet

12. PB pipe shall be supported at maximum intervals of _____ when installed horizontally.

    A. 32 inches
    B. 36 inches
    C. 60 inches
    D. 72 inches

13. A fixture tail piece for a laundry tub shall be a minimum of _____ in diameter.

    A. 1 inch
    B. 1 ¼ inches
    C. 1 ½ inches
    D. 2 inches

14. Unless provided with an approved arrangement for access purposes, a fixture with a concealed slip-joint connection shall be provided with an access panel or utility space a minimum of _____ inches in its smallest dimension.

    A. 12
    B. 18
    C. 30
    D. 36

15. Standpipes shall extend a minimum of _____ inches and a maximum of _____ inches above the trap weir.

    A. 18; 30
    B. 18; 42
    C. 24; 30
    D. 24; 42

16. The outlet of a laundry tray shall be a maximum horizontal distance of _____ from the standpipe trap.

    A. 18 inches
    B. 30 inches
    C. 42 inches
    D. 60 inches

17. In general, shower compartments shall have a minimum interior cross-sectional area of _____ square inches.

   A. 900
   B. 1,080
   C. 1,296
   D. 1,440

18. A water closet shall be set a minimum of _____ inches from its center to any side wall, partition or vanity.

   A. 15
   B. 16
   C. 18
   D. 20

19. A lavatory shall have a waste outlet a minimum of _____ in diameter.

   A. 1 inch
   B. 1 ¼ inches
   C. 1 ½ inches
   D. 2 inches

20. Unless an approved alternative is provided, flush valve seats in tanks for flushing water closets shall be a minimum of _____ above the flood-level rim of the bowl to which it is connected.

   A. ½ inch
   B. 1 inch
   C. 1 ½ inches
   D. 2 inches

21. The waste outlet and overflow outlet for a bathtub shall be connected to waste tubing or piping a minimum of _____ in diameter.

   A. 1 inch
   B. 1 ¼ inches
   C. 1 ½ inches
   D. 2 inches

22. Sinks shall have a waste outlet a minimum of _____ in diameter.

   A. 1 ¼ inches
   B. 1 ½ inches
   C. 2 inches
   D. 3 ½ inches

23. Food waste disposers shall be connected to a drain having a minimum diameter of _____ in diameter.

   A. 1 ¼ inches
   B. 1 ½ inches
   C. 2 inches
   D. 3 ½ inches

24. Floor drains shall have waste outlets a minimum of _____ in diameter.

   A. 1 ¼ inches
   B. 1 ½ inches
   C. 2 inches
   D. 3 ½ inches

25. What is the minimum size drain required for a macerating toilet system?

   A. ¾ inch
   B. 1 ¼ inches
   C. 1 ½ inches
   D. 2 inches

26. Where a smoke test is utilized to verify gas tightness of the DWV system, a pressure equivalent to a 1-inch water column shall be applied and maintained for a minimum time period of _____ minutes.

   A. 10
   B. 15
   C. 30
   D. 60

27. Where an air test of the rough plumbing installation requires a gauge pressure of 5 psi, the testing gauge shall have increments of _____ psi.

   A. 0.10
   B. 0.50
   C. 1.00
   D. 2.00

28. Trenches used for the installation of piping that are excavated parallel to footings shall extend a maximum of _____ below the bearing plane of the bottom edge of the footing.

   A. 30 degrees
   B. 45 degrees
   C. 12 inches
   D. 30 inches

29. Each compartment of a laundry tub shall be provided with a waste outlet a minimum of _____ in diameter.

    A. 1 inch
    B. 1 ¼ inch
    C. 1 ½ inch
    D. 2 inches

30. There shall be a minimum of _____ inches clearance in front of a water closet to any wall, fixture or door.

    A. 18
    B. 21
    C. 24
    D. 27

31. The access and egress opening for a shower compartment shall have a minimum and unobstructed clear width of _____ inches.

    A. 22
    B. 24
    C. 30
    D. 32

32. A water-temperature-limiting device shall be provided to limit the hot water supplied to a bathtub or whirlpool bathtub to a maximum of _____ °F.

    A. 110
    B. 115
    C. 120
    D. 125

33. The combined discharge from a dishwasher and a two-compartment sink, with a food-waste disposer, shall be served by a trap having a minimum outside diameter of _____ inches.

    A. 1 ¼
    B. 1 ½
    C. 2
    D. 2 ½

34. Where the manufacturer's instructions do not specify the minimum required size of a field-fabricated access opening to the circulation pump of a whirlpool bathtub, a minimum _____ opening shall be installed.

   A. 10-inch by 10-inch
   B. 12-inch by 12-inch
   C. 10-inch by 16-inch
   D. 12-inch by 18-inch

35. The discharge water temperature from a bidet fitting shall be limited to a maximum of _____ by a water-temperature-limiting device.

   A. 98 °F
   B. 105 °F
   C. 110 °F
   D. 112 °F

International Residential Code, 2018
Chapter 25, 26, and 27 - Answers

1.	D	Sec. P2503.4
2.	B	Sec. P2503.5.1, #2
3.	D	Sec. P2503.7
4.	C	Sec. P2603.2.1
5.	C	Sec. P2603.2.1
6.	D	Sec. P2603.4
7.	B	Sec. P2603.5
8.	B	Sec. P2603.5
9.	D	Sec. P2604.1
10.	B	Sec. P2604.3
11.	D	Table P2605.1
12.	A	Table P2605.1
13.	C	Sec. P2703.1
14.	A	Sec. P2704.1
15.	B	Sec. P2706.1.2
16.	B	Sec. P2706.1.2.1
17.	A	Sec. P2708.1
18.	A	Sec. P2705.1, #5
19.	B	Sec. P2711.3
20.	B	Sec. P2712.4
21.	C	Sec. P2713.1
22.	B	Sec. P2714.1
23.	B	Sec. P2716.1
24.	C	Sec. P2719.1
25.	A	Sec. P2723.2
26.	B	Sec. P2503.5.2, #2.1
27.	A	Sec. P2503.9
28.	B	Sec. P2604.4
29.	C	Sec. P2715.1
30.	B	Sec. P2705.1, #5
31.	A	Sec. P2708.1.1
32.	C	Sec. P2713.3
33.	B	Sec. P2717.2
34.	B	Sec. P2720.1
35.	C	Sec. P2721.2

International Residential Code, 2015
Chapter 28, 29, and 30 - Questions and Answers

1. A required overflow pan for a water heater shall be a minimum of _____ in depth and of sufficient size and shape to collect all dripping and condensate.

   A. 1 inch
   B. 1 ½ inches
   C. 2 inches
   D. 3 inches

2. Where the termination of a drain pan for a water heater extends to the exterior of the building, it shall terminate a minimum of _____ and a maximum of _____ above the adjacent ground surface.

   A. 3 inches, 12 inches
   B. 3 inches, 24 inches
   C. 6 inches, 12 inches
   D. 6 inches, 24 inches

3. Where installed in a garage, water heaters having an ignition source shall be elevated such that the source of ignition is a minimum of _____ above the garage floor unless the appliance is listed as flammable vapor ignition resistant.

   A. 6 inches
   B. 12 inches
   C. 18 inches
   D. 24 inches

4. A water heater pressure-relief valve shall be set to open at not less than _____ above the system pressure but not over _____.

   A. 15 psi, 125 psi
   B. 15 psi, 150 psi
   C. 25 psi, 125 psi
   D. 25 psi, 150 psi

5. A water heater temperature-relief valve shall be set to open at a maximum temperature of _____.

   A. 150°F
   B. 165°F
   C. 180°F
   D. 210°F

6. Where located close to a wall, what is the minimum required air gap for a lavatory with an effective opening of 1/2 inch?

   A. 1 inch
   B. 1 ½ inches
   C. 2 inches
   D. 3 inches

7. A temperature-relief valve installed in a water heater shall be installed such that the temperature-sensing element monitors the water within the top _____ of the tank.

   A. one-sixth
   B. one-fourth
   C. 6 inches
   D. 12 inches

8. In determining the peak demand for the water service and water distribution service, a flow rate of _____ and a flow pressure of _____ shall be used for a bathtub at the point of outlet discharge.

   A. 3 gpm, 20 psi
   B. 4 gpm, 20 psi
   C. 4 gpm, 8 psi
   D. 5 gpm, 8 psi

9. A water closet shall have a maximum consumption of _____ gallons per flushing cycle.

   A. 1.0
   B. 1.6
   C. 2.0
   D. 2.3

10. A handheld shower spray shall have a maximum flow rate of _____.

   A. 2.2 gpm at 60 psi
   B. 2.2 gpm at 80 psi
   C. 2.5 gpm at 60 psi
   D. 2.5 gpm at 80 psi

11. What is the maximum static pressure required for a water service?

    A. 80 psi
    B. 90 psi
    C. 100 psi
    D. 110 psi

12. When sizing a water distribution system, a tank-type water closet shall have a water-supply fixture unit value of _____.

    A. 1.0
    B. 1.4
    C. 2.2
    D. 2.7

13. Where a fire sprinkler system is installed, sprinklers are not required in bathrooms having a maximum floor area of _____ square feet.

    A. 40
    B. 50
    C. 55
    D. 65

14. Pipe and fittings used in the water supply system shall have a maximum of _____ lead content.

    A. 1 percent
    B. 2 percent
    C. 5 percent
    D. 8 percent

15. Bends of polyethylene pipe shall have a minimum installed radius of pipe curvature greater than _____ pipe diameters.

    A. 15
    B. 20
    C. 25
    D. 30

16. Hot-water-distribution piping within dwelling units shall have a minimum pressure rating of _____ at 180°F.

    A. 80 psi
    B. 100 psi
    C. 110 psi
    D. 125 psi

17. Where changing direction, what is the minimum required radius for bends in copper tubing used for water distribution?

   A. four tube diameters
   B. six tube diameters
   C. 4 inches
   D. 6 inches

18. What is the calculated load on DWV-system piping for two bath groups, a kitchen group, a laundry group and a clothes washer standpipe?

   A. 15 d.f.u.
   B. 16 d.f.u.
   C. 18 d.f.u.
   D. 20 d.f.u.

19. Building sewer cleanouts shall be installed a maximum of _____ apart in horizontal drainage lines for building sewers smaller than 8 inches.

   A. 40 feet
   B. 60 feet
   C. 80 feet
   D. 100 feet

20. Unless located on a stack, the minimum size of a cleanout serving a 3-inch pipe shall be _____.

   A. 3 inches
   B. 2 ½ inches
   C. 2 inches
   D. 1 ½ inches

21. Cleanouts for 8-inch drainage piping shall be provided with a minimum clearance of _____ inches from, and perpendicular to, the face of the opening to any obstruction.

   A. 18
   B. 24
   C. 30
   D. 36

22. What is the minimum required clearance in front of a cleanout for a 6-inch drainage pipe?

   A. 12 inches
   B. 18 inches
   C. 24 inches
   D. 30 inches

23. Three-inch horizontal drainage piping shall be installed at a minimum uniform slope of _____ per foot.

    A. 1/8 inch
    B. 3/16 inch
    C. ¼ inch
    D. 5/16 inch

24. What is the maximum number of fixture units allowed to be connected to a 3-inch building drain branch sloped at ¼-inch per foot?

    A. 24
    B. 36
    C. 42
    D. 50

25. What is the maximum number of fixture units allowed to be connected to a 3-inch-diameter vertical drain stack?

    A. 10
    B. 12
    C. 20
    D. 48

26. A water heater discharge pipe serving a pressure-relief valve shall terminate atmospherically a maximum of _____ inch(es) above the floor or waste receptor.

    A. 1
    B. 2
    C. 4
    D. 6

27. A hose connection backflow preventer shall conform to which of the following applicable standards?

    A. ASSE 1012, CSA B64.3
    B. ASSE 1020, CSA B64.1.2
    C. ASSE 1052, CSA B64.2.1.1
    D. ASSE 1056, CSA B64.1.3

28. Water service pipe installed underground and outside of a structure shall have a minimum working pressure rating of _____ psi at 73°F.

    A. 100
    B. 140
    C. 160
    D. 175

29. Back-to-back water closet connections to double sanitary tee patterns are permitted provided the horizontal developed length between the outlet of the water closet and the connection to the double sanitary tee is a minimum of _____ inches.

   A. 18
   B. 24
   C. 30
   D. 36

30. The area of coverage of a single fire sprinkler is limited to a maximum of _____ square feet and shall be based on the sprinkler listing and the manufacturer's installation instructions.

   A. 225
   B. 300
   C. 350
   D. 400

31. Where chemicals are intended to be introduced into a lawn irrigation system, the potable water supply shall be protected against backflow by a(n) _____.

   A. atmospheric-type vacuum breaker
   B. double check-valve assembly
   C. pressure-type vacuum breaker assembly
   D. reduced pressure principle backflow prevention assembly

32. Where polyethylene plastic pipe is used in water service piping, bends must occur a minimum of _____ pipe diameters from any fitting or valve.

   A. 4
   B. 6
   C. 10
   D. 12

33. Galvanized steel DWV pipe used within a building shall be maintained a minimum of _____ inches above ground.

   A. 2
   B. 3
   C. 4
   D. 6

34. A quarter-bend fitting is permitted for a vertical to horizontal change in direction in drainage piping provided the fixture drain is a maximum of _____ inches in diameter.

    A. 1 ¼
    B. 1 ½
    C. 2
    D. 3

35. Where a fire sprinkler system is installed in a one-story dwelling with a floor area of 2,600 square feet, the water supply shall have the capacity to provide the required design flow rate for sprinklers for a minimum of _____ minutes.

    A. 7
    B. 10
    C. 12
    D. 15

International Residential Code, 2015
Chapter 28, 29, and 30 - Answers

1.	B	Sec. P2801.6.1
2.	D	Sec. P2801.6.2
3.	C	Sec. P2801.7
4.	D	Sec. P2804.3
5.	D	Sec. P2804.4
6.	B	Table P2902.3.1
7.	C	Sec. P2804.4
8.	B	Table P2903.1
9.	B	Table P2903.2
10.	D	Table P2903.2, Note a
11.	A	Sec. P2903.3.1
12.	C	Table P2903.6
13.	C	Sec. P2904.1.1, Exception 3
14.	D	Sec. P2906.2
15.	D	Sec. P2906.3
16.	B	Sec. P2906.5
17.	A	Sec. P2907.1
18.	A	Table P3004.1
19.	D	Sec. P3005.2.2
20.	A	Sec. P3005.2.5
21.	D	Sec. P3005.2.9
22.	B	Sec. P3005.2.9
23.	A	Sec. P3005.3
24.	C	Table P3005.4.2
25.	D	Table P3005.4.1
26.	D	Sec. P2804.6.1, #10
27.	C	Table P2902.3
28.	C	Sec. P2906.4
29.	A	Sec. P3005.1.1, Exception
30.	D	Sec. P2904.2.4.1
31.	D	Sec. P2902.5.3
32.	C	Sec. P2906.3
33.	D	Sec. P3002.1
34.	C	Table P3005.1, Note a
35.	B	Sec. P2904.5.2, #2

1. Where the accumulation of snow is not a concern and the roof is not used for assembly purposes, open vent pipes shall extend a minimum of _____ inches above a roof used solely for weather protection.

   A. 6
   B. 12
   C. 18
   D. 24

2. Where a vent extension through a roof is increased in size due to cold climatic conditions, the size increase shall occur inside the structure a minimum of _____ inches inside the thermal envelope of the building.

   A. 6
   B. 12
   C. 24
   D. 36

3. Horizontal vent pipes forming branch vents shall be a minimum of _____ inches above the flood level rim of the highest fixture served.

   A. 3
   B. 4
   C. 6
   D. 12

4. Where a roof is to be used for assembly, such as a promenade or observation deck, a vent extension shall terminate a minimum of _____ above the roof.

   A. 2 feet
   B. 5 feet
   C. 7 feet
   D. 10 feet

5. Unless located a minimum of _____ above the top of the opening, an open vent terminal from a drainage system shall be located at least 10 feet horizontally from a door, openable window or other air intake opening of the building.

   A. 12 inches
   B. 24 inches
   C. 36 inches
   D. 60 inches

6. Every dry vent shall rise vertically a minimum of _____ above the flood level rim of the highest trap or trapped fixture being vented.

   A. 1 inch
   B. 2 inches
   C. 4 inches
   D. 6 inches

7. What is the maximum permitted developed length of the fixture drain from the trap weir to the vent fitting for a self-siphoning fixture such as a water closet?

   A. 6 feet
   B. 8 feet
   C. 12 feet
   D. no limit

8. A maximum distance of _____ is permitted between a 1 1/2 -inch fixture trap and the vent fitting.

   A. 4 feet
   B. 5 feet
   C. 6 feet
   D. 8 feet

9. The total fall in a fixture drain due to pipe slope is limited to a maximum of _____.

   A. 1 inch
   B. one pipe diameter
   C. 2 inches
   D. two pipe diameters

10. A fixture vent shall be installed a minimum of _____ from the trap weir.

   A. 1 inch
   B. one pipe diameter
   C. 2 inches
   D. two pipe diameters

11. An individual vent may vent a maximum of _____ trap(s) or trap fixture(s) as a common vent.

   A. one
   B. two
   C. three
   D. four

12. Where fixture drains connect at different levels and the vent connects as a vertical extension of the vertical drain, the vertical drain pipe connecting the two fixture drains shall be considered the vent for the lower fixture drain. If the vent pipe size is 2 inches, what is the maximum permitted discharge from the upper fixture drain?

   A. 1 d.f.u.
   B. 4 d.f.u.
   C. 6 d.f.u.
   D. 8 d.f.u.

13. A vertical wet vent shall have a minimum pipe size of _____ where serving a total fixture unit load of 9 d.f.u.

   A. 2 inches
   B. 2 1/2 inches
   C. 3 inches
   D. 4 inches

14. A 3-inch waste stack vent may be used for a maximum total discharge to the stack of _____.

   A. 8 d.f.u.
   B. 12 d.f.u.
   C. 24 d.f.u.
   D. 32 d.f.u.

15. What is the maximum number of fixtures connected to a horizontal branch drain that are permitted to be circuit vented?

   A. two
   B. four
   C. six
   D. eight

16. Which one of the following fixtures shall not be served by a combination waste and vent system?

    A. sink
    B. floor drain
    C. standpipe
    D. lavatory

17. The maximum permitted slope of a horizontal combination waste and vent pipe shall be _____ unit vertical in 12 units horizontal.

    A. one-eighth
    B. one-fourth
    C. one-half
    D. one

18. A 2 1/2-inchdiameter pipe used as a combination waste and vent shall serve a maximum of _____ fixture units where connected to a horizontal branch.

    A. 3
    B. 6
    C. 12
    D. 26

19. Vents having a minimum developed length exceeding _____ shall be increased by one nominal pipe size for the entire developed length of the vent pipe.

    A. 25
    B. 40
    C. 50
    D. 60

20. Where used in a vent system, an individual air admittance valve shall be located a minimum of _____ above the horizontal branch drain or fixture drain being vented.

    A. 1 inch
    B. 2 inches
    C. 4 inches
    D. 6 inches

21. Traps shall have a minimum liquid seal of   inches and a maximum seal of _____ inches.

    A.   2, 4
    B.   2, 6
    C.   3, 4
    D.   3, 6

22. Where a fixture is separately trapped, what is the maximum vertical distance permitted from the fixture outlet to the trap weir?

  A. 6 inches
  B. 12 inches
  C. 18 inches
  D. 24 inches

23. Where common trapped fixture outlets are permitted, they shall be located a maximum of _____ apart.

  A. 18 inches
  B. 24 inches
  C. 30 inches
  D. 36 inches

24. Unless otherwise approved, a sump pit shall be a minimum of _____ inches in diameter and _____ inches deep.

  A. 12, 15
  B. 15, 18
  C. 18, 24
  D. 24, 36

25. The minimum required size for a trap arm serving a clothes washer standpipe shall be

  A. 1 1/4 inches
  B. 1 1/2 inches
  C. 2 inches
  D. 2 1/2 inches

26. An open vent terminal extending through an exterior wall shall terminate a minimum of _____ feet from the lot line.

  A. 4
  B. 5
  C. 6
  D. 10

27. In circuit venting, the maximum slope of the vent section of the horizontal branch drain shall be _____ unit(s) vertical in 12 units horizontal.

  A. ¼
  B. ½
  C. 1
  D. 2

28. What is the maximum vertical distance between the fixture drain of a sink and a horizontal combination waste and vent pipe?

   A. 30 inches
   B. 4 feet
   C. 6 feet
   D. 8 feet

29. The vent or branch vent for multiple island fixture vents shall extend a minimum of _____ inch(es) above the highest island fixture being vented before connecting to the outside vent terminal.

   A. 1
   B. 2
   C. 4
   D. 6

30. Stack-type air admittance valves shall be located a minimum of _____ inches above the flood level rim of the highest fixture being vented.

   A. 4
   B. 6
   C. 12
   D. 15

31. Offsets in a stack vent installed for the waste stack shall be located a minimum of _____ inches above the flood level of the highest fixture.

   A. 2
   B. 4
   C. 6
   D. 8

32. Plumbing vent pipes shall be a minimum of _____ inches in diameter.

   A. 1 ¼
   B. 1 ½
   C. 2
   D. 2 ½

33. The air pressure relief pipe from a pneumatic sewage ejector shall be a minimum of _____ inch(es) in size.

   A. ¾
   B. 1
   C. 1 ¼
   D. 1 ½

34. Where the developed length of a sump vent is 110 feet, what is the minimum required vent size for a sump with a sewage pump having a discharge capacity of 60 gallons per minute?

    A. 1 1/4 inches
    B. 1 1/2 inches
    C. 2 inches
    D. 2 1/2 inches

35. The horizontal distance from a fixture outlet to the trap weir shall be a maximum of _____ inches measured from the centerline of the fixture outlet to the centerline of the trap inlet.

    A. 24
    B. 30
    C. 36
    D. 48

International Residential Code, 2018
Chapter 31, 32, and 33 - Answers

1.	A	Sec. P3103.1.1
2.	B	Sec. P3103.2
3.	C	Sec. P3104.5
4.	C	Sec. P3103.1.2
5.	C	Sec. P3103.5
6.	D	Sec. P3104.4
7.	D	Sec. P3105.1, Exception
8.	C	Table P3105.1
9.	B	Sec. P3105.2
10.	D	Sec. P3105.3
11.	B	Sec. P3107.1
12.	B	Table P3107.3
13.	C	Table P3108.3
14.	C	Table P3109.4
15.	D	Sec. P3110.1
16.	C	Sec. P3111.1
17.	C	Sec. P3111.2.1
18.	B	Table P3111.3
19.	B	Sec. P3113.1
20.	C	Sec. P3114.4
21.	A	Sec. P3201.2
22.	D	Sec. P3201.6
23.	C	Sec. P3201.6, #2
24.	C	Sec. P3303.1.2
25.	C	Table P3201.7
26.	A	Sec. P3103.5
27.	C	Sec. P3110.3
28.	D	Sec. P3111.2
29.	D	Sec. P3112.2
30.	B	Sec. P3114.4
31.	C	Sec. P3109.3
32.	A	Sec. P3113.1
33.	C	Sec. P3113.4.2
34.	C	Table P3113.4.1
35.	B	Sec. P3201.6

International Residential Code, 2018
Chapters 34, 35, and 37 – General Electrical Requirements
Questions and Answers

1. Energized parts operating at a minimum of _____ shall be guarded against accidental contact by people through the use of approved enclosures.

A. 50 volts
B. 60 volts
C. 90 volts
D. 110 volts

2. An electrical panelboard requiring access while energized shall be provided with a minimum of _____ in depth measured in the direction of access.

A. 30 inches
B. 36 inches
C. 42 inches
D. 48 inches

3. Work space in front of an electrical panelboard shall be a minimum of _____ in width, but no less than the width of the panelboard.

A. 30 inches
B. 36 inches
C. 42 inches
D. 48 inches

4. The dedicated indoor space above an electrical panelboard shall be a minimum of _____ high or to the structural ceiling, whichever is lower.

A. 4 feet
B. 5 feet
C. 6 feet
D. 6.5 feet

5. The minimum size of electrical conductors for feeders and branch circuits, when of copper, shall be _____ AWG.

A. NO. 16
B. NO. 14
C. NO. 12
D. NO. 10

6. Where electrical conductors are to be spliced, terminated or connected to fixtures or devices, a minimum length of _____ of free conductor shall be provided at each outlet, junction or switch point.

A. 4 inches
B. 6 inches
C. 8 inches
D. 12 inches

7. Insulated grounded conductors of sizes 6 AWG and smaller may be identified by all but which one of the following methods?

A. Continuous white outer finish
B. Continuous gray outer finish
C. Continuous black outer finish
D. Three continuous white stripes (on other than green insulation)

8. Equipment grounding conductors of sizes 6 AWG and smaller may be identified by all but which one of the following methods?

A. Continuous white color
B. Continuous green color
C. Bare
D. Continuous green color with one or more yellow stripes

9. In general, which of the following continuous colors is permitted for the insulation on ungrounded conductors?

A. Gray
B. White
C. Green
D. Red

10. Where it is impractical to locate the service head or gooseneck above the point of attachment of the service-drop or overhead service conductors to the building, the service head or gooseneck shall be location shall be a maximum of _____ inches from the point of attachment.

A. 12
B. 18
C. 24
D. 36

11. An open service conductor without an overall outer jacket shall have a minimum clearance of _____ from the sides of doors, porches and openable windows.

A. 3 feet
B. 4 feet
C. 6 feet
D. 8 feet

12. An overhead service conductor shall have a minimum clearance above a 3:12 roof of _____.

A. 3 feet
B. 6 feet
C. 7 feet
D. 8 feet

13. Overhead service conductors shall have a minimum clearance of _____ over residential property and driveways.

A. 8 feet
B. 10 feet
C. 12 feet
D. 15 feet

14. In all cases, the point of attachment of service-drop conductors to a building shall be a minimum of _____ above finished grade.

A. 8 feet
B. 10 feet
C. 12 feet
D. 14 feet

15. A metal underground water pipe used as part of the grounding electrode system shall be in direct contact with the earth for a minimum of _____ .

A. 8 feet
B. 10 feet
C. 15 feet
D. 20 feet

16. Where more than one rod, pipe or plate electrode is used in one grounding electrode system, each electrode shall be located a minimum of _____ from any other electrode of another grounding system.

A. 5 feet
B. 6 feet
C. 10 feet
D. 20 feet

17. Where a grounding electrode is made of a stainless steel rod, the rod shall be a minimum of _____ in diameter and a minimum of _____ in length unless listed.

A. 1/2 inch, 8 feet
B. 1/2 inch, 10 feet
C. 5/8 inch, 8 feet
D. 5/8 inch, 10 feet

18. Where used outside, an aluminum or copper-clad aluminum grounding electrode conductor shall be installed a minimum of _____ from the earth.

A. 6 inches
B. 12 inches
C. 18 inches
D. 30 inches

19. The rating of any one cord- and plug-connected utilization equipment not fastened in place shall be a maximum of _____ of the branch-circuit ampere rating.

A. 80 percent
B. 100 percent
C. 110 percent
D. 125 percent

20. A minimum of _____ branch circuit(s) shall be provided to serve receptacles located in the kitchen, pantry, breakfast area and dining area.

A. One 15-ampere-rated
B. One 20-ampere-rated
C. Two 15-ampere-rated
D. Two 20-ampere-rated

21. A minimum of _____ branch circuit(s) shall be provided for receptacles located in the laundry room and a minimum of _____ branch circuit(s) shall be provided to supply the bathroom receptacle outlet(s).

A. One 15-ampere-rated, one 15-ampere-rated
B. One 20-ampere-rated, one 20-ampere-rated
C. One 15-ampere-rated, two 15-ampere-rated
D. One 20-ampere-rated, two 20 ampere-rated

22. In the calculation of electrical feeder loads, an electric clothes dryer load shall be considered _____ VA for each dryer circuit or the nameplate rating load of each dryer, whichever is greater.

A. 4,000
B. 5,000
C. 5,500
D. 6,000

23. When sizing feeder conductors, a minimum unit load of _____ shall constitute the minimum lighting and convenience receptacle load for each square foot of floor area.

A. Two volt-amperes
B. Three volt-amperes
C. Five volt-amperes
D. Six volt-amperes

24. What is the maximum overcurrent-protection-device rating permitted for No. 12 copper conductors?

A. 15 amps
B. 20 amps
C. 25 amps
D. 30 amps

25. Which one of the following ratings is not a standard ampere rating for fuses and inverse time circuit breakers?

A. 25 amperes
B. 50 amperes
C. 75 amperes
D. 100 amperes

26. Where metallic plugs or plates are used with nonmetallic electrical enclosures to close unused openings, they shall be recessed a minimum of _____ inch from the outer surface of the enclosure.

A. 1/8
B. 1/4
C. 3/8
D. 1/2

27. Electrical panelboards and overcurrent protection devices shall not be located in _____.

A. Clothes closets
B. Sleeping rooms
C. Garages
D. Storage rooms

28. Where the opening to an outlet, junction, or switch point is less than 8 inches in any dimension, each electrical conductor shall be long enough to extend a minimum of _____ inches outside of such opening.

A. 2
B. 3
C. 4
D. 6

29. Electrical service disconnecting means shall not be installed in _____.

A. Storage closets
B. Laundry rooms
C. Sleeping rooms
D. Bathrooms

30. In order to be used as a part of the grounding electrode system, interior metal water pipe shall be located a maximum of _____ feet from the entrance to the building.

A. 3
B. 5
C. 6
D. 10

31. Electrical conductors located above a roof shall be installed with a minimum vertical clearance of _____ feet where the roof has a slope of 8:12.

A. 3
B. 4
C. 6
D. 7

32. Service-entrance cables shall be supported by straps or other approved means within _____ inches of every electrical service head and at maximum intervals of _____ inches.

A. 8, 30
B. 8, 36
C. 12, 30
D. 12, 36

33. A plate electrode installed as a part of a grounding electrode system shall be located a minimum of _____ inches below the surface of the earth.

A. 12
B. 18
C. 24
D. 30

34. Where an electrical branch circuit has multiple outlets, what is the minimum required size of circuit conductors for a circuit rated at 30 amps?

A. 14 awg
B. 12 awg
C. 10 awg
D. 8 awg

35. An overcurrent protection device shall be installed so that the center of the grip of the operating handle of the switch or circuit breaker, when in its highest position, is located a maximum of _____ above the floor or working platform.

A. 5 feet, 0 inches
B. 6 feet, 4 inches
C. 6 feet, 7 inches
D. 7 feet, 0 inches

International Residential Code, 2018
Chapters 34, 35, and 37 – General Electrical Requirements
Answer Key

No.	Answer	Sec.
1.	A	E3404.9
2.	B	E3405.2
3.	A	E3405.2
4.	C	E3405.3
5.	B	E3406.3
6.	B	E3406.11.3
7.	C	E3407.1
8.	A	E3407.2
9.	D	E3407.3
10.	C	E3605.9.3, Exception
11.	A	E3604.1
12.	D	E3604.2.1
13.	C	E3604.2.2, #2
14.	B	E3604.3
15.	B	E3608.1.1
16.	B	E3608.3
17.	C	E3608.1.4, #2
18.	C	E3610.2
19.	A	E3702.3
20.	D	E3703.2
21.	B	E3703.3, E3703.4
22.	B	Table E3704.2(1)
23.	B	E3704.4
24.	B	Table E3705.5.3
25.	C	E3705.6
26.	B	E3404.6
27.	A	E3405.5
28.	B	E3406.11.3
29.	D	E3601.6.2
30.	B	E3608.1.1.1
31.	A	E3604.2.1, Exception
32.	C	E3605.7
33.	D	E3608.1.5
34.	C	Table E3702.14
35.	C	E3705.7, #6

International Residential Code, 2018
Chapters 38, 39, 40, 41 and 42
Lighting, Appliance Installation, and Swimming Pools
Questions and Answers

1. Electrical nonmetallic tubing is an allowable wiring method in all but which one of the following applications?

A. Feeders
B. Branch circuits
C. Embedded in masonry
D. Direct burial

2. Unless installed parallel to framing members, NM wiring run in an attic accessed by a portable ladder shall be protected from damage where located within _____ of the nearest edge of the attic entrance.

A. 6 feet
B. 7 feet
C. 8 feet
D. 10 feet

3. Type NM wiring shall be supported a maximum of _____ on center.

A. 3 feet
B. 41/2 feet
C. 6 feet
D. 12 feet

4. In general, direct burial cable installed below a driveway serving a one-family dwelling unit shall have a minimum burial depth of _____ .

A. 6 inches
B. 12 inches
C. 18 inches
D. 24 inches

5. Direct buried conductors and cables emerging from the ground shall be protected by enclosures or raceways extending to a minimum height of _____ above finished grade or the point of entrance to the building.

A. 7 feet
B. 8 feet
C. 10 feet
D. 12 feet

6. Receptacle outlets shall be installed so that all points along the floor line of any wall space are a maximum of _____ from an outlet in that space when measured horizontally.

A. 4 feet
B. 6 feet
C. 8 feet
D. 12 feet

7. An unbroken wall space having a minimum width of _____ shall be considered a wall space for the purpose of determining receptacle outlet distribution.

A. 12 inches
B. 18 inches
C. 24 inches
D. 48 inches

8. Floor receptacle outlets cannot be counted as part of the required number of receptacle outlets unless located within _____ of the wall.

A. 4 inches
B. 6 inches
C. 12 inches
D. 18 inches

9. At a kitchen counter, countertop receptacle outlets shall be installed with a maximum horizontal distance of _____ from any point along the wall line to an outlet.

A. 12 inches
B. 18 inches
C. 24 inches
D. 36 inches

10. In a bathroom, at least one receptacle outlet shall be located a maximum of_____ from the outside edge of each lavatory.

A. 18 inches
B. 24 inches
C. 30 inches
D. 36 inches

11. A hallway a minimum of _____ in length shall be provided with at least one receptacle outlet.

A. 6 feet
B. 8 feet
C. 10 feet
D. 12 feet

12. All 125-volt, single-phase, 20-ampere receptacles shall be provided with ground-fault circuit-interrupter protection where located within _____ of the outside edge of a sink.

A. 2 feet
B. 3 feet
C. 4 feet
D. 6 feet

13. Where nonmetallic-sheathed cable is used, the cable assembly including the sheath shall extend into the box a minimum of _____ through a nonmetallic-sheathed cable knockout opening.

A. 1/4 inch
B. 3/8 inch
C. 1/2 inch
D. 3/4 inch

14. Electrical outlet boxes that do not enclose devices or utilization equipment shall have a minimum internal depth of _____ .

A. 1/2 inch
B 5/8 inch
C. 15/16 inch
D. 1 inch

15. What is the maximum number of No. 12 conductors permitted for a 4-inch by 11/2-inch standard round metal box not marked with a cubic-inch capacity?

A. 4
B. 6
C. 9
D. 10

16. In a wall constructed of wood or other combustible material, outlet boxes shall be installed so that the front edge of the box is set back a maximum of _____ from the finished surface.

A. 0 inches; (the box must be flush or project outward)
B. 1/8 inch
C. 1/4 inch
D. 1/2 inch

17. All switches shall be installed so that the center of the grip of the operating handle, in its highest position, shall be located a maximum of _____ above the floor or working platform.

A. 6 feet, 0 inches
B. 6 feet, 6 inches
C. 6 feet, 7 inches
D. 6 feet, 9 inches

18. What is the required receptacle rating for a 20-ampere branch circuit supplying two or more receptacles or outlets?

A. 15 amperes only
B. 20 amperes only
C. 30 amperes only
D. 15 amperes or 20 amperes

19. Cord-connected luminaires, lighting track and pendants shall be located a minimum of_____ horizontally and _____ vertically from the top of a bathtub rim or shower stall threshold.

A. 2 feet, 7 feet
B. 2 feet, 8 feet
C. 3 feet, 7 feet
D. 3 feet, 8 feet

20. Where installed in a storage closet, a recessed fluorescent luminaires shall be located so as to provide a minimum clearance of _____ between the fixture and the nearest point of the storage space.

A. 3 inches
B. 6 inches
C. 8 inches
D. 12 inches

21. A luminaires that weighs more than _____ or exceeds _____ in any dimension shall not be supported by the screw shell of a lampholder.

A. 4 pounds, 14 inches
B. 4 pounds, 16 inches
C. 6 pounds, 14 inches
D. 6 pounds, 16 inches

22. Ceiling-suspended paddle fans weighing a maximum of _____ are permitted to be supported by outlet boxes identified for such use.

A. 25 pounds
B. 35 pounds
C. 42 pounds
D. 70 pounds

23. 125-volt receptacles located _____ from the inside walls of a swimming pool do not need to be protected by a ground-fault circuit-interrupter.

A. 10 feet
B. 15 feet
C. 20 feet
D. 30 feet

24. At least one 125-volt receptacle shall be located a minimum of _____ from the inside walls of indoor spas and hot tubs.

A. 5 feet
B. 6 feet
C. 10 feet
D. 12 feet

25. Receptacles shall be located a minimum of _____ feet from the inside walls of a storable pool.

A. 5
B. 6
C. 10
D. 20

26. Where three or more conductors of minimum size _____ AWG are run at angles with joists in unfinished basements, additional protection is not required if the cable assembly is attached directly to the bottom of the joists.

A. 6
B. 8
C. 10
D. 12

27. Underground service conductors not encased in concrete and buried 18 inches or more below grade shall have their location identified by a warning ribbon placed a minimum of _____ above the underground installation.

A. 4
B. 6
C. 8
D. 12

28. The receptacle outlet required in a bathroom, where located on the side of the basin cabinet, shall be located a maximum of _____ inches below the top of the basin.

A. 8
B. 12
C. 15
D. 18

29. Wall-mounted luminaires weighing a maximum of _____ pounds are permitted to be supported on boxes other than those specifically designed for luminaires, provided the luminaires are secured to the box with at least two No. 6 or larger screws.

A. 6
B. 10
C. 14
D. 18

30. Lighting track shall be located a minimum of _____ above the finished floor unless protected from physical damage or the track operates at less than 30 volts rms open-circuit voltage.

A. 5 feet, 0 inches
B. 6 feet, 0 inches
C. 6 feet, 4 inches
D. 6 feet, 8 inches

31. A receptacle outlet installed to serve a washing machine shall be installed a maximum of _____ feet from the intended location of the washing machine.

A. 2
B. 3
C. 4
D. 6

32. For other than evaporative coolers, a receptacle outlet shall be installed for the servicing of HVAC equipment a maximum of _____ feet from such equipment.

A. 20
B. 25
C. 40
D. 50

33. Unless the outlet box is listed for the weight to be supported, an outlet box in a wall may support a luminaire having a maximum weight of _____ pounds.

A. 28
B. 35
C. 50
D. 70

34. Noncombustible surfaces that are broken or incomplete shall be repaired so that gaps or open spaces at the edge of a panelboard employing a flush-type cover are a maximum of _____ inch in size.

A. 0 (no gaps permitted)
B. 1/16
C. 1/8
D. 1/4

35. A flexible cord for a cord-and-plug-connected range hood shall have a minimum length of _____ inches and a maximum length of _____ inches.

A. 18, 36
B. 18, 48
C. 30, 36
D. 36, 48

International Residential Code, 2018
Chapters 38, 39, 40, 41 and 42
Lighting, Appliance Installation, and Swimming Pools
Answer Key

No.	Answer	Sec.
1.	D	Tables E3801.2, E3801.4
2.	A	E3802.2.1
3.	B	Table E3802.1
4.	C	Table E3803.1
5.	B	E3803.3
6.	B	E3901.2.1
7.	C	E3901.2.2, #1
8.	D	E3901.2.3
9.	C	E3901.4.1
10.	D	E3901.6
11.	C	E3901.10
12.	D	E3902.7
13.	A	E3905.3.1
14.	A	E3905.4.1
15.	B	Table E3905.12.1
16.	A	E3906.5
17.	C	E4001.6
18.	D	Table E4002.1.2
19.	D	E4003.11
20.	B	E4003.12, #4
21.	D	E4004.4
22.	D	E4101.6, E3905.8
23.	D	E4203.1.4
24.	B	E4203.1.5
25.	B	E4207.4
26.	B	E3802.4
27.	D	E3803.2
28.	B	E3901.6
29.	A	E3905.6.1, Exception
30.	A	E4005.4, #8
31.	D	E3901.5
32.	B	E3901.12
33.	C	E3905.6.1
34.	C	E3907.4
35.	B	Table E4101.3

1. In concrete walls a cold joint occurs when _____.

    A. Concrete batches are mixed differently
    B. Fresh concrete poured on top of or next to concrete that has already begun to cure
    C. Too much air is in the concrete
    D. There is too much moisture in the concrete and the temperature is below 30°F

2. The first priority for underground excavation in any developed area is _____.

    A. Notify all owners
    B. Notify Sunshine
    C. Locate existing ground utilities
    D. Site preparation and material layout

3. If there is a conflict in the code between a general requirement and a specific requirement, the _____ requirement shall apply.

    A. General
    B. Specific
    C. Least restrictive
    D. Most restrictive

4. To what depth should a control joint be cut into a concrete slab?

    A. One-eight the slab thickness
    B. One-fourth the slab thickness
    C. 10% of the slab thickness
    D. Up to 60% of the slab thickness

5. When precise information is needed about a small or complex portion of the building, what would you look for on a plan?

    A. Section views
    B. A detail drawing
    C. Engineering drawings
    D. Mechanical plan

6. Used materials may be utilized under which one of the following conditions?

    A. They meet the requirements for new materials
    B. When approved by the building official
    C. Used materials may never be used in new construction
    D. A representative sampling is tested for compliance

7. _____ mortar joints are recommended in areas exposed to high winds and heavy rains.

    A. Weathered
    B. Concave
    C. Troweled
    D. Raked

8. In _____ splice, the bars are lapped next to each other at a certain length and securely wired together with tie wire.

    A. Lap
    B. Welded
    C. Mechanical
    D. None of the above

9. Habitable rooms other than kitchens shall have a minimum floor area of _____ square feet.

    A. 70
    B. 100
    C. 120
    D. 150

10. A six-foot wide sheep foot roller, .75 operator skill, .83 efficiency, 12-inch fill layers compacted to 8 inch layers requiring eight passes of the roller at the speed of 2.5 miles per hour. Using only the given information, according to Pipe and Excavating Contracting, the maximum number of cubic yards is _____.

    A. Less than 155
    B. Between 155 and 160
    C. Between 160 and 165
    D. More than 165

11. In general, the minimum required ceiling height of all habitable rooms is _____.

    A. 6 feet, 8 inches
    B. 7 feet, 0 inches
    C. 7 feet, 6 inches
    D. 8 feet, 0 inches

12. Forms and shores in concrete shall not be removed until _____.
    A. Directed by the architect or engineer
    B. The removal time stated in the specifications has elapsed
    C. The concrete has attained the specified compressive strength
    D. The concrete has gained sufficient strength to support its weight and superimposed loads

13. For concrete cast against and permanently exposed to earth (such as footings), minimum cover for bundled bars is _____ inch(es).

    A. 1
    B. 2
    C. 3
    D. 4

14. The _____ is the part of a window that holds the glazing.

    A. Muntin
    B. Sash
    C. Casing
    D. Mounting flange

15. Asphalt shingles can be installed on roofs as steep as _____.

    A. 5:12
    B. 18:12
    C. 21:12
    D. 20:12

16. The minimum width of a hallway shall be _____ feet.

    A. 2.5
    B. 3
    C. 3.5
    D. 4

17. Trenches over _____ feet deep should be provided with some kind of cave-in protection.

    A. 4
    B. 5
    C. 8
    D. 10

18. Stairways shall have a maximum riser height of _____ inches and a minimum tread run of _____ inches.

    A. 8 ¼, 9
    B. 8, 9
    C. 7 ¾, 10
    D. 7 ½, 10

19. Type _____ mortar is best suited for use below grade.

    A. S
    B. N
    C. M
    D. O

20. Soil that is excavated from its original state, increases in volume due to swell and is called _____.

    A. Loose
    B. Medium consistency
    C. Cycled
    D. Useable

21. _____ footings are often used on a lot that slopes.

    A. Pier
    B. Rabbeted
    C. Monolithic
    D. Stepped

22. When lifting concrete slabs, operation of jacks shall be synchronized in such a manner as to insure even and uniform lifting of the slab. All points of the slab support shall be kept level within _____ inches.

    A. ½
    B. 1
    C. 1 ½
    D. 2

23. The minimum thickness of a solid masonry wall for a single-story dwelling is _____ inches.

    A. 6
    B. 8
    C. 10
    D. 12

24. A _____ is a transit that reads horizontal and vertical angles electronically.

    A. Vernier scale
    B. Theodolite
    C. Electronic transit level
    D. Electronic layout device

25. For the mortar set method, on roof slopes from 4:12 to 6:12, the roofer must nail each eaves tile with _____.

    A. Two nails and additional bulling
    B. One nail only
    C. Three nails
    D. One nail in additional to using mortar

26. The lack of roof expansion joints will cause roofing felt to _____.

    A. Slip
    B. Split
    C. Blister
    D. Bubble

27. The maximum distance for placing control joints in a wall without openings is _____ feet.

    A. 18
    B. 20
    C. 24
    D. 25

28. The minimum and maximum required footing projections for a concrete footing having a thickness of 8 inches are _____.

    A. 2 inches, 4 inches
    B. 2 inches, 8 inches
    C. 4 inches, 8 inches
    D. 8 inches, 12 inches

29. Eye protection near dangerous working conditions _____.

    A. Is required at the employee's cost
    B. Is required at the employer's cost
    C. Can only be required by union regulations
    D. Is not required

30. A _____ is a board fastened horizontally to stakes placed to the outside where the corners of the building will be located.

    A. Corner board
    B. Batter board
    C. Starter strip
    D. Foundation board

31. A 10ft x 100ft single wythe brick wall is to be constructed and will have 655 non modular brick per 100 sq ft and 3/8-inch mortar joints. _____ cubic feet of mortar will need to be purchased.

    A. 32
    B. 34
    C. 50
    D. 58

32. Low humidity and wind are the primary causes of rapidly evaporating surface moisture that causes the surface tension resulting in _____.

    A. Shrinkage cracks
    B. Crazing
    C. Plastic shrinkage cracks
    D. Blistering

33. An area of sitework where a contractor should be over prepared is _____.

    A. Workers compensation
    B. Drilling insurance
    C. Groundwater knowledge
    D. Hidden utilities

34. All exterior footings shall be placed a minimum of _____ inches below the undisturbed ground surface.

    A. 6
    B. 8
    C. 9
    D. 12

35. _____ is a measure of how well the soil can support the weight of a house.

    A. Load capacity
    B. Bearing capacity
    C. Load resistance
    D. None of the above

36. To prevent chimneys from leaking, the contractor should apply a _____.

    A. Generous amount of roofing cement
    B. Small amount of roofing cement
    C. Flue collar
    D. Flue cap

37. When masonry blocks are stacked higher than _____ feet, the stack shall be tapered back one-half block per tier above the six-foot level.

    A. 4
    B. 6
    C. 8
    D. 10

38. The minimum distance from the point of excavation that batter boards can be placed is _____ feet.

    A. 2
    B. 3
    C. 4
    D. 5

39. Where masonry veneer is used, concrete and masonry foundations shall extend a minimum of _____ inches above adjacent finished grade.

    A. 4
    B. 6
    C. 8
    D. 12

40. _____ work best in unstable soil.

    A. Steel sheets
    B. Trench boxes
    C. Shoring jacks
    D. Angle of repose

41. Where wood studs having an Fb value of 1320 are used in a wood foundation wall, the minimum stud size shall be _____ and the maximum stud spacing shall be _____ on center.

    A. 2 inches by 4 inches, 24 inches
    B. 2 inches by 4 inches, 16 inches
    C. 2 inches by 6 inches, 24 inches
    D. 2 inches by 6 inches, 16 inches

42. Extended periods of _____ will discolor panel face paper.

    A. High humidity
    B. Low humidity
    C. Cold weather
    D. Strong sunlight

43. The sides of footings are molded by boards referred to as _____ boards.

    A. Batter
    B. Backer
    C. Haunch
    D. Form

44. Wall ties in a brick masonry cavity wall should be placed _____-inch from either edge of the masonry unit.

    A. 3/16
    B. 3/8
    C. 5/8
    D. ½

45. The maximum allowable girder span for an interior bearing wall using a built-up girder consisting of three hem fir 2 by 10s and supporting one floor in a building having a width of 36 feet is _____.

    A. 5 feet, 5 inches
    B. 6 feet, 9 inches
    C. 7 feet, 7 inches
    D. 8 feet, 10 inches

46. Lumber that is handled manually shall not be stacked more than _____ feet high.

    A. 14
    B. 16
    C. 18
    D. 20

47. A _____ clip is used to hold foundation wall forms together.

    A. Snap ties
    B. Bracket
    C. 6d nails
    D. Wales

48. Where a vapor retarder is required between a concrete floor slab and the prepared subgrade, the joints of the vapor retarder shall be lapped a minimum of _____ inches.

    A. 2
    B. 4
    C. 6
    D. 8

49. What procedure is used to prevent segregation of concrete components when pouring a slab?

    A. The concrete should be spread as it is deposited
    B. Deposit the concrete in a pile and then spread with a vibrator
    C. Addition of an admixture
    D. None of the above

50. If a base course is required for a concrete floor slab installed below grade, the minimum thickness of the base course shall be _____ inches.

    A. 3
    B. 4
    C. 6
    D. 8

51. A _____ support is used over window and door openings in a concrete block wall.

    A. Lintel
    B. Girder
    C. Collar beam
    D. Bond beam

52. All pneumatically driven nailers provided with automatic fastener feed, which operate at more than 100 psi pressure at the tool shall have a _____.

    A. Slight angle to the decking
    B. Safety device installed at the muzzle
    C. Regulated pressure to not exceed 110 psi
    D. Regulated pressure not to have less than 90 psi

53. The benchmark is 37.89. A back sight reading of 4.8 is taken. A front swing of 9.8 is also taken. The elevation at the second reading is _____.

    A. 32.89
    B. 52.49
    C. 23.29
    D. 42.89

54. Where reinforcement is provided in concrete slab-on-ground floors, the reinforcement shall be supported to remain within the _____ of the slab during the concrete placement.

    A. Middle one-third
    B. Middle one-half
    C. Center to the upper one-third
    D. Center to the upper one-fourth

55. The proper location of welded wire mesh in a concrete slab is _____.

    A. 1" below the slab surface, in the upper half of the slab
    B. 1.5" below the slab surface, in the upper third of the slab
    C. 2" below the slab surface, in the upper third of the slab
    D. 2" below the slab surface, in the upper half of the slab

56. The maximum center-to-center stud spacing permitted for a 2-inch by 6-inch, 8-foot-high wood stud bearing wall supporting two floors, roof and ceiling is _____ inches.

    A. 8
    B. 12
    C. 16
    D. 24

57. Horizontal members that carry the heaviest load of attached horizontal members are called _____.

    A. Girders
    B. Floor joists
    C. Collar beams
    D. Lally columns

58. Wall ties in a brick masonry cavity wall should be placed _____ inch from either edge of the masonry unit.

    A. 3/16
    B. 3/8
    C. 5/8
    D. ½

59. Screws for attaching gypsum board to wood framing shall penetrate the wood a minimum of _____ inch.

    A. ¼
    B. 3/8
    C. ½
    D. 5/8

60. What is the best way to reduce lateral pressure on concrete forms when placing concrete?
    A. Slower placement or rate of pour
    B. Faster placement or rate of pour
    C. Distributing concrete as it pours out
    D. None of the above

61. Roll roofing end laps should be offset _____ inches.

    A. 4
    B. 6
    C. 7
    D. 8

62. When using roll roofing, the strip should be nailed so that it overhangs the edge by a minimum of _____ inch.

    A. ¼
    B. ½
    C. 1/8
    D. 3/16

63. When reroofing with asphalt shingles, fasteners should be long enough for the shank to penetrate through the roofing materials and at least _____ inch into the deck sheathing.

    A. 1/4
    B. 1
    C. 3/4
    D. 1/2

64. Where the top plate of an interior load-bearing wall is notched by more than _____ percent of its width to accommodate piping, a complying metal tie shall be installed.

    A. 25
    B. 33 1/3
    C. 40
    D. 50

65. The proper installation of drip edge calls for it to be installed _____.

    A. It is applied to the fascia and under the underlayment at the eaves, but over the underlayment at the rake
    B. It is applied to the sheathing and under the underlayment at the rake, but over the underlayment at the eaves
    C. It is applied to the sheathing and under the underlayment at the eaves, but over the underlayment at the rake
    D. None of the above

66. On a new shingle roof, nails should be _____ inches long.

    A. 1
    B. 1 ¼
    C. 1 ½
    D. 2 ½

67. The warning line erected around all sides of the roof work area shall not be less than _____ feet from the roof edge when mechanical equipment is not being used.

    A. 3
    B. 4
    C. 5
    D. 6

68. The ends of a ceiling joist shall have a minimum of _____ inches bearing on wood and metal and a minimum of _____ inches on masonry or concrete.

    A. 1 ½; 1 ½
    B. 1 ½; 3
    C. 3; 1 ½
    D. 3; 3

69. When installing shingles, no nails should be placed within _____ inches of a valley.

    A. 2
    B. 4
    C. 6
    D. 8

70. An opening in a wood framed roof system may be framed with a single header and single trimmer joists provided the header joist is located a maximum of _____ feet from the trimmer joist bearing.

    A. 3
    B. 4
    C. 6
    D. 12

71. Gutters are fastened to the _____ of a house.

    A. Soffit
    B. Roof eave
    C. Gable end
    D. Fascia

72. Double underlayment is required for an asphalt shingle application where the roof has a slope of up to _____ .

    A. 2:12
    B. 2 ½:12
    C. 3:12
    D. 4:12

73. Wood flooring should be stored in the building in which it is going to be installed in for _____ to allow for acclimation.

    A. At least 3 days
    B. At least 4 days
    C. At least 7 days
    D. 14 days

74. Valley flashing used for metal roofs is preformed _____.

    A. Aluminum
    B. Terne
    C. Stainless steel
    D. Galvanized iron

75. The first board of tongue and groove flooring should be installed _____ inches from the frame wall and with the _____ end of the board facing the wall.

    A. 1/4" to 5/8"; Tongue
    B. 1/2" to 5/8"; Tongue
    C. 1/2" to 5/8"; Grooved
    D. 1/2" to 3/8"; Grooved

76. In the framing of an opening in ceiling construction, approved hangers are not required for the header joist to trimmer joist connections where the header joist span is a maximum of _____ feet.

    A. 4
    B. 6
    C. 8
    D. 12

77. A benchmark is a/an _____.

    A. Point of known distance
    B. Point of known elevation
    C. Grade stake gradient
    D. Topographic mark

78. _____ is used as a base for tile and in shower stalls.

    A. Backerboard
    B. Sheathing
    C. Plywood
    D. Fiberglass

79. For roll roofing on a new deck, nails to be used will be _____ inch(es) in length.

    A. 7/8
    B. 1
    C. ¼
    D. ½

80. A system of framing where the floor joists of each story rest on the top of the plates of the story below _____ is called framing.

    A. Stud
    B. Balloon
    C. Platform
    D. Post and beam

81. Roll roofing material in open valley flashing shall be installed by cementing the layers together with a/an _____.

    A. 18-inch strip face down and a 36-inch strip face up
    B. 36-inch strip face up
    C. 36-inch strip face down and an 18-inch strip face down
    D. 18-inch strip face up and a 36-inch strip face down

82. Mechanical and gravity outdoor air intakes shall be located a minimum of _____ feet from any hazardous or noxious contaminants.

    A. 10
    B. 15
    C. 20
    D. 25

83. When an emergency situation requires the replacement or repair of equipment, the permit application must be submitted within _____ working day(s) to the building official.

    A. The next
    B. 2
    C. 3
    D. 4

84. The top and bottom horizontal members of a wall frame are called _____.

    A. Headers
    B. Plates
    C. Trimmers
    D. Sills

85. Maximum frame spacing for 3/8 inch single-layer ceiling application is _____ inches on center.

    A. 12
    B. 16
    C. 24
    D. In compliance with local building codes

86. Which one of the following building projects is required to have a permit?
    A. New deck, 300 square feet and 5 feet off the ground
    B. New one-story accessory building, 180 square feet
    C. New privacy fence, 6 feet tall
    D. New retaining wall, 2.5 feet tall

87. When dewatering a trench, the contractor should _____ to prevent the blockage of a pump's intake hose from drain rock and silt.

   I. Weld a mesh screen on the end of the last pipe
   II. Use a dewatering bag
   III. Filter the water through a baffle tank or sump before it's discharged to the pump

      A. I only
      B. II only
      C. I and II
      D. I and III

88. Which one of the following jobs requires the contractor get a permit for the work?

      A. Fences less than 7 feet tall
      B. Retaining walls not over 4 feet tall
      C. One-story detached accessory building less than 200 square feet
      D. Installing a new shingle roof

89. When working in firm soil, the best choice for shoring is _____.

      A. A repose angle of 45 degrees
      B. Shoring jacks
      C. Benching
      D. Firm soils do not require shoring

90. The roofer should allow _____ inch(es) of overhang along the rake fascia for the installation of wood shakes.

      A. .5
      B. 1
      C. 2
      D. 3

91. A dwelling that contains two-family dwelling units shall have a _____ fire-resistance rating between units.

      A. 30-minute
      B. 1-hour
      C. 90-minute
      D. 2-hour

92. Maintain a minimum temperature of _____ °F during gypsum board application.

      A. 30
      B. 40
      C. 50
      D. 60

93. A _____-inch corrosion-resistant mesh screen shall be used for protecting exterior air intakes supplying combustion air to a fireplace.

    A. 1/16
    B. 1/8
    C. ¼
    D. 3/8

94. What is the minimum nominal size wood column used for support in a residential house?

    A. 4" x 4"
    B. 4" x 6"
    C. 6" x 6"
    D. 6" x 8"

95. Which of the following is a true statement concerning OSHA regulations?

    A. Manually stacked lumber piles shall not be more than 16 feet in height
    B. Material stored inside the building may not be placed within 2 feet of doors
    C. Brick stacks shall not be more than 6 feet in height
    D. Masonry blocks shall not be stacked more than 7 feet in height

96. A minimum clearance of _____ inches is required in front of a water closet in a residential home.

    A. 21
    B. 22
    C. 23
    D. 24

97. Where screw application is used for attaching gypsum panel to either wood or steel framing, screwhead shall be driven _____ but not deep enough to break the paper.

    A. To just above
    B. Flush with
    C. Slightly below the face of the panel
    D. Deep enough to just slight break

98. Interior spaces intended for human occupancy shall have a heating system capable of maintain a temperature of _____°F when measured 3 feet off the floor.

    A. 68
    B. 69
    C. 70
    D. 71

99. The base area is 47 feet by 58 feet. Elevations show corner heights of 3 feet, 5 feet, 9 feet, and 7 feet. The cubic yards of excavation required is _____.

  A. Less than 600
  B. Between 600 and 610
  C. Between 610 and 620
  D. More than 620

100. All of the following information shall be included on the Certificate of Occupancy except the _____.

  A. Building permit number
  B. Name of the building official
  C. Address of the dwelling
  D. Legal description of the property

****Please see Answer Key on the following page****
3/23/23

288

Tennessee BC – A Residential
Practice Exam
Answer Key

	Answer	Reference	Page # / Section #
1.	B	Carpentry and Building Construction	266
2.	C	Pipe and Excavation Contracting	137
3.	D	International Residential Code, 2012 International Residential Code, 2018	102.1 102.1
4.	B	Contractors Guide to Quality Concrete Construction, 4th Contractors Guide to Quality Concrete Construction, 3rd	121 88
5.	B	Carpentry and Building Construction	55
6.	B	International Residential Code, 2012 International Residential Code, 2018	104.9.1 104.9.1
7.	B	Modern Masonry, 9th Edition Modern Masonry, 8th Edition	131-132 99
8.	A	Contractors Guide to Quality Concrete Construction, 4th Contractors Guide to Quality Concrete Construction, 3rd	105 76
9.	A	International Residential Code, 2012 International Residential Code, 2018	304.2 304.1
10.	A	Pipe and Excavation Contracting 6 x 2.5 x 8 x 16.3 = 1956 1956 ÷ 8 = 244.5 244.5 x 83% x .75 = 152.2	192-193
11.	B	International Residential Code, 2012 International Residential Code, 2018	305.1 305.1
12.	D	Code of Federal Regulations (OSHA)	1926.703 (e)(2)
13.	C	Contractors Guide to Quality Concrete Construction, 4th Contractors Guide to Quality Concrete Construction, 3rd	100 73
14.	B	Carpentry and Building Construction	577
15.	C	Roofing Construction and Estimating, Revised 2022 Roofing Construction and Estimating, 1995	74 76
16.	B	International Residential Code, 2012 International Residential Code, 2018	311.6 311.6
17.	B	Pipe and Excavation Contracting	171
18.	C	International Residential Code, 2012 International Residential Code, 2018	311.7.5.1, 311.7.5.2 311.7.5.1, 311.7.5.2
19.	C	Modern Masonry, 9th Edition Modern Masonry, 8th Edition	191 152

	Answer	**Reference**	**Page # / Section #**
20.	A	Pipe and Excavation Contracting	61
21.	D	Carpentry and Building Construction	259
22.	A	Code of Federal Regulations (OSHA)	1926.705(g)
23.	A	International Residential Code, 2012 International Residential Code, 2018	606.2.1 606.4.1
24.	B	Carpentry and Building Construction	238
25.	D	Roofing Construction and Estimating, Revised 2022 Roofing Construction and Estimating, 1995	194 204
26.	B	Roofing Construction and Estimating, Revised 2022 Roofing Construction and Estimating, 1995	307 319
27.	C	Contractors Guide to Quality Concrete Construction, 4th Contractors Guide to Quality Concrete Construction, 3rd	110 80
28.	B	International Residential Code, 2012 International Residential Code, 2018	403.1.1 403.1.1
29.	B	Code of Federal Regulations (OSHA)	1926.102(a)(1)
30.	B	Carpentry and Building Construction	244
31.	D	Modern Masonry, 9th Edition Choose the row with 655 per 100 square ft and would require 5.8 cuft per 100 sq ft of mortar 5.8 cuft / 100 square ft x (10 ft x 100 ft) = 58 cubic feet	197-198, Figure 10-11
		Modern Masonry, 8th Edition	159, Figure 8-8
32.	C	Contractors Guide to Quality Concrete Construction, 4th Contractors Guide to Quality Concrete Construction, 3rd	196 135
33.	C	Pipe and Excavation Contracting	290
34.	D	International Residential Code, 2012 International Residential Code, 2018	403.1.4 403.1.4
35.	B	Carpentry and Building Construction	247
36.	D	Roofing Construction and Estimating, Revised 2022 Roofing Construction and Estimating, 1995	388 382
37.	B	Code of Federal Regulations (OSHA)	1926.250(b)(7)
38.	C	Carpentry and Building Construction	244-245
39.	A	International Residential Code, 2012 International Residential Code, 2018	404.1.6 404.1.6
40.	B	Pipe and Excavation Contracting	172
41.	D	International Residential Code, 2012 International Residential Code, 2018	404.2.2 404.2.2
42.	D	Gypsum Construction Handbook, 7th Edition	355
43.	C	Carpentry and Building Construction	258

<u>Answer</u>		<u>Reference</u>	<u>Page # / Section #</u>
44.	C	Modern Masonry, 9th Edition	244
		Modern Masonry, 8th Edition	200
45.	B	International Residential Code, 2012	502.5, Table 502.5(1)
		International Residential Code, 2018	502.5, Table 602.7(2)
46.	B	Code of Federal Regulations (OSHA)	1926.250(b)(8)(iv)
47.	A	Carpentry and Building Construction	265
48.	C	International Residential Code, 2012	506.2.3
		International Residential Code, 2018	506.2.3
49.	A	Contractors Guide to Quality Concrete Construction, 4th	176
		Contractors Guide to Quality Concrete Construction, 3rd	123
50.	B	International Residential Code, 2012	506.2.2
		International Residential Code, 2018	506.2.2
51.	A	Carpentry and Building Construction	287
52.	B	Code of Federal Regulations (OSHA)	1926.302(b)(3)
53.	A	Pipe and Excavation Contracting	114-115
		BM + BS − FS = Elevation	
54.	C	International Residential Code, 2012	506.2.4
		International Residential Code, 2018	506.2.4
55.	C	Contractors Guide to Quality Concrete Construction, 4th	127
		Contractors Guide to Quality Concrete Construction, 3rd	93
56.	C	International Residential Code, 2012	Table 602.3(5)
		International Residential Code, 2018	Table 602.3(5)
57.	A	Carpentry and Building Construction	396
58.	C	Modern Masonry, 9th Edition	244
		Modern Masonry, 8th Edition	200
59.	D	International Residential Code, 2012	702.3.6
		International Residential Code, 2018	702.3.5.1
60.	A	Contractors Guide to Quality Concrete Construction, 4th	74-75
		Contractors Guide to Quality Concrete Construction, 3rd	55
61.	B	Carpentry and Building Construction	629
62.	A	Carpentry and Building Construction	629
63.	C	Roofing Construction and Estimating, Revised 2022	102
		Roofing Construction and Estimating, 1995	106
64.	D	International Residential Code, 2012	602.6.1
		International Residential Code, 2018	602.6.1
65.	C	Carpentry and Building Construction	634

	Answer	**Reference**	**Page # / Section #**
66.	B	Roofing Construction and Estimating, Revised 2022 Roofing Construction and Estimating, 1995	102, Figure 4-78 106, Figure 4-78
67.	D	Code of Federal Regulations (OSHA)	1926.502(f)(1)(i)
68.	B	International Residential Code, 2012 International Residential Code, 2018	802.6 802.6
69.	C	Carpentry and Building Construction	641
70.	A	International Residential Code, 2012 International Residential Code, 2018	802.9 802.9
71.	D	Carpentry and Building Construction	651
72.	D	International Residential Code, 2012 International Residential Code, 2018	905.2.6 905.2.3, Table 905.1.1(2)
73.	B	Carpentry and Building Construction	975
74.	D	Roofing Construction and Estimating, Revised 2022 Roofing Construction and Estimating, 1995	250 261
75.	C	Carpentry and Building Construction	979
76.	B	International Residential Code, 2012 International Residential Code, 2018	802.9 802.9
77.	B	Pipe and Excavation Contracting	111
78.	A	Carpentry and Building Construction	993
79.	B	Roofing Construction and Estimating, Revised 2022 Roofing Construction and Estimating, 1995	102, Figure 4-78 106, Figure 4-78
80.	B	Carpentry and Building Construction	370
81.	A	Roofing Construction and Estimating, Revised 2022 Roofing Construction and Estimating, 1995	66 68
82.	A	International Residential Code, 2012 International Residential Code, 2018	303.5.1 303.5.1
83.	A	International Residential Code, 2012 International Residential Code, 2018	105.2.1 105.2.1
84.	B	Carpentry and Building Construction	432
85.	B	Gypsum Construction Handbook, 7th Edition	73
86.	A	International Residential Code, 2012 International Residential Code, 2018	105.2 (Building, #10) 105.2 (Building, #10)
87.	D	Pipe and Excavation Contracting Note: This questions asks both "drain rock and silt."	292
88.	D	International Residential Code, 2012 International Residential Code, 2018	105.2 (Building, #1 – 3) 105.2 (Building, #1 – 3)
89.	B	Pipe and Excavation Contracting	172

	Answer	Reference	Page # / Section #
90.	A	Roofing Construction and Estimating, Revised 2022	154
		Roofing Construction and Estimating, 1995	164
91.	B	International Residential Code, 2012	302.3
		International Residential Code, 2018	302.3
92.	C	Gypsum Construction Handbook, 7th Edition	105
93.	C	International Residential Code, 2012	1006.2
		International Residential Code, 2018	1006.2
94.	A	International Residential Code, 2012	407.3
		International Residential Code, 2018	407.3
95.	A	Code of Federal Regulations, (OSHA)	1926.250(b)(1)
			1926.250(b)(6)
			1926.250(b)(7)
			1926.250(b)(8)(iv)
96.	A	International Residential Code, 2012	Figure 307.1
		International Residential Code, 2018	Figure 307.1
97.	C	Gypsum Construction Handbook, 7th Edition	107
98.	A	International Residential Code, 2012	303.9
		International Residential Code, 2018	303.10
99.	B	Pipe and Excavation Contracting	256
		Average Depth x L x W ÷ 27 = Cubic Yards	
		(58 x 47 x 6) ÷ 27 = 605.7	
		(3 + 5 + 9 + 7) ÷ 4 = 6	
100.	D	International Residential Code, 2012	110.3
		International Residential Code, 2018	110.3

GENERAL MATH FOR PASSING

Your math and problem solving skills will be a key element in achieving a passing score on your exam. It will be necessary to brush up on your math and problem solving skills. To help you, *1 Exam Prep* has prepared this math review. Work through the examples on the following pages to gain the math experience you will need. The purpose of this unit is to learn or relearn general math rules and skills you need. Do not skip this unit.

Construction math deals mostly with areas, volumes, and time calculations. The purpose of this unit is to give you an overview of general math; the specific math skills for each facet of the trade will be covered in the section dealing with that facet.

Note: Your specific trade math is covered in its own unit.

THE ROSE OF PROBLEM SOLVING

R - Read for understanding
O - Organize the information given:

Setting the problem up: When you set up a problem (get ready to solve it), remember the following steps, and take them one at a time:

- Always write the formula you will be using before doing anything else.
- Write down the values for each letter in the formula.
- Show each step of your work
- Write in a logical sequence.
- Always label your answer in the units.
- Keep your work neat.
- Avoid division when you can multiply.
- Avoid working with large numbers

S - Solve the problem

E - Evaluate the answers (Does it look right? Remember, matching an answer does not mean it's right.)

ROUNDING DECIMALS

How many places should you carry an answer beyond the decimal point? The rule of thumb is three (3) places unless you see that one more place will make your answer even. When you round your answer, the rule is as follows:

- If the number is below 5, round down.
- If the number is 5 or more, add one to the number to the left.

For example, 1.743 rounded to two decimal places would be 1.74, but 1.747 rounded to 2 places would be 1.75

DO NOT ROUND ANY NUMBERS UNTIL YOU HAVE THE FINAL ANSWER.

PARENTHESIS AND BRACKETS

In the previous example, we used the expression (3' x 3') + (4' x 4'). What do the parentheses mean? They simply mean to do whatever is inside them first. In other words, we are to take 3 times 3 (9) and add it to 4 times 4 (16). If we ignored the parentheses, we would get 3 x 3 + 4 x 4 = 52 which is very different from 25.

The rule for working complex math problems is as follows. Use the acronym PEMDAS - Please Excuse My Dear Aunt Sally to help you remember

1st   Parentheses - groupings are always done from the innermost set outward – inside to outside
2nd   Exponents - Applying an exponent is different than just multiplying - 2^3 means 2 x 2 x 2 = 8
3rd   Multiply and Divide - These operations are done in the order from left to right. They are done together because they have the same importance.
4th   Add and Subtract - Here again, they are done together because they have the same importance. These are done in the order left to right.

For example, 5 x 3 + 4 = 19. But if the problem calls for us to add 3 and 4 first, then multiply by 5, we would write 5 x (3 + 4). The answer is 35, because 3 + 4 = 7 and 5 x 7 = 35.

Sometimes, brackets are used to surround parentheses. If this happens, you do whatever is inside the parentheses first, then the brackets from left to right, then everything else from left to right. 7 x [(6 + 4) + (8 -3)] = 105, because 6 + 4 = 10, 8 - 3 = 5, 10 + 5 = 15, and 7 x 15 = 105. Follow this through, and make sure you understand. If you ignore the parentheses and brackets, you get 7 x 6 + 4 + 8 - 3 = 51, which is the wrong answer. Pay attention to the parentheses and brackets, and you'll be OK.

SYMBOLS

Math is a system of numbers, signs, and symbols, each of which has a unique and consistent meaning that you must understand before proceeding further. Formulas are stated using letters to represent numbers, which you must substitute into the formulas to solve them. In solving problems, first write the formula (with the letters), then replace any letters you already know with their values.

Here are some examples of the way formulas might be stated. In the following examples, A is always 9", and B is always 6". C is the unknown quantity we will be solving for:

ADDITION: $C = A + B$ $C = 9" + 6"$ $C = 15"$

SUBTRACTION: $C = A - B$ $C = 9" - 6"$ $C = 3"$

MULTIPLICATION: $C = A \times B$ $C = 9" \times 6"$ C = 54 square inches

$C = A \cdot B$ $C = 9" \times 6"$ C = 54 square inches

$C = AB$ $C = 9" \times 6"$ C = 54 square inches

Note the usage in the multiplication problems above. All of the above forms are seen in formulas, with "x" being by far the most common. The dot (•) is seldom seen, but you need to know what it means when it happens. Sometimes the sign is omitted altogether.

DIVISION: $C = A \div B$ $C = 9" \div 6"$ $C = 1.5"$

$C = \dfrac{A}{B}$ $C = \dfrac{9}{6}$ $C = 1.5"$

$C = B\overline{)A}$ $C = 6\overline{)9}$ $C = 1.5"$

All three signs for division are acceptable; you just have to know what they mean.

A ÷ B   Means A divided by B $\frac{A}{B}$ Means A divided by B

$B\overline{)A}$ Means B divided into A, or A divided by B

EXPONENTS

When a number is multiplied by itself a certain number of times, as in 4 x 4, an exponent is often used 4 x 4 can be abbreviated as 4^2. This is read as "four squared" or "four to the second power. The exponent is the little number above and to the right of the number and tells you how many times the number is being multiplied by itself.

For example: 5^3= 5 x 5 x 5 = 125 and 6^4 is the same as writing 6 x 6 x 6 x 6 = 1296. Why would anyone want to write out 8 x 8 x 8 x 8 x 8 x 8 x 8 x 8 x 8 x 8 when they could just write 8^{10}? They wouldn't! That's why we have exponents.

Exponents are also used to abbreviate certain measurements. Square feet (Sq. ft.) is often abbreviated ft^2. As we will see, areas are always measured in square units, so this shorthand will come in very handy.

Volumes are measured in cubic units. A number to, the third power is often called the "cube" of that number. So in^3, ft^3, and yd^3 are common abbreviations for cubic inches, cubic feet, and cubic yards. For example, how many cubic feet are in a cubic yard? yd3 = 3 ft/yd x 3 ft/yd x 3 ft/yd = 27 ft^3/yd^3.

SQUARE ROOTS

Square roots are related to exponents. The square of 4 is 16; therefore the square root of 16 is 4. Another way to say this is that the square root of any number "A" is the number that you have to multiply by itself to get "A". If we call the square root "B", we would write "the square root of A is B" this way: $B\sqrt{A}$ The symbol is called the "square root sign."

Squares and square roots are frequently used in the trades. Often, we need to find the length of the third side of a right triangle. As long: we know that one of the angles is 90°, and we know the length of the two sides that form that angle, we can find the length of the third side.

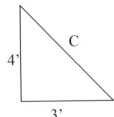

Suppose we need to know the length of side C in the following triangle. This triangle could represent the corner of a lot, the corner of a house, or anything else. Here is the triangle:

Now, a very smart Greek guy was sitting around thinking about triangles one day and figured out a way to find the length of the unknown side. His name was Pythagorean, and his way of figuring out the length of that side is called the Pythagorean Theorem. It still works today, 3,000 years later. In fact, it's the only easy way to find the length of that side. Here it is $C = \sqrt{a^2 + b^2}$

A and B are the sides that we know about, and C is the one we need to know. Let's plug in the values for the triangle that we know about, and solve for C.

$$C = \sqrt{a^2 + b^2} \qquad C = \sqrt{(3 \times 3) + (4 \times 4)} \qquad C = \sqrt{9 + 16} \qquad C = \sqrt{25} \qquad C = 5$$

Reverse to find A or B $\qquad A = \sqrt{C^2 + B^2} \qquad\qquad A = \sqrt{5^2 + 4^2} \qquad A = \sqrt{(5 \times 5) - (3 \times 3)}$

$$A = \sqrt{25 - 9} \qquad\qquad A = \sqrt{16} \qquad\qquad A = 4$$

THE CALCULATOR

The calculator pictured is an example of a good basic model which you can purchase for around $5.00 in discount stores. In addition to the standard keys (+, x, and ÷), it has a square root key (1) and a percent key (%). When buying a calculator to use during the exam, make sure that it has square root and percent keys. Memory is important to have on a calculator. It can help you store values while you are working on something else. There are three memory buttons on the above calculator. The M+ button adds the number in the display to the number in memory and the - button subtracts the number in the display from the number in the memory. The MRC button recalls the contents of memory to the display. Also make sure that the calculator you take to the exam is not too fancy Besides the fact that it may be difficult to find what you are looking for amid a maze of tiny little buttons, so-called "contractor's calculators" that have conversion formulas and programmable calculators are prohibited. You don't want to spend all of this time and money just to be kicked out of the exam because of your calculator.

Many calculators have two clear buttons, CE and C. The CE button clears the last number you entered. This can be handy; it keeps you from having to start all over again if you accidentally hit a wrong number. The C key wipes the whole mess out, so you can start over When using a calculator, you generally input the information just as you read it on the page. For example, if you saw this:

5+ 4 =? You would enter: $\boxed{5}$ $\boxed{+}$ $\boxed{4}$ $\boxed{=}$

On your calculator, the answer **9** would be displayed on the screen.

Some calculations require a little different approach. If you want to take the square root of a number, you hit the number, then the square root key. To find the square root of 9, enter:

$\boxed{9}$ $\boxed{\surd}$ $\boxed{=}$ The answer is 3.

The percent key is a bit tricky to get used to, but once you understand it, it becomes one of your best friends. Let's say you are estimating the cost of materials which you are going to pay 7% sales tax on. What is the total material cost if the cost before taxes is 10,000? Here's what you would do:

$\boxed{1}$ $\boxed{0}$ $\boxed{0}$ $\boxed{0}$ $\boxed{0}$ $\boxed{+}$ $\boxed{7}$ $\boxed{\%}$ The answer would be **$10,700.**

FRACTIONS

A fraction is some part of a whole. The word fraction comes from the Latin root fract-, which means "to break."When something is divided into two or more equal parts, those parts are called fractions.

Suppose you own and operate a pie shop. You sell three different kinds of pie: apple, key lime, and pecan. You sell your pie by the slice or by the whole pie. Apple pie costs $4.00; key lime costs $5.00; and pecan costs $6.00. The prices are for whole pies only. You cut your apple and key lime pies into 6 slices, and your pecan pie into 8, because pecans are more expensive. Here's what they look like:

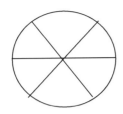
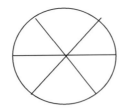
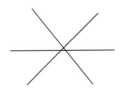

| APPLE | KEY LIME | PECAN |

So, you're sitting there one day, and a customer walks in. He asks you for a piece of apple pie. What do you charge him?

Since apple pie is cut into six pieces, the price per slice would be: $4.00 + 6 = $0.67. Note that we rounded off 0.666 to 0.67. If the customer wanted 2 slices of apple pie the charge would have been 2 x 0.666 = $1.33, not 2 x 0.67 = $1.34. This is why you should not round off numbers until the end of the calculation.

The next customer wants 2 slices of key lime pie and 1 slice of apple pie. The price per slice of key lime pie is $5.00 + 6 = $0.833. So you would charge him (2 x 0.833) + 0.67 = $2.34.

You seem to be having a good day, so you go in the back and bake more pies. The next customer walks in and asks for two slices of apple, three slices of key lime, and four slices of pecan. In the following formulas, "a" stands for the price of the apple, "k" for the key lime, and "p" for the pecan. Here are the formulas:

$$a = 2 \times (\$4.00 + 6) = \$1.33 \qquad k = 3 \times (\$5.00 + 6) = \$2.50 \qquad p = 4 \times (\$6.00 + 8) = \$3.00$$

Total Price = a + k + p = 1.33 + 2.50 + 3.00 = $ 6.83:

By now you are really tired of selling pie and decide to learn more about fractions.

TYPES OF FRACTIONS

There are three basic types of fractions, proper, improper, and mixed. EXAMPLES:

$$\text{Proper: } \frac{1}{3} \qquad\qquad \text{Improper: } \frac{3}{2} \qquad\qquad \text{Mixed: } 3\frac{1}{3}$$

When the numerator of a fraction is smaller than the denominator, the fraction is proper. Proper fractions have a value of less than one. If the numerator is greater than the denominator, the fraction is said to be improper. When the numerator denominator are equal, the value of the fraction is ONE. (Neither proper nor improper) Remember that last sentence, it becomes very important later.

Mixed fractions have a whole number part and a fractional part. The fraction is proper. A mixed number can always be converted to an improper fraction by multiplying the whole number by the denominator, adding the numerator, and putting the result over the denominator:

Improper fractions can be converted to mixed numbers by dividing the numerator by the denominator, taking the result as the whole number, and the remainder as the numerator:

17/3 is an improper fraction. 3 goes into 17 five times with two left over. 2 is the remainder:

$$\frac{17}{3} = 5\frac{2}{3}$$

MULTIPLYING FRACTIONS

To multiply two fractions, multiply the numerators and denominators, then reduce:

$$\frac{1}{2} \times \frac{2}{3} \times \frac{2}{6} = \frac{1}{9}$$

298

$$\frac{1}{4} \times \frac{1}{2} = \frac{1}{8}$$

To multiply mixed numbers, first convert them to improper fractions, and then multiply as usual:

$$3\frac{1}{2} \times 2\frac{1}{3} = \frac{(3 \times 2)+1}{2} \times \frac{(2 \times 3)=1}{3} = \frac{7}{2} \times \frac{7}{3} = \frac{49}{6} = 8\frac{1}{6}$$

ADDING AND SUBTRACTING FRACTIONS

Adding and subtracting fractions is easy, provided the denominators are the same. Since they hardly ever are, you must first find a common denominator. You obtain this number by finding a number that all of the denominators will go into evenly. Once you find this number, you multiply the numerator of the fractions by the number of times each denominator goes into the common denominator. A picture is worth a thousand words:

$$\frac{1}{2} + \frac{2}{3}$$

The common denominator is 6, since both 2 and 3 go into 6 evenly.

$$\frac{?}{6} + \frac{?}{6}$$

To find the new numerators, we multiply each old numerator by the number of times its denominator goes into 6.2 goes into 6 three times, and 3x1 = 3, so the first fraction is .The second fraction is , since 3 goes into 6 two times, and 2x2 = 4. Once you have the two new fractions, just add the numerators and keep the same denominator. Reduce, if necessary.

$$\frac{3}{6} + \frac{4}{6} = \frac{7}{6} = 1\frac{1}{6}$$

To subtract fractions, use the same procedure, subtracting the numerators instead of adding them:

$$\frac{2}{3} - \frac{1}{2} = \frac{4}{6} - \frac{3}{6} = \frac{1}{6}$$

CONVERTING FRACTIONS TO DECIMALS

To convert a fraction to a decimal, you will divide the part by the whole. Remember, a decimal is also a percent. Example:

$$.25 = \frac{25}{100} \qquad 25 \div 100 = 25\%$$

Examples: Part ÷ Whole

$$\frac{6"}{12"} = 6" \div 12" = .5' \quad .5 \times 100 = 50\% \text{ of a foot}$$

$$\frac{30 \, min.}{60 \, min.} = 30 \, min \div 60 \, min. = .5 \, hr.$$

$$1/_2" = 1 \div 2 = .5$$

CONVERTING DECIMALS TO FRACTIONS OR WHOLE NUMBERS

Remember, to get the decimal you divide the part by the whole. Now we will multiply the decimal part times the whole to get the fraction or whole number. For example:

.5" x 12" = 6"
.5 hr, x 60 min. = 30 min.
.5 of an inch x 16 = 8 inches
.5 of an inch x 4 = 2 inches

$$\frac{0.75"}{1} \; X \; \frac{16"}{16} = \frac{12"}{16} = \frac{3"}{4}$$

What you are doing is multiplying the "parts times the whole." This is an extremely important concept because when you are dealing with rulers, you are dealing with fractions, but when you are dealing with calculators, you are dealing with decimals. Being able to convert between one and the other is'very important. Let's do another one. What is 0.25' expressed as a fraction?

$$\frac{0.25'}{1} \; X \; \frac{12}{12} = \frac{3}{12} = \frac{1}{4} = 3"$$

Note: With inches, any number can be a whole inch: 16/16, 8/8, 4/4, etc.
B.T.E.S. uses a 16th because this is the smallest part of a construction ruler.

Here are some examples:

       6" is what % of a whole foot?
       6" is 6 parts of a foot or 12" (remember the whole needs to be in the same unit.)
       6" ÷ 12" = .5 or 50% of a foot
       15 min. is what % of an hour?
       15 min. ÷ 60 min. = 25%

There are a few decimals that you should just know. Stick them in your mind. The most common are:

0.0625" = 1/16"	0.3125" = 5/16"	0.565" = 9/16	0.1875" = 3/16"
0.125" = 1/8"	0.375" = 3/8"	0.625" = 5/8"	0.875" = 7/8"
0.1875" = 3/16"	0.4375" = 7/16"	0.6875" = 11/16"	0.9375" = 15/16"
0.25" = 1/4"	0.5" = 1/2"	0.75" = 3/4"	1 " = 1"

PERCENTAGES

A percentage is like a fraction or decimal. It is part of the whole. The word percent comes from two Latin words: per, meaning for and centum meaning one-hundred. A percent, therefore, is a part of 100.

Let's suppose that we have a very large pizza that is cut into 100 equal pieces. If you eat 10 pieces of this pizza, you have eaten 10 percent (10%) of the pizza. If your neighbor, Joe, eats 43 pieces, not only is he a pig, but he has eaten 43% of the pizza. After you and Joe get through, 53% of the pizza is gone, and 47% is left. Why? Because 100 — 53 = 47. *Remember, percentages always relate to 100.*

It is often easier to multiply a number by a percentage rather than by a fraction and it is always easier than dividing. In this section, we will show you a couple of little tricks to make your fractions and division easier. But first, let's learn how to convert a fraction to a percentage.

CONVERTING FRACTIONS TO PERCENT OR DECIMAL

Remember, a fraction and a percent are the same. It is how they are expressed or put on paper that is different. For example: With money, would you say you had 50% of a dollar or simply say a half dollar or 50 cents. Or was the price 50% lower or 1/2 as much. Each have their own place in the scheme of things. Percent will always be found by dividing a part of a whole by the whole in the same unit. Example: 50 cents is 50 parts of thewhole 100 cents. Percent = 50 ÷ 100 = .50 x 100 = 50%. With todays calculator, % = 50 ÷ 100. Hit the % key and decimal is moved. 50. or 50%. There are two steps to converting a fraction to a percent.

1. Divide the fraction out on your calculator.
2. Multiply the result by 100.

Here are some examples: **1/2 = 1 ÷ 2 = 0.50 and .5 x 100 = 50%**
3/5 = 3 ÷ 5 = 0.6 and 0.6 x 100 = 60%
5/8 = 5 8 = 0.625 and 0.625 x 100 = 62.5%

In summary, to get a percent, the part of something is divided by the whole something. So asking what 1/2 of something is the same as asking what 50% of something is 60% of a gallon is the same as 3/5ths of a gallon. 5/8 of an inch is 62.5% of an inch.

Here are some problems using percentages:

1. A job costing $5,000.00 is figured to have 12% overhead. What is the total cost of the job?

| 5 | 0 | 0 | 0 | | + | | 1 | 2 | | % |

The calculator reads **5600,** *so the cost of the job is $5,600.00*

2. If sales tax is 7%, what is the cost, including tax, of an item with a price of $34.50?

| 3 | 4 | . | 5 | 0 | | + | | 7 | | % |

The calculator reads **36.915.** *We round to the nearest cent, and get* **$36.92.**

3. If a job requires 200 pounds of lead, and you figure on 6% waste, what will be the total job need in pounds of lead ?

| 2 | 0 | 0 | | + | | 6 | | % |

The calculator reads **212,** *so you will need* **212** *lbs of lead.*

4. You get a deal on a quantity of lead 10% less than the going rate, which is $150 for that quantity. What will you pay?

| 1 | 5 | 0 | | - | | 1 | 0 |

You will be paying **$135.**

5. Joe Invested $20,000 and Bill invested $30,000. What percent does Joe own? What is the relationship or part and whole.

Solution: It is Joe's part of the total investment, so 20,000 is to 50,000; (is to) is a key phrase for division: 20 000 ÷ 50 000 = 40%.

GENERAL MATH TEST QUESTIONS

Adding fractions:

1. $\dfrac{2}{4} + \dfrac{12}{16}$

2. $\dfrac{3}{16} + \dfrac{7}{8} + \dfrac{3}{64}$

3. $\dfrac{3}{5} + \dfrac{3}{4}$

Subtracting fractions:

4. $\dfrac{3}{8} - \dfrac{3}{16}$

5. $\dfrac{4}{5} - \dfrac{1}{2}$

6. $\dfrac{1}{4} - \dfrac{1}{16}$

Converting fractions to decimals:

7. $\dfrac{3}{8}$

8. $\dfrac{1}{16}$

9. $\dfrac{2}{5}$

Converting inches into decimals of a foot:

10. 3"

11. $1\dfrac{1}{2}$"

12. 8"

Converting decimal feet to inches and fractions of an inch:

13. .25'

14. .125'

15. .375'

Converting decimal inches to a fraction of an inch:

16. .25"

17. .60 to the nearest 1/8th

18. .80 to the nearest 1/16th

Percentages:

19. 6" is what % of a yard?

20. 2' is what % of a yard?

21. 20 minutes is what % of an hour?

22. 12" of fall in a 100', is what % per 100.

Converting decimals to fractions or wholes:

23. .25"

24. .25'

25. .25 hour

Numbers and Powers:

26. 4^2 27. $3^{\prime 2}$ 28. $3^{\prime 3}$

Square Roots:

29. $\sqrt{25}$ 30. $\sqrt{144}$ 31. $\sqrt{289}$

ANSWERS TO GENERAL MATH TEST

1. $1\frac{1}{4}$ 2. $1\frac{7}{64}$ 3. $1\frac{7}{20}$

4. $\frac{3}{16}$ 5. $\frac{3}{10}$ 6. $\frac{3}{16}$

7. .375   8. .0625   9. .400

10. .25'   11. .125'   2. .666'

13. 3"   14. 1 ½"   15. 4 ½"

16. $\frac{4}{16}$" or $\frac{1}{4}$"   17. $\frac{5}{8}$"   18. $\frac{13}{16}$"

19. 16.66%   20. 66.66%   21. 33.33%   22. 1%

23. $\frac{4}{16}$" or $\frac{1}{4}$"   24. 3"   25. 15 minutes

26. 16   27. 9'   28. 27'

29. 5   30. 12   31. 17

303

How to Determine the Number of Blocks to Build a Wall
Questions and Answers

1. If you are building a wall using 8x8x16 concrete block, and the wall is 40 feet long and 6 feet high. How many blocks will you need to build the wall?

    A. 30
    B. 270
    C. 688
    D. 1,920

2. If you are building a wall using 12x12x16 concrete block, and the wall is 20 feet long and 6 feet high. How many blocks will you need to build the wall?

    A. 1920
    B. 1440
    C. 900
    D. 90

3. If you are building a wall using 6x6x12 concrete block, and the wall is 25 feet long and 10 feet high. How many blocks will you need to build the wall?

    A. 50
    B. 500
    C. 1500
    D. 3000

4. If you are building a wall using 8x8x16 concrete block, and the wall is 100 feet long and 6 feet high. How many blocks will you need to build the wall?

    A. 67
    B. 75
    C. 675
    D. 4800

5. If you are building a wall using 12x12x12 concrete block, and the wall is 18 feet long and 6 feet high. How many blocks will you need to build the wall?

    A. 1920 blocks
    B. 1080 blocks
    C. 108 blocks
    D. 90 blocks

6. If you are building a wall using 8x8x16 concrete block, and the wall is 40 feet long and 6 feet high. How many blocks will you need to build the wall?

    A. 70
    B. 270
    C. 1,920
    D. 2,700

7. If you are building a wall using 6x6x12 concrete block, and the wall is 36 feet long and 8 feet high. How many blocks will you need to build the wall?

    A. 3456
    B. 1,728
    C. 576
    D. None of the above

8. If you are building a wall using 8w x4h x 16lng concrete block, and the wall is 12 feet long and 6 feet high. How many blocks will you need to build the wall?

    A. 576
    B. 288
    C. 162
    D. 152

9. If you are building a wall using 8x8x16 concrete block, and the wall is 60 feet long and 4 feet high. How many blocks will you need to build the wall?

    A. 70
    B. 270
    C. 1,920
    D. 2,700

10. If you are building a wall using 10w x 9h x 15lng concrete block, and the wall is 50 feet long and 12 feet high. How many blocks will you need to build the wall?

    A. 5400
    B. 640
    C. 540
    D. None of the above

Please see Answer Key on the following page

ABC 09/20/2021

305

How to Determine the Number of Blocks to Build a Wall
Questions and Answers
Answer Key

Answer	Solution:

1. B

Convert 40 feet into inches:
40 feet x 12 = 480 inches
480 inches divided by 16 inches length = 30 blocks long

Convert 6 feet into inches:
6 x 12 = 72 inches
72 inches divided by 8 inches height= 9 blocks high

Multiply 9 blocks by 30 blocks = 270 blocks

2. D

Convert 20 feet into inches:
20 feet x 12 = 240 inches
240 inches divided by 16 inches length = 15 blocks long

Convert 6 feet into inches
6 x 12 = 72 inches
72 inches divided by 12 inches height = 6 blocks

Multiply 6 blocks by 15 blocks = 90 blocks high

3. B

Convert 25 feet into inches:
25 feet x 12 = 300 inches
300 inches divided by 12 inches length = 25 blocks long

Convert 10 feet into inches
10 x 12 = 120 inches
120 inches divided by 6 inches height = 20 blocks high

Multiply 25 blocks by 20 blocks = 500 blocks

4. C

Convert 100 feet into inches:
100 feet x 12 = 1,200 inches
1,200 inches divided by 16 inches length = 75 blocks long

Convert 6 feet into inches
6 x 12 = 72 inches
72 inches divided by 8 inches height = 9 blocks high

Multiply 75 blocks by 9 blocks = 675 blocks

	Answer	**Solution:**

5. C

Convert 18 feet into inches:
18 feet x 12 = 216 inches
216 inches divided by 12 inches length = 18 blocks long

Convert 6 feet into inches
6 x 12 = 72 inches
72 inches divided by 12 inches height = 6 blocks high

Multiply 18 blocks by 6 blocks = 108 blocks

6. B

Convert 40 feet into inches:
40 feet x 12 = 480 inches
480 inches divided by 16 inches length = 30 blocks long

Convert 6 feet into inches
6 x 12 = 72 inches
72 inches divided by 8 inches height = 9 blocks high

Multiply 30 blocks by 9 blocks = 270 blocks

7. C

Convert 36 feet into inches:
36 feet x 12 = 432 inches
432 inches divided by 12 inches length = 36 blocks long

Convert 8 feet into inches
8 x 12 = 96 inches
96 inches divided by 6 inches height = 16 blocks high

Multiply 36 blocks by 16 blocks = 576 blocks

8. C

Convert 12 feet into inches:
12 feet x 12 = 144 inches
144 inches divided by 16 inches length = 9 blocks long

Convert 6 feet into inches
6 x 12 = 72 inches
72 inches divided by 4 inches height = 18 blocks high

Multiply 9 blocks by 18 blocks = 162 blocks

9. B

Convert 60 feet into inches:
60 feet x 12 = 720 inches
720 inches divided by 16 inches length = 45 blocks long

Convert 4 feet into inches
4 x 12 = 48 inches
48 inches divided by 8 inches height = 6 blocks high

Multiply 45 blocks by 6 blocks = 270 blocks

Answer	Solution:

10. B   Convert 50 feet into inches:
50 feet x 12 = 600 inches
600 inches divided by 15 inches long = 40 blocks long

Convert 12 feet into inches
12 x 12 = 144 inches
144 inches divided by 9 inches height = 16 blocks

Multiply 16 blocks by 40 blocks = 640 blocks

Purchasing Drywall
Practice Exam 1

Note: The best answer may be closest answer.

You are the subcontractor for a home that will need 83 sheets of drywall. Supplier # 1 Sells the drywall at $7.31 per sheet, plus 6% sales tax. Supplier # 2 is in another state, sells the same drywall for $6.95 per sheet and charges no sales tax. However, supplier # 2 does charge $.50 per sheet for delivery.

1. How much will be paid in state tax for supplier #1?

    A. $35.14
    B. $36.40
    C. $36.82
    D. $37.14

2. What is the total cost for drywall from Supplier #1?

    A. $528
    B. $609
    C. $627
    D. $640

3. What is the delivery cost only from Supplier #2?

    A. $41.50
    B. $46.00
    C. $52.50
    D. $83.00

4. What is the total cost for drywall from Supplier #2?

    A. $611
    B. $618
    C. $627
    D. $650

5. Supplier #1, offers an 8% discount on the full total of all orders of over 50 sheets of drywall. Which of the following is now true?

   A. Supplier #2 is less expensive than Supplier #1
   B. Supplier #1 has a final price of more than $600
   C. Supplier #1 has a final price between $575 and $599
   D. Supplier #1 has a final price between $550 and $574

****Please see Answer Key on the following page****

3/31/22

Purchasing Drywall
Practice Exam 1
Answer Key

<u>Answer</u>		<u>Solution</u>
1.	B	83 sheets at $7.31 per sheet: 83 x 7.31 = $606.73 Tax is 6%: $606.73 x .06 = $36.40
2.	D	83 sheets at $7.31 per sheet: 83 x 7.31 = $606.73 Tax is 6%: $606.73 x .06 = $36.40 Total drywall cost from Supplier #1: $606.73 + $36.40 = $643.13 (select closest answer)
3.	A	Drywall is delivery cost is 83 sheets at $.50 per sheet: 83 x $.50 = $41.50
4.	B	Drywall cost is 83 sheets at $6.95 per sheet: 83 x $6.95 = $576.85 Drywall is delivery cost is 83 sheets at $.50 per sheet: 83 x $.50 = $41.50 Total drywall cost from Supplier #2: $576.85 + $41.50 = $618.35 (select closest answer)
5.	C	83 sheets at $7.31 per sheet: 83 x 7.31 = $606.73 Tax is 6%: $606.73 x .06 = $36.40 Total drywall cost from Supplier #1: $606.73 + $36.40 = $643.13 (select closest answer) Discount of 8%: $643.13 x .08 = $51.45. New total cost with volume discount from Supplier #1: $643.13 - $51.45 = $591.68

Purchasing Drywall
Practice Exam 2

Note: The best answer may be closest answer.

You are the subcontractor for a home that will need 109 sheets of drywall. The supplier sells the drywall at $8.47 per sheet, plus a delivery charge of $.42 per sheet, plus 6% sales tax on the total, including delivery.

1. The delivery cost only from the supplier is _____.

    A. $56.33
    B. $45.78
    C. $59.62
    D. $41.30

2. The total cost for drywall delivered to the site is_____.

    A. $953
    B. $972
    C. $988
    D. $1,027

3. _____ will be paid in sales tax.

    A. $58.14
    B. $59.71
    C. $61.60
    D. $62.94

4. You just bought a truck. You will pick up the drywall, eliminating the delivery charge. The new total cost of the drywall, including tax is _____.

    A. $979
    B. $985
    C. $1,007
    D. $1,014

5. After buying the truck, you are informed that the supplier offers a 5% discount on the full total of all orders (before tax) of over 50 sheets of drywall for those who pick up their own orders. Your final cost of the drywall is now _____.

    A. $974.31
    B. $944.08
    C. $929.69
    D. $916.59

****Please see Answer Key on the following page****

ABC 09/21/2021

Purchasing Drywall
Practice Exam 2
Answer Key

	Answer	Solution

1.   B

109 sheets at $.42 per sheet delivery:
109 x $.42 = $45.78

2.   D

109 sheets at $8.47 per sheet, plus $.42 per sheet delivery:
$8.47 + $.42 = $8.89;   109 x $8.89 = $969.01
Tax is 6%: $969.01 x .06 = $58.14;
$969.01 + $58.14 = $1,027.15 (select closest answer)

3.   A

109 sheets at $8.47 per sheet, plus $.42 per sheet delivery:
$8.47 + $.42 = $8.89;   109 x $8.89 = $969.01
Tax is 6%: $969.01 x .06 = $58.14

4.   A

109 sheets at $8.47 per sheet:
$109 x 8.47 = $923.23
Tax is 6%: $923.23 x .06 = $55.39
$923.23 + $55.39 = $978.62

5.   C

109 sheets at $8.47 per sheet:
$109 x 8.47 = $923.23
Discount of 5%:
$923.23 x .05 = $46.16.
Total cost before tax with volume discount:
$923.23 - $46.16 = $877.07
Tax is 6%:
$877.07 x .06 = $52.62
$877.07 + $52.62 = $929.69

Drywall Math Calculations
Practice Test – 1

Please refer to diagram #1 as needed for the following ten questions.
Do not worry about doors, windows, closets, bathrooms, and halls. Assume the house is rectangular.
Best answer may be closest answer.

1. The total four wall perimeter for Bedroom (BR) 1 is _____ feet.

   A. 35
   B. 60
   C. 70
   D. 90

2. Excluding ceiling and floor, the four kitchen walls are a total of _____ square feet.

   A. 240
   B. 960
   C. 1224
   D. 1400

3. The total outside perimeter of this home is _____ feet

   A. 220
   B. 240
   C. 360
   D. 380

4. Sheets of drywall measure 4' x 12' x ½". _____ sheets will be needed for the kitchen.

   A. 20
   B. 22
   C. 24
   D. 18

5. In question 4, if drywall costs $8.27, per sheet, the drywall for the four kitchen walls will cost _____.

   A. $122.80
   B. $147.64
   C. $165.40
   D. $218.54

6. In the dining room, the total area of the four walls and the ceiling is _____ square feet.

    A. 1,660
    B. 1,892
    C. 2,020
    D. 2,282

7. In question 6, above, if the drywall is sold in 4' x 12' x ½" sheets, _____ sheets will be needed for the four walls and ceiling.

    A. 39
    B. 40
    C. 41
    D. 43

8. We see at the supply store that the drywall cost is up to $8.48 per sheet, and that they now must charge 6% sales tax on our drywall purchase. In questions 6 and 7, the total purchase price is _____.

    A. $122.80
    B. $147.64
    C. $165.40
    D. $386.52

9. The total amount of wall area for all three bedrooms (including ceilings but not floors) is between _____ square feet.

    A. 3,000 and 3,499
    B. 3,500 and 3,999
    C. 4,000 and 4,499
    D. 4,500 and 4,999

10. It is determined that the entire home will require 215 sheets of drywall.
    45 sheets of drywall are on hand from a previous job and will be used.
    The drywall contractor charges $2.85 per sheet to hang and finish each sheet.
    The supplier charges $7.45 per sheet of drywall, inclusive of sales tax.
    The total amount to be to the contractor by both the supplier and drywall contractor is _____.

    A. $1,880
    B. $1,900
    C. $2,126
    D. $2,280

DRYWALL CALCULATIONS - DIAGRAM #1

All Ceilings are 12'
Drawing not to scale

70'

30'		15'
Living Room 20'	Master Bedroom 20'	BR 1 20'
	25'	**40'**
20'		
Kitchen	Dining Room	BR 2
	35'	

Please see Answer Key on the following page**

ABC 09/21/2021

Drywall Math Calculations
Practice Test – 1
Answer Key

	Answer	**Solution**
1.	C	There are two walls 15' in length, and two walls 20' feet in length $15 + 15 + 20 + 20 = 70$
2.	B	One kitchen wall is 20', as is the opposite wall The other kitchen walls are also 20', because we see the short outside wall is 40' and living room is 20' of that 40' So, four kitchen walls are each 20' x 12'. $20 \times 12 = 240$ square feet $240 \times 4 = 960$ square feet
3.	A	Rectangular home with length 70' and width 40' $70 + 70 + 40 + 40 = 220$'
4.	A	From question 2, we know that total sf of kitchen is 960 Dry wall is 4' x 12' = 48 square feet per sheet $960 \div 48 = 20$ So, 20 sheets are needed
5.	C	$8.27 x 20 (sheets needed) = $165.40
6.	C	The dining room is 35' long, 20' wide, and 12' high Two of the walls are each: 35' x 12' = 420 sf Two of the walls are each: 20' x 12' = 240 sf Ceiling is 35' x 20' = 700 square feet Total square footage of four walls and ceiling $420 + 420 + 240 + 240 + 700 = 2,020$
7.	D	From question 6., we know that the dining room walls and ceiling total 2,020 sf Drywall is 12' x 4' 12 x 4 = 48 square feet per sheet $2,020 \div 48 = 42.083$ sheets So, 43 sheets are needed Note that we must have the extra sheet, even if only part of the sheet will be used
8.	D	$8.48 x 43 = $364.64 subtotal for drywall 6% sales tax is $364.64 x .06 = $21.88. $364.64 + $21.88 = $386.52

	Answer	Solution

9. B
Bedroom 1 is 20' x 15' with a height of 12'
Two walls are 15' x 12' = 180 square feet each
Two walls are 20' x 12' = 240 square feet each
Ceiling is 15' x 20' = 300 square feet
180 + 180 + 240 + 240 + 300 = 1,140 total square feet for Bedroom 1

Bedroom 2 is identical to Bedroom 1, so BR 2 is also 1,140 square feet

Master Bedroom is 20' x 25' with a height of 12'
Two walls are 20' x 12' = 240 square feet each
Two walls are 25' x 12' = 300 square feet each
Ceiling is 20' x 25' = 500 square feet
240 + 240 + 300 + 300 + 500 = 1,580 total square feet for Master Bedroom

Three-bedroom total square feet is 1,140 + 1,140 + 1,580 = 3,860

10. A
215 sheets of drywall to be hung
215 x $2.85 = $612.75
215 sheets needed, but already have 45
215 – 45 = 170
170 x $7.45 = $1,266.50
The total amount to be invoiced for this is $612.75 + $1,266.50 = $1,879.25

Drywall Math Calculations
Practice Test – 2

Please refer to Diagram # 2 as needed for the following ten questions.
Do not worry about doors, windows, closets, bathrooms, and halls. Assume the house is rectangular.
Best answer may be closest answer.

1. The total four wall perimeter for Bedroom (BR) 1 is _____ feet.

    A. 35
    B. 40
    C. 45
    D. 54

2. Excluding ceiling and floor, the four kitchen walls are a total of _____ square feet (sf).

    A. 1,128
    B. 1,206
    C. 1,434
    D. 1,877

3. The total square footage of this home is _____ square feet.

    A. 2,500
    B. 3,600
    C. 4,000
    D. 4,800

4. Sheets of drywall measure 4' x 12' x ½". _____ sheets will be needed for the kitchen.

    A. 21.5
    B. 21.25
    C. 22.75
    D. 23.5

5. In question 4, if drywall is sold by the sheet, and costs $8.17 per sheet, the drywall for the four kitchen walls will cost _____.

    A. $122
    B. $181
    C. $196
    D. $208

6. In the dining room, the total area of the four walls and the ceiling is _____ square feet.

    A. 1,500
    B. 1,530
    C. 1,684
    D. 1,930

7. In question 6, above, if the drywall is sold in 4' x 12' x ½" sheets, _____ sheets will be needed for the four walls and ceiling.

    A. 29
    B. 30
    C. 32
    D. 44

8. We see at the supply store that the drywall cost is up to $8.39 per sheet, and that they now must charge 6% sales tax on our drywall purchase. Per questions 6 and 7, the total purchase price of the drywall is _____.

    A. $207.96
    B. $242.18
    C. $268.48
    D. $284.59

9. The total amount of wall area for all three bedrooms (including ceilings but not floors) is between _____ square feet.

    A. 3,000 and 3,499
    B. 3,500 and 3,999
    C. 4,000 and 4,499
    D. 4,500 and 4,999

10. It is determined that the entire home will require 145 sheets of drywall.
65 sheets of drywall are on hand from a previous job and will be used.
The drywall contractor charges $2.95, inclusive of all taxes, per sheet to hang and finish each sheet.
The supplier charges $.8.39 per sheet of drywall, plus 6% sales tax.
The total amount to be invoiced to the contractor by both the supplier and drywall contractor is _____.

    A. $1,139
    B. $1,176
    C. $1,426
    D. $1,489

All Ceilings are 12'
Drawing not to scale

80'

30'

Kitchen

17'

Master
Bedroom

15'

BR 1   12'

15'

Dining Room

BR 2   12'

50'

18'

Living Room

Foyer

Family Room

26'

34'

****Please see Answer Key on the following page****
ABC 09/21/2021

322

Drywall Math Calculations
Practice Test – 2
Answer Key

	Answer	Solution
1.	D	There are two walls 15' in length, and two walls 12' feet in length. 15' + 15' + 12' + 12' = 54'
2.	A	One kitchen wall is 30' long x 12' high, as is the opposite wall. The other kitchen walls are each 17' long x 12' high. 30' x 12' = 360 square feet. 360 x 2 walls: 360 square feet + 360 square feet = 720 square feet. 17' x 12' = 204 square feet. 204 x 2 walls. 204 square feet + 204 square feet = 408 square feet. 720 square feet + 408 square feet = 1,128 square feet total for kitchen walls w/out ceiling and floor
3.	C	Rectangular home with length 80' and width 50'. 80' x 50' = 4,000 square feet
4.	D	From question 2, we know that total square feet of kitchen is 1,128 square feet. Dry wall is 4' x 12' = 48 square feet per sheet. 1,128 ÷ 48 = 23.5. 23.5 sheets are needed.
5.	C	$8.17 x 24 (we need 23.5 but it's sold by the sheet) = $196.08
6.	B	Dining room is 30' long, 15' wide, and 12' high. Two of the walls are each: 30' x 12' = 360 square feet. Two of the walls are each: 15' x 12' = 180 square feet. Ceiling is 30' x 15' = 450 square feet. Total square footage of four walls and ceiling: 360 + 360 + 180 + 180 + 450 = 1,530 square feet
7.	C	From question 6., we know that the dining room walls and ceiling total 1,530 square feet. Drywall is 12' x 4'. 12 x 4 = 48 square feet per sheet. 1,530 sf ÷ 48 sf = 31.88 sheets. So, 32 sheets are needed. Note that we must have the full extra sheet, even if only a fraction of the sheet will be used
8.	D	$8.39 x 32 = $268.48 subtotal for drywall. 6% sales tax is $268.48 x .06 = $16.11. $268.48 + $16.11 = $284.59

	Answer	Solution

9. B

Bedroom 1 is 12' x 15' with a height of 12'
Two walls are 12' x 12' = 144 square feet each
Two walls are 15' x 12' = 180 square feet each
Ceiling is 12' x 15' = 180 square feet
144 + 144 + 180 + 180 + 180 = 828 total square feet for Bedroom 1

Bedroom 2 is identical to Bedroom 1, so BR 2 is also 828 square feet

Master Bedroom is 35' x 24' with a height of 12'
(We get 35' length because length of home is:
80' – 15' – 30' ((of known other rooms)) = 35')
(We get 24 width' because combined width of BRs 1 & 2 = 24')
Two walls are 35' x 12' = 420 square feet each
Two walls are 24' x 12' = 288 square feet each
Ceiling is 35' x 24' = 840 square feet
420 + 420 + 288 + 288 + 840 = 2,256 total wall/ceiling square feet for Master Bedroom.

Three-bedroom total wall/ceiling square feet is 828 + 828 + 2,256 = 3,912 square feet

10. A

145 sheets of drywall to be hung:
145 x $2.95 = $427.75
145 sheets needed, but already have 65:
145 – 65 = 80
80 x $8.39 = $671.20
Sales Tax 6%
$671.20 x .06 = $40.27
$671.20 + $40.27 = $711.47 total paid for 80 sheets
The total amount to be invoiced for this is $427.75 + $711.47 = $1,139.22

Excavation and Hauling
Questions and Answers

1. Your job calls for you to excavate a perimeter trench around a pool area that is 3' wide x 4' deep and runs 160 lineal feet. The soil is comprised of heavy soil and clay. You have no option but to excavate this trench by hand and you only have 1 day to get this accomplished. Approximately _____ cubic yards of soil must be excavated. (Select closest answer)

    A. 25
    B. 27
    C. 64
    D. 71

2. For the above question, you will have to hire _____ laborers if an average laborer can excavate an average of 5 cubic yards of heavy soil/clay per day. (Select closest answer)

    A. 15
    B. 17
    C. 22
    D. 24

3. In question 1, _____ laborers would be needed if the soil to be excavated was sandy loam, if a laborer can excavate an average of 6 cubic yards of sandy loam per day. (Select closest answer)

    A. 9
    B. 12
    C. 16
    D. 24

4. In the example in question 1, _____ laborers would be needed if the trench to be excavated was 120 linear feet of heavy soil/clay. (Select closest answer)

    A. 11
    B. 12
    C. 16
    D. 20

5. In question 1, if the 160-foot trench forms a 50' x 30' rectangle, the area inside the rectangle is _____ square feet. (Select closest answer)

    A. 900
    B. 1,200
    C. 1,500
    D. 2,400

6. Your job calls for you to excavate a pit for a pool. The pit must be 30' wide x 50 long and be 12' deep. The soil is comprised of wet clay. You will be using a hydraulic backhoe tractor with a 1.0 cubic yard bucket. _____ cubic yards of material must be removed. Round up any partial cubic yards. (Select closest answer)

    A. 525
    B. 624
    C. 666
    D. 667

7. In the example in question 6, taking into account the swell factor, _____ eight cubic yard capacity truckloads will be required to remove all the material excavated. (Select closest answer)

    A. 21
    B. 78
    C. 84
    D. 100

8. In the example in question 6, the project has to be delayed after excavation. Municipal code requires warning tape be placed around the perimeter of the pit, and that the pit be covered. _____ feet of tape will be needed to surround the pit. (Select closest answer)

    A. 80
    B. 100
    C. 160
    D. 1,500

9. If in the above question, tape comes in 50' rolls costing $11.00 per roll plus 3% tax, _____ must be spent on tape. (Select closest answer)

    A. $11.33
    B. $33.00
    C. $45.32
    D. $67.98

10. In question 6, _____ square feet of material would be required to exactly cover the pit (no overlap). (Select closest answer)

    A. 1,500
    B. 1,560
    C. 1,600
    D. 2,000

Questions 11 – 16 refer to the following job:

A construction job will require a trench for PVC pipe 3' wide, 3'deep, and 250 yards long. Because of accessibility issues, the trench must be hand excavated. The soil is sandy loam. The job must be completed in two regular work days (8 hours per person per day). The labor cost, per man, per whole day, is $110. The trench, by municipal code, must have yellow fluorescent tape around the entire perimeter of the trench after normal working hours. (Select closest answers)

11. _____ cubic yards of material must be excavated.

     A. 198
     B. 225
     C. 250
     D. 750

12. _____ laborers will be needed to complete the job within the required time if a laborer can excavate an average of 6 cu yds of sandy loam per day.

     A. 20
     B. 21
     C. 28
     D. 32

13. The cost of manpower would be _____. (Laborers only, no partial day payments)

     A. $3,220
     B. $3,690
     C. $4,620
     D. $4,880

14. _____ feet of tape will be required for perimeter of the trench.

     A. 276
     B. 1,506
     C. 2,280
     D. 2,800

15. In the above job, if the labor cost was increased to $120.00 per day per man, instead of $110, _____ extra would have to be spent.

     A. $320
     B. $420
     C. $462
     D. $488

16. An excavation job was completed, leaving 24 cubic yards of wet gravel that has a swell factor of 15%. You've been hired to remove the gravel in your truck, which can carry 6 cubic yards per load. Allowing for swell, you will need _____ loads to haul all the gravel.

    A. 2
    B. 4
    C. 5
    D. 7

17. In the above example, if the load were Topsoil, allowing for swell factor of 30%, _____ trips will be needed.

    A. 3
    B. 4
    C. 5
    D. 6

18. Your job calls for you to excavate a pit for a foundation. The pit must be 40' wide x 64' long and be 10' deep. The soil is comprised of wet earth (moist loam). You will be using a Hydraulic Backhoe Tractor with a 1.0 Cubic Yard Bucket. Your trucks can haul 10 cubic yards in one load. _____ cubic yards of material must be removed. Round up any partial cubic yards.

    A. 895
    B. 927
    C. 949
    D. 971

19. The excavation should take _____ days. Backhoe can excavate an average of 720 cu. yds of moist loam per day

    A. 1
    B. 2
    C. 3
    D. 5

20. For the above question, allowing for a swell factor of 10%, you will need _____ loads to haul all the gravel.

    A. 86
    B. 97
    C. 101
    D. 105

****Please see Answer Key on the following page****

3/31/22

Excavation and Hauling
Questions and Answers
Answers Key

	Answer	**Solution**

1.   D

3 x 4 x 160 = 1,920 cu ft.
1,920 cu ft. ÷ 27 = 71.11 cu yds
(Note: Cubic feet ÷ 27 = cubic yards)

2.   A

3 x 4 x 160 = 1,920 cu. ft.
1,920 cu. ft. ÷ 27 = 71.11 cu. yds.
71.11 ÷ 5 = 14.22
So, 15 workers needed.

3.   B

3 x 4 x 160 = 1,920 cu. ft.
1,920 cu. ft. ÷ 27 = 71.11 cu. yds.
71.11 ÷ 6 = 11.85
So, 12 workers needed

4.   A

3 x 4 x 120 = 1,440 cu. ft.
1,440 cu. ft. ÷ 27 = 53.33 cu. yds.
53.33 ÷ 5 = 10.67
So, 11 workers needed

5.   C

30 x 50 = 1,500
(Side x Adjoining side = Area of a rectangle)

6.   D

30 x 50 x 12 = 18,000 cu ft.
18,000 ÷ 27 (27 cu ft per cu yd) = 666.67
(Remember the instruction to round up)

7.   D

Total cu. yds. to be hauled is 30 x 50 x 12 = 18,000 cu. ft.
18,000 ÷ 27 (27 cu. ft. per cu. yd.) = 666.67
Add swell factor of 20% or 133.333 (666.67 x .2)
133.33 + 666.67 = 800
800 ÷ 8 (capacity of truck) = 100

8.   C

Perimeter of a rectangle = sum of all four sides
30 + 50 + 30 + 50 = 160

9.   C

Perimeter of a rectangle = sum of all four sides
30 + 50 + 30 + 50 = 160
So, 4 rolls are needed even though 40 feet will be left over
(3 rolls would only contain 150 feet)
Each roll is $11.00, 11 x 4 = $44.00
Add tax of 3% or $1.32
Total due is $45.32

	Answer	Solution

10. A

One side x Adjoining side = Area of a rectangle
30 x 50 = 1,500

11. C

3 x 3 x 750 (250 yd x 3 to get feet) = 6,750 cu. ft.
6,750 cu. ft. ÷ 27 = 250 cu. yds.
(Note: Cubic feet ÷ 27 = Cubic yards)

12. B

3 x 3 x 750 = 6,750 cu. ft.
6,750 cu. ft. ÷ 27 = 250 cu. yds.
250 ÷ 6 = 41.67
So, 42 workers needed to do the job in one day
But, given two days, it will take 20.83, or 21 workers.

13. C

3 x 3 x 750 = 6,750 cu. ft.
6,750 cu. ft. ÷ 27 = 250 cu. yds.
250 ÷ 6 = 41.67
So, 42 laborers needed to do the job in one day
But, given two days, it will take 20.83, or 21 laborers
21 x $110.00/day = $2,310.00 x 2 days = $4,620.00

14. B

Perimeter of a rectangle = sum of all four sides
First convert the length of the trench from yards to feet: (multiply yards by 3)
250 yards x 3 = 750 feet
Add the sum of all four sides: 750 ft. + 750 ft. + 3 ft. + 3 ft. = 1,506 ft

15. B

Given: a laborer can excavate an average of 6 cu yds. of sandy loam per day
3 x 3 x 750 = 6,750 cu. ft.
6,750 cu. ft. ÷ 27 = 250 cu. yds.
250 ÷ 6 = 41.67
So, 42 laborers needed to do the job in one day.
But, given two days, it will take 20.83, or 21 laborers.
21 x $110.00/day = $2,310.00
$2,310.00 x 2 days = $4,620.00
Substitute $120.00 per day and it's 21 x $120.00 = $2,520
$2,520 x 2 days = $5,040
The difference between 5,040 and 4,620 = 420

16. C

Total cu. yds. to be hauled is 24.
Add swell factor of 15% or 3.6 cu. yds. (24 x .15)
24 + 3.6 = 27.6.
27.6 ÷ 6 (capacity of truck) = 4.6.
So, 5 trips will be needed, with the last trip being a partial load

17. D

Total cu. yds. to be hauled is 24
Add swell factor of 30% or 7.2 cu. yds. (24 x .30).
24 + 7.2 = 31.2
31.2 ÷ 6 (capacity of truck) = 5.2.
So, 6 trips will be needed, with the last trip being a partial load.

18. C

40 x 64 x 10 = 25,600 cu ft.

25,600 cu ft. ÷ 27 = 948.15 cu yds.
(Note: cubic feet ÷ 27 = cubic yards)

Answer	Solution

19.   B   Per table in Walker's, the described Backhoe can excavate an average of 720 cu. yds of moist loam per day. So, if we determined that there are 948.15 cu. yds. to be excavated, it will take 2 days (1,440 cu. yds. possible, but one day is too little – 720 cu. yds.)

20.   D   Total cu. yds. to be hauled is 949
Add swell factor of 10% or 94.9 cu. yds. (949 x .10)
949 + 94.9 = 1,043.9
1,043.9 ÷ 10 (capacity of truck) = 104.39
So, 105 trips will be needed, with the last trip being a partial load.

Concrete Calculations
Practice Exam – 1

1. You are a contractor that is estimating a job for a homeowner that has a driveway measuring 18 feet wide by 50 yards long. The driveway will be 6 inches thick. _____ cubic yards of concrete will need to be ordered.

    A. 20
    B. 45
    C. 50
    D. 60

2. In the above example, if concrete costs $75.00 per cubic yard, the total cost of concrete will be

    _____.

    A. $3,750
    B. $3,780
    C. $4,000
    D. $4,275

3. You are a contractor that is estimating a job for a homeowner that has a driveway that measures 6 yards wide by 100 yards long. The driveway will be 4 inches thick. _____ cubic yards of concrete will need to be ordered.

    A. 66
    B. 76
    C. 112
    D. A, B, and C are wrong

4. In the above example, if concrete costs $50.00 per cubic yard, the cost of concrete will be _____.

    A. $1,650
    B. $3,300
    C. $3,450
    D. $5,250

5. You are a contractor that is estimating a job for a homeowner that has a driveway that measures 12 feet wide by 300 yards long. The driveway will be 6 inches thick. _____ cubic yards of concrete will need to be ordered.

    A. 90
    B. 160
    C. 200
    D. 220

332

6. In the above example, if concrete costs $75.00 per cubic yard, the cost of concrete will be _____.

    A. $12,000
    B. $13,000
    C. $14,000
    D. $15,000

7. You are a contractor that is estimating a job for a homeowner that has a driveway that measures 12 feet wide and 120 feet long. The driveway will be 6 inches thick. _____ cubic yards of concrete will need to be ordered.

    A. 22
    B. 24
    C. 26
    D. 27

8. In the above example, if concrete costs $60.00 per cubic yard, the cost of concrete will be _____.

    A. $1,600
    B. $1,620
    C. $1,640
    D. $4,000

9. You are a contractor that is estimating a job for a homeowner that has a driveway that measures 12 yards wide by 12 yards long. The driveway will be 8 inches thick. _____ cubic yards of concrete will need to be ordered.

    A. 20
    B. 25
    C. 28
    D. 33

10. In the above example, if concrete costs $80.00 per cubic yard, the cost of the concrete will be

_____.

    A. $1,960
    B. $2,640
    C. $2,700
    D. $3,220

11. You are a contractor that is estimating a job for a homeowner that has a driveway that measures 16 yards wide by 60 yards long. The driveway will be 5 inches thick. _____ cubic yards of concrete will need to be ordered.

    A. 106
    B. 128
    C. 135
    D. A, B, and C are wrong

12. In the above example, if concrete costs $75.00 per cubic yard, the cost of concrete will be _____.

    A. $1,065
    B. $1,240
    C. $2,720
    D. $10,125

13. You are a contractor that is estimating a job for a homeowner that has a driveway that measures 6 yards feet wide by 900 feet long. The driveway will be 6 inches thick. _____ cubic yards of concrete will need to be ordered?

    A. 280
    B. 300
    C. 420
    D. 620

14. In the above example, if concrete costs $55.00 per cubic yard, the cost of concrete be will be

_____.

    A. $16,500
    B. $17,000
    C. $17,200
    D. $10,125

15. You are a contractor that is estimating a job for a homeowner that has a walkway that measures 30 feet wide by 50 yards long. The driveway will be 1 foot thick. _____ cubic yards of concrete will need to be ordered.

    A. 98
    B. 106
    C. 167
    D. 168

16. In the above example, if concrete costs $50.00 per cubic yard, the cost of concrete will be _____.

    A. $6,300
    B. $8,200
    C. $8,350
    D. $9,900

17. You are a contractor that is estimating a job for a homeowner that has a driveway that measures 18 feet wide by 250 yards long. The concrete will be 6 inches thick. If the surface coating costs the contractor $.95, the cost of resurfacing material will be _____.

    A. $9,288
    B. $10,660
    C. $12,825
    D. $13,825

18. You are a contractor that is estimating a job for a homeowner that has a driveway that measures 20 feet wide by 75 yards long. The driveway will be 4 inches thick. _____ cubic yards of concrete will need to be ordered.

    A. 55
    B. 85
    C. 134
    D. 135

19. In the above example, if concrete costs $75.00 per cubic yard, the cost of concrete will be _____.

    A. $3,070
    B. $4,125
    C. $4,525
    D. $5,095

20. You are a contractor that is estimating a job for a homeowner that has a driveway that measures 7 yards wide by 20 yards long. The driveway will be 6 inches thick. _____ cubic yards of concrete will need to be ordered.

    A. 17
    B. 22
    C. 24
    D. 32

****Please see Answer Key on the following page****

Concrete Calculations
Practice Exam – 1
Answer Key

	Answer	**Solution**

1.   C   18 feet x 150 feet (50 yards x 3 feet per yard) x .5 feet (6 inches = 1/2 foot and 1 divided by 2 = .5) = 1,350 cubic feet
1,350 cubic feet divided by 27 (27 cubic feet = 1 cubic yard) = 50 cyd

2.   A   50 cubic yards x $75.00 per cubic yard = $3,750

3.   A   18 feet (6 yards x 3 feet per yard) x 300 feet (100 yards x 3 feet per yard) x .33 feet (4 inches = 1/3 or 4/12 of a foot and 4 divided by 12 = .33) = 1,782 cubic feet.
1,782 cubic feet divided by 27 (27 cubic feet = 1 cubic yard) = 66 cyd

4.   B   66 cubic yards x $50.00 per cubic yard = $3,300

5.   C   12 feet x 900 feet (300 yards x 3 feet per yard) x .5 feet (6 inches = 1/2 foot and 1 divided by 2 = .5) = 5,400 cubic feet
5,400 cubic feet divided by 27 (27 cubic feet = 1 cubic yard) = 200 cyd

6.   D   200 cubic yards x $75.00 per cubic yard = $15,000

7.   D   12 feet x 120 feet x .5 feet (6 inches = 1/2 foot and 1 divided by 2 = .5) = 720 cubic feet.
720 cubic feet divided by 27 (27 cubic feet = 1 cubic yard) = 26.67.
Round up to 27 cyd

8.   B   27 cubic yards x $60.00 per cubic yard = $1,620

9.   D   36 feet (12 yards x 3 feet per yard) x 36 feet (12 yards x 3 feet per yard) x .67 feet (8 inches = 8/12 0r 2/3 foot - 8 divided by 12 = .67) = 868.32 cubic feet
868.32 cubic feet divided by 27 (27 cubic feet = 1 cubic yard) = 32.16 cyd – round up to 33 cyd

10.   B   33 cubic yards x $80.00 per cubic yard = $2,640

11.   C   48 feet (16 yards x 3 feet per yard) x 180 feet (60 yards x 3 feet per yard) x .42 feet (5/12 inches = 5 divided by 12 = .42) = 3,628.88 or 3,629 cubic feet
3,629 cubic feet divided by 27 (27 cubic feet = 1 cubic yard) = 134.4 cyd – round up 135 cyd

12.   D   135 cubic yards x $75.00 per cubic yard = $10,125

	Answer	**Solution**
13.	B	18 feet (6 yards x 3 feet per yard) x 900 feet x .5 feet (6/12 inches = 6 divided by 12 = .5) = 8,100 cubic feet 8,100 cubic feet divided by 27 (27 cubic feet = 1 cubic yard) = 300 cyd
14.	A	300 cubic yards x $55.00 per cubic yard = $1,650
15.	C	30 feet x 150 feet (50 yards x 3 feet per yard) x 1 foot = 4,500 cubic feet 4,500 cubic feet divided by 27 (27 cubic feet = 1 cubic yard) = 166.67 cyd Round up to 167 cyd
16.	C	167 cubic yards x $50.00 per cubic yard = $8,350
17.	C	18 feet x 750 feet (250 yards x 3 feet per yard) = 13,500 square feet x $.95 = $12,835
18.	A	20 feet x 225 feet (75 yards x 3 feet per yard) x .33 feet (4 inches = 1/3 or 4/12 of a foot and 1 divided by 3 = .33) = 1,485 cubic feet 1,485 cubic feet divided by 27 (27 cubic feet = 1 cubic yard) = 55 cyd
19.	B	55 cubic yards x $75.00 per cubic yard = $4,125
20.	C	21 feet (7 yards x 3 feet per yard) x 60 feet(20 yards x 3 feet per yard) x .5 (6 inches is 1/2 or 6/12 foot and 6 divided by 12 = .5) = 630 cubic feet 630 cubic feet divided by 27 (27 cubic feet = 1 cubic yard) = 23.33 cyd Round up 24 cyd

Concrete Calculations
Practice Exam – 2

1. You are a contractor that is estimating a job for a homeowner that has a driveway that measures 18 feet wide and 50 yards long. The driveway will be 6 inches thick. What will the cost of resurfacing material be, if the surface coating costs the contractor $.95 per square foot?

    A. $1,990
    B. $2,010
    C. $2,565
    D. $2,600

2. In the above example, what will the cost of surface material be, if surface material costs $.75 per square foot?

    A. $1,080
    B. $2,025
    C. $4,000
    D. $4,275

3. You are a contractor that is estimating a job for a homeowner that has a driveway that measures 6 yards wide and 100 yards long. The driveway will be 4 inches thick. What will the cost of resurfacing material be, if the surface coating costs the contractor $.80 per square foot?

    A. $4,320
    B. $4,360
    C. $4,400
    D. None of the above

4. In the above example, what will the cost of surface material be, if surface material costs $.76 per square foot?

    A. $4,000
    B. $4,104
    C. $4,450
    D. $5,250

5. You are a contractor that is estimating a job for a homeowner that has a driveway that measures 12 feet wide and 300 yards long. The driveway will be 6 inches thick. What will the cost of resurfacing material be, if the surface coating costs the contractor $1.15 per square foot?

    A. $10,080
    B. $12,025
    C. $12,420
    D. $13,275

6. In the above example, what will the cost of surface material be, if surface material costs $1.20 per square foot?

    A. $12,000
    B. $12,420
    C. $12,560
    D. $12,960

7. You are a contractor that is estimating a job for a homeowner that has a driveway that measures 12 feet wide and 120 feet long. The driveway will be 6 inches thick. What will the cost of resurfacing material be, if the surface coating costs the contractor $.78 per square foot?

    A. $980.82
    B. $1,000.00
    C. $1,005.99
    D. $1,123.20

8. In the above example, what will the cost of surface material be, if surface material costs $.85 per square foot?

    A. $1,110
    B. $1,224
    C. $1,640
    D. $2,125

9. You are a contractor that is estimating a job for a homeowner that has a driveway that measures 12 yards wide and 12 yards long. The driveway will be 8 inches thick. What will the cost of resurfacing material be, if the surface coating costs the contractor $.95 per square foot? (round to the nearest dollar)

    A. $1,110
    B. $1,125
    C. $1,231
    D. $1,232

10. In the above example, what will the cost of surface material be, if surface material costs $.1.02 per square foot (round to the nearest dollar)?

    A. $1,230
    B. $1,322
    C. $1,422
    D. $1,888

11. You are a contractor that is estimating a job for a homeowner that has a driveway that measures 48 feet wide and 60 yards long. The driveway will be 5 inches thick. What will the cost of resurfacing material be, if the surface coating costs the contractor $.65 per square foot?

    A. $5,082
    B. $5,525
    C. $5,608
    D. $5,616

12. In the above example, what will the cost of surface material be, if surface material costs $.75 per square foot?

    A. $5,765
    B. $5,998
    C. $6,028
    D. $6,480

13. You are a contractor that is estimating a job for a homeowner that has a driveway that measures 6 yards feet wide and 900 feet long. The driveway will be 6 inches thick. What will the cost of resurfacing material be, if the surface coating costs the contractor $1.25 per square foot?

    A. $20,185
    B. $20,250
    C. $20,750
    D. $22,120

14. In the above example, what will the cost of surface material be, if surface material costs $1.20 per square foot?

    A. $19,440
    B. $19,600
    C. $19,720
    D. $20,025

15. You are a contractor that is estimating a job for a homeowner that has a walkway that measures 30 feet wide and 50 yards long. The driveway will be 1 foot thick. What will the cost of resurfacing material be, if the surface coating costs the contractor $.85 per square foot?

    A. $3,600
    B. $3,820
    C. $3,825
    D. $3,975

16. In the above example, what will the cost of surface material be, if surface material costs $.80 per square foot?

    A. $3,400
    B. $3,500
    C. $3,600
    D. $3,700

17. You are a contractor that is estimating a job for a homeowner that has a driveway that measures 18 feet wide and 250 yards long. The concrete will be 6 inches thick. What will the cost of resurfacing material be, if the surface coating costs the contractor $.55 per square foot?

   A. $6,288
   B. $7,366
   C. $7,425
   D. $7,825

18. In the above example, what will the cost of surface material be, if surface material costs $.77 per square foot?

   A. $12,150
   B. $12,200
   C. $12,330
   D. $12,900

19. You are a contractor that is estimating a job for a homeowner that has a driveway that measures 7 yards wide and 20 yards long. The driveway will be 6 inches thick. What will the cost of resurfacing material be, if the surface coating costs the contractor $1.00 per square foot?

   A. $1,070
   B. $1,260
   C. $1,280
   D. $1,300

20. In the above example, what will the cost of surface material be, if surface material costs $.70 per square foot?

   A. $780
   B. $800
   C. $882
   D. $890

****Please see Answer Key on the following page****

ABC 09/20/2021

341

Concrete Calculations - 2
Questions and Answers
Answer Key

	Answer	Solution
1.	C	18 feet x 150 feet (50 yards x 3 feet per yard) = 2,700. 2,700 x $.95 = $2,565
2.	B	2,700 x $.75 per square foot = $2,025
3.	A	18 feet (6 yards x 3 feet per yard) x 300 feet (100 yards x 3 feet per yard) = 5,400 5,400 x $.80 per square foot = $4,320
4.	B	5,400 x $.76 per square foot = $4,104
5.	C	12 feet x 900 feet (300 yards x 3 feet per yard) x = 10,800 10,800 x $1.15 per square foot = $12,420
6.	D	10,800 square feet x $1.20 per square foot = $12,960
7.	D	12 feet x 120 feet x $.78 = $1,123.20
8.	B	1,440 x $.85 per square foot = $1,224
9.	C	36 feet (12 yards x 3 feet per yard) x 36 feet (12 yards x 3 feet per yard) x $.95 =$1,231.20
10.	B	1,296 x $1.02 per square foot = $1,321.92
11.	D	48 feet x 180 feet (60 yards x 3 feet per yard) x $.65 = $5,616
12.	D	8,640 x $.75 per square foot = $6,480
13.	B	18 feet (6 yards x 3 feet per yard) x 900 feet x $1.25 = $ 20,250
14.	A	16,200 x $1.20 per square foot = $19,440
15.	C	30 feet x 150 feet (50 yards x 3 feet per yard) x $.85 = $3,825
16.	C	4,500 x $.80 per square foot = $3,600
17.	C	18 feet x 750 feet (250 yards x 3 feet per yard) = 13,500 square feet x $.55 = $7,425
18.	A	13,500 square feet x $.90 per square foot = $12,150
19.	B	21 feet (7 yards x 3 feet per yard) x 60 feet (20 yards x 3 feet per yard) = 1,260 sq. feet 1,260 sq. feet x $1.00 = $1,260
20.	C	1,260 x $.70 per square foot = $882

Made in the USA
Columbia, SC
18 March 2025